I sat hidden, absolutely motionless. I had my rifle cradled in front of me, but pointed forward toward the front. But what if they came toward me from the side? I wouldn't be able to see them. The voices came on. It would be a matter of seconds before whoever was talking would pass right in front of me. Then there was silence. They had stopped moving and talking. What now?

I caught the movement off to my left side, it was a dark green color moving slowly toward me. I recognized it as the outline of a pith helmet, not more than ten feet away. I tried to make myself small without moving. I just wanted him to go away, but the helmet continued to come forward slowly until it was directly in front of me. Then the outline of his face began to show. His left hand reached forward and began to part the branches of the bush. He leaned forward.

The orange muzzle flash was the last thing he ever saw. . . .

Also by B. H. Norton
Published by Ivy Books:

FORCE RECON DIARY, 1970

FORCE RECON DIARY, 1969

B. H. Norton

IVY BOOKS • NEW YORK

Ivy Books
Published by Ballantine Books
Copyright © 1991 by B. H. Norton

All rights reserved under International and Pan-American Copyright Conventions. Published in the United States by Ballantine Books, a division of Random House, Inc., New York, and simultaneously in Canada by Random House of Canada Limited, Toronto.

Grateful acknowledgment is made to William Krasilovsky, Esq., for permission to reprint three poems by Robert Service: "Just Think!" copyright 1921 by Dodd Mead and Company; "The Call" and "My Mate" copyright 1921 by Dodd Mead and Company.

Library of Congress Catalog Card Number: 91-91828

ISBN 0-8041-0671-1

Manufactured in the United States of America

First Edition: May 1991
Third Printing: June 1992

ACKNOWLEDGMENTS

I am forever grateful to my friend, the Reverend Ray W. Stubbe (Cmdr. USN ret.), for his encouragement and personal involvement in getting me to write this account of the superb officers and brave men of the 3d Force Recon Company, in Vietnam, during 1969 and 1970.

My thanks to Mr. Owen A. Lock, who knew that I had a story worth telling.

Force Recon Diary, 1969
is dedicated

To the Marines of 3d Force Reconnaissance Company. They were the best.

To the memory of Cpl. Ted Jason Bishop, Cpl. Donnell Kegler, Sgt. Arthur Martinez Garcia, LCpl. James Michael Furhman, and Maj. Norman Hisler. They are not forgotten.

To Lt. Col. Alex Lee, USMC, Lt. Col. "Bucky" Coffman, Jr., USMC, Lt. Col. Wayne Morris, USMC, and to my teammates, "Ol' Man" Paul Keaveney and Guillermo Silva. "Anytime, anywhere, no questions asked."

To my wife Deaine—my best friend—and our daughter, Michelle.

To my family, George, Rosalba, Marilyn, and Carolyn.

To the hospital corpsmen who serve the Fleet Marine Force.

To the corporals and sergeants of the United States Marine Corps.

FOREWORD

Bruce "Doc" Norton is a unique individual. The former U.S. Navy Force Recon corpsman, now a field-grade Marine officer, performed as an exceptional team member while in 3d Force Recon in Vietnam, 1969 to 1970. We who worked and fought with him admire him.

The accounts in *Force Recon Diary, 1969* are, unlike many Vietnam "experiences," accurate and factual, lacking any self-aggrandizement. They are, in short, *professional,* which is important to all of us from Alex Lee's 3d Force Recon Company because he had no patience whatsoever with inaccuracy, dishonesty, or lack of balls. Mistakes are paid for—witness Singleton and Garcia. Doc hasn't held it back and this account of his tour in our company is, like his performance in the bush, *well done!*

Bucky the Igor
C. C. Coffman, Jr.
Lt. Col. USMC (Ret.)

—— PROLOGUE ——

BY GOING BACK IN TIME, THIRTY-THREE YEARS AGO, to 1957, I hope to explain how the early years of my childhood, spent in the woods of the small New England township of North Scituate, Rhode Island, served to educate and prepare me for a truly adventurous and exciting period of my life. I cannot recapture all of the many thrills and disappointments of my youth, but I do believe that sharing some of my more interesting childhood experiences will serve to demonstrate how the lessons of sportsmanship and woodsmanship which I learned as a young man helped me to stay alive when I went to Vietnam.

In 1969 and 1970 I was a United States Navy hospital corpsman serving in Marine Force Recon teams with both 3d Force and 1st Force Reconnaissance Companies, on twenty-four long-range combat missions. A Marine Force Recon team, which conducts combat reconnaissance patrols, has always been considered an elite unit, even outside the Marine Corps.

Serving alongside Marines in combat is a common tradition for Navy corpsmen because the Marine Corps has no trained medical personnel that are organic to its organization. The Navy provides the corpsmen to the Marine Corps' Fleet Marine Force (FMF) units. To have served as a team member within two Force Recon companies while I was in Vietnam was the greatest of personal honors.

This is my account of how I happened to serve with these two Marine Force Recon units, and what occurred on patrols during that time. I have not embellished any of the events, nor have I exaggerated the truth for the sake of enhancing the story. There really isn't any need to do that. I have tried to name the people, places, and dates that influenced my life, whether they were in a positive manner or not. I have also tried to give credit where that credit was due.

Hopefully, many of my lessons learned while patrolling against the North Vietnamese will prove to be useful and positive to those small-unit leaders who may someday be tasked to carry out difficult patrolling assignments in combat.

To those military men of the present, and to those of the future, I will pass on to you the first of several truisms, "It is the man on the ground with his rifle who ultimately wins the war."

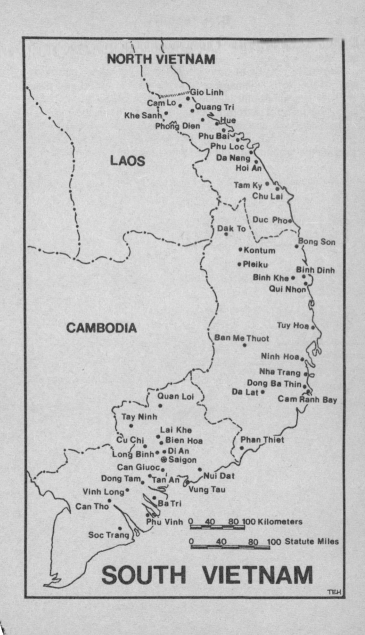

JUST THINK!

Just think! some night the stars will gleam
　　Upon a cold, grey stone,
And trace a name with silver beam,
　　And lo! 'twill be your own.

That night is speeding on to greet
　　Your epitaphic rhyme.
Your life is but a little beat
　　Within the heart of Time.

A little gain, a little pain
　　A laugh, lest you may moan;
A little blame, a little fame,
　　A star-gleam on a stone.

Rhymes of a Rolling Stone
(Robert Service)

—— THE WOODS ——

DEEP IN THE THOUGHTS OF NEARLY ALL YOUNG BOYS is the belief that there is something mysterious, fascinating, and powerful about owning a real gun. It makes no difference whether it is a rifle, a pistol, or a shotgun. As a youngster growing up in the 1950s in the small rural town of North Scituate, Rhode Island, I was no exception.

To possess my own rifle meant many things to me. It meant that I could be trusted, and it meant that I was expected to know the difference between what was right and what was wrong. It also meant that I would be held responsible for my actions with that rifle.

I learned that a rifle could take a life, but it could never bring a life back.

My very first rifle was given to me by my father when I was nine years old. It was a Crossman model 140-B, pneumatic, .22 caliber pellet rifle. The rifle had to be pumped up by hand at least a dozen times so that the solid lead pellet would have enough velocity behind it to make it to the target, whether that was a marked piece of paper, a squirrel high up in an oak tree, or some unsuspecting rabbit that had exposed itself in the open.

The Crossman was a single-shot rifle, and that one important characteristic would later prove to be a very useful teaching point some ten years later in Vietnam.

Looking back on those times, it seems as though I spent every idle moment in those quiet pine forests of North Scituate.

The property that surrounded our old family home on three sides was owned by the city of Providence, and all of those thousands of acres were fenced off and "posted," to keep trespassers from ruining the land or fouling the pristine waters of the reservoir.

The entire area was made up of farmland, pine and hardwood forests, and the great body of water that was the reservoir. All of the property was under the control of the Providence Water Supply Board. It is still an extremely valuable watershed for our small state because the Scituate reservoir provides all of the fresh water to the city of Providence.

To me, at the age of nine, it was a place of dreams and made for adventure. The forest was there to be explored, the reservoir was there to be fished, and the open areas of old farmland were there to be hunted. The only obstacle that separated me from the woods was a three-foot-high stone wall.

The heavily wooded areas were the perfect place for any small boy to learn what nature had to reveal to one who was curious. It was there that I learned how to track small game animals and how to move slowly and silently through the forest. I learned how to tell when the New England weather was about to change quickly, and I learned how to prepare for it. I was taught how to live-trap muskrat and mink, using catfish for bait.

It was one great learning place. It was better than any school classroom imaginable.

No matter the season of the year, I was to be found in the woods with my pellet rifle, and I practiced with it constantly.

Through trial and error, I came to realize that because I had a single-shot rifle I would always have to make the very first shot count; given the length of time it took to reload and repump the damned thing, a second shot was usually impossible. The pumping up of the rifle made it very noisy and always gave away my presence. Any living thing that I shot at, and missed, usually did not wait around for me to reload and try again.

I practiced with that rifle constantly. Within a month I was able to take careful aim, squeeze the trigger, and nine out of ten times, shatter an aspirin tablet held in the bark of a pine tree, at a distance of about thirty paces.

I could hardly realize then that the skills of marksmanship, patience, and practice would prove so useful in the preparation for a much more serious type of shooting game that I would be playing in the years to come. The target would change from the aspirin tablets, paper, and small game, to man-size targets in the form of North Vietnamese soldiers. Paper targets and small game do not return fire. The NVA did.

My pellet rifle later gave way to a *real* rifle. I was thirteen years old when I received a Winchester .22 caliber, bolt-action rifle. It had a five-shot magazine and accommodated .22 short, long, and long-rifle cartridges. The only changes that I made to it were in adding a leather sling and a Bushnell 4X scope.

It was perfect: not as difficult to use as the pellet rifle and the increased range, four additional shots, and the advantage provided by the scope made up for the shortcomings of the Crossman pellet rifle.

A boy named Gerry Curran lived about a mile from me, and he, too, had a .22 caliber rifle. We were the same age and we always palled around together because we shared similar interests: hunting and fishing. What that really means is that we always got into trouble together.

The only time that we could spend in the woods was during the weekends or in the summertime between school sessions. Gerry attended a parochial school in the city, and I attended the local elementary school.

Gerry had two brothers, John and Bill, and they, too, knew the secrets of how to hunt successfully and fish in the large area of the Scituate woods. We learned skills from one another, and we shared what we had learned after each outing. When I became old enough to join the local chapter of the Boy Scouts I thought that I was pretty well schooled in the art of camping and in knowing all there was to know about survival in the out-of-doors. I had never gotten myself lost in the woods, or at least I would never admit to anyone of having done so.

The key to my better than average success in hunting or fishing on the reservoir property was *stealth*. The reason was simple: the city of Providence had the reservoir property constantly patrolled by state officers whose sole purpose in life was to catch us hunting, fishing, or swimming within the boundaries of the posted city property.

To get caught by one of these officers meant not only the possibility of a stiff fine for trespassing, but also the far greater penalty of loss of face before all of the other kids in our small town who had successfully eluded capture by the "city guys," year after year.

It was a great game. It was taken quite seriously by both sides, and we were all good at it. We learned the traveling patterns and the routes and patrol times of the officers. We were better at hiding from them than they ever were at catching us.

During the ten years that I spent roaming the woods of North Scituate, I was only caught by the city officers twice. The first time, there were too many of us in a group; we made too much noise while swimming, which masked the sound of the approaching officer until he was upon us. We were all caught when we tried to get dressed. He had gathered up our clothes and waited for us to come out of the water.

The second time, I was caught when I unknowingly silhouetted myself against the setting sun on an autumn skyline while bass fishing. I stood out against the tree line. That's all it took. That time the officer was clever enough to ambush me on the path that led out of the cove where I thought I would be undetected. There was no escape.

I gave a phony name to the officer. That was the standard practice. He let me go with only a stern lecture and a warning as to what would happen to me if I was ever caught again. He also kept the fish.

I was lucky to have been let go, and even though I lost the fish, I realized that I would have to get better at not being seen if I were to chance going into the woods again.

Here was another lesson that would repeat itself time and again in Vietnam.

On one particular late September afternoon, my buddy Gerry and I were headed home through the woods with our rifles. We had been squirrel hunting, but without success. We happened to cross the land that was used as the dump site for Scituate's garbage and trash, which was brought there by the townspeople. The dump was a breeding place for rats, and we could see and hear them as they moved around the trash piles looking for food.

On that particular occasion, it was our good fortune to have each had an extra box of .22 shorts. There were just too many targets of opportunity for us to pass up, and we emptied our guns on the rats.

The number of rats went far beyond the infrequent rabbits or the squirrels that we might have encountered during a full day of hunting in the woods. There were literally hundreds of rats waiting to be shot. It wasn't long before we were both out of ammunition, but certainly not out of rats.

The many return trips that we made to the town dump after closing hours developed into periods of competition among the few boys who were allowed to go there to shoot. The truth is that none of us ever had permission from our parents to be there, but it was the best game in town; it was exciting and not to be missed.

For night shooting, we learned to tape flashlights to the front stocks of our rifles. The rats usually "froze" when the bright light hit their eyes, making them an easier target, so we centered the point of bullet impact with the center of the flashlight beam. Then it was possible to shoot the rats without taking particularly good aim. We just placed the center of the light beam on the body of the rat and pulled the trigger.

That was an old trick used by poachers to shoot deer at night, and usually out of season.

On more than one occasion I took my older sister Marilyn along with me to the dump site. She was, to some degree, fascinated with what we were doing, and not to be outdone by her younger brother, she demanded the opportunity to shoot at the rats. After a short lesson in how to hold the rifle, aim, fire, and reload she was ready. Needless to say, she hit the mark more than a few times, and when we were finished, she walked home with us, triumphant in her newly acquired status as "one of the guys."

The many days and nights that I spent in the woods of North Scituate hunting and fishing were always special. I spent the majority of this time alone. There were only a few boys who lived near us, and no normal thirteen-year-old boy ever took his sisters out into the one place where he, alone, was king.

I never found on any football field, baseball diamond, or golf course the excitement, peacefulness, or education that the forest offered.

My fascination with being in the woods and the enjoyment that I received from living in that kind of natural and unspoiled environment may be difficult to explain to those who grew up in the inner city, but my experiences were all self-made and not "manufactured." We had no gaming arcades or video centers to go to with pockets full of dollars to waste. In the fifties there were no great shopping malls or day-care centers where parents now routinely drop off their kids for the day. My arcade was the forest, my sisters and the friends who lived close by were my gang members.

What I learned while hunting and fishing alone and within the confines of the Scituate reservoir property has proved to be invaluable to me.

This book will tell my story of how these simple childhood lessons learned were later refreshed and put to use on combat reconnaissance patrols against the North Vietnamese Army in South Vietnam.

─── BOSTON ───

TO UNDERSTAND THE REASONS FOR MY LEAVING COLlege and enlisting in the United States Navy early in 1968, it is necessary for me to describe the many events that influenced my decision to abandon the relative safety of being a draft-deferred, full-time college student for entry into the new, dark, and uncertain world of the Navy "enlisted puke."

After I graduated from public high school in 1966, I left North Scituate, Rhode Island, and moved into a student boardinghouse on Carlton Street, in Boston, Massachusetts. I was there to attend an institution of higher learning.

The immediate problem was that this was a little higher than anything that I had ever encountered before, and it became a very difficult struggle for me to keep up with the studying that was regularly required of any student attending this renowned school of anatomy.

The mediocre study habits that I had refined so well as a high school student had left their indelible mark, and I now see that I was not very well prepared for the rigors of mastering seventeen credits per semester, as well as working at a part-time job in order to help pay for books, tuition, and the weekly rent.

My first year at college went by quickly, and I finished the year with a C+ average. I hoped that the second school year might be to some degree easier, but I was sadly mistaken.

By then it was now apparent to me that it was more important for my parents to say that they had a son in his second year of college than it was for me to be there. As one professor put it, "Mr. Norton, never have I seen anyone work so hard, yet have so little to show for it."

Unfortunately, in the late 1960s the same was true for more than a few students who were heavily pressured into attending college at the insistence of their parents. Perhaps it was a family status symbol to have a son in college. In my case it was a family's veiled attempt to keep their only son out of a service uniform and from eventually having to serve his country in a combat zone.

My full-time "part-time" job had consisted of working after school for a prominent funeral director who happened to own two large funeral homes. One of them was located in Jamaica Plains and the second one was located in the town of West Roxbury.

I had left the old student boardinghouse on Carlton Street after my freshman year and moved into the upstairs apartment at the West Roxbury funeral home, but I worked at the funeral home in Jamaica Plains each day after classes in Boston.

It was not uncommon for an anatomy student to take that type of position. I was not licensed to perform any of the technical mortuary procedures, but I did keep myself occupied by answering the telephones, cleaning the massive home and outside grounds, and by driving the hearse on different occasions. Unlike the boardinghouse, there were never any outside disturbances to detract from my studying. I wish there had been. Studying in a funeral home was lonely.

The most difficult part of my apprenticeship was getting accustomed to taking out the hearse and picking up a "customer." No two experiences were ever the same. On most occasions the deceased had passed away from natural causes and was to be removed from one of the many local hospital morgues and brought back to the funeral home. Other times, this was not the case.

The work was a unique experience, and it was a strange profession for me to be involved with, but it did help pay the costs of my going to college, and it was somewhat related to the field in which I was interested at the time, medicine. I had thought that becoming a doctor of medicine was at least an honorable profession and that attending anatomy school and working, even as an assistant, in a mortuary would be a good step in the right direction. It was simply not to be; the job had a few drawbacks.

I remember driving that shiny black Superior hearse over to an old three-story brownstone apartment building one cold January day. It was in the old Back Bay area of Boston, and at the address I was given, several Boston city policemen were standing around outside the apartment building with white handkerchiefs held loosely to their mouths. They looked ill.

The funeral director had driven his own car to the address, ahead of me, to make sure that everything was ready for the removal of the deceased to the funeral home in Jamaica Plains.

What I had not known at the time of the initial telephone call was that the people who lived in the building had not seen their neighbor, Mrs. Murphy, for several days; they had found it necessary to call the police when a very disturbing odor emanated from within her third-floor apartment and spread rapidly throughout the entire building. I had to traverse three levels of banister stairs with a collapsible stretcher, and when I entered the apartment Mrs. Murphy was dead on the kitchen floor, the telephone receiver still held to her ear. Her face was totally blackened. She had died of a heart attack.

Because it was the middle of winter, she had turned the steam radiators to high; the temperature of her apartment was close to ninety-five degrees. The steaming radiators emitted a hot and humid mist which had spread throughout the entire apartment. She must have weighed three hundred pounds, if she weighed an ounce. The buttons on her dress had popped off as her body expanded. She was as bloated as any dead African hippo that had ever graced the pages of *National Geographic* magazine.

My boss, who was a most serious gentleman, told me that he and I would pick up Mrs. Murphy, place her body into the body bag on the stretcher, zip it up, and then maneuver the stretcher back down the three flights of stairs to the waiting hearse. Right!

I positioned myself by her feet, and when, on the count of three, we started to lift her onto the stretcher, her skin started to separate, quickly, from the bones of her legs. Her body had been slowly cooked during the previous four days in that overheated apartment.

It was all I could do to keep myself from bolting out of that hot and stinking little room. Seeing that we were unable to lift the bloated body, two of Boston's finest helped us get her onto the stretcher, down the three flights of stairs, and out to the waiting hearse.

It was shortly after this event that I discovered that nature can play a cruel trick on someone who has recently experienced the ripe smell of death. Several days later as I was relating this unpleasant story to a friend of mine, the smell of the dead woman and the stench of her apartment came rushing back to me, and they were just as powerful and overwhelming then as they had been before. I was sick to my stomach for what seemed no apparent reason.

Shortly thereafter came the event that quickly led to my decision to find a new profession. I had received a late-night call to take the hearse to the scene of an accident just outside of the blue-collar town of South Boston.

It seems that two local street gangs had been waging war upon each other for several years, and on that particular winter night one of the gang members was celebrating his sixteenth birthday with a small party of friends in an old, run-down apartment. Several members of the rival gang found out about it and "crashed" his birthday party. Then they kidnapped the honored guest, brought him to a section of tracks that was routinely used by the New Haven Railroad line. They waited until a diesel-electric locomotive approached them, and then they pushed the birthday boy in front of the oncoming train. "Happy birthday to you."

The Suffolk County medical examiner had quickly determined the cause of death (genius), and now it was up to me and several others to assist in the gruesome task of removing the boy's body from under the wheels of the engine. The poor victim lay in a number of large and seemingly unrelated pieces. I did what was required, but once the work was finished, I brought the remains of that boy back to the funeral home and announced my immediate retirement. I thought that I had seen enough to give me nightmares for a lifetime. The next morning I went into Boston to see the Marine Corps recruiter.

As I rode the subway toward Boston from West Roxbury, I remember passing by the Unicorn Coffee House, which was located on Boylston Street next to Peter Lane's Jazz Workshop. The Unicorn was one of Boston's better known semiunderground meeting places for music lovers, student activists, and hippies.

I had been there more than once because it was not an expensive place to get into, and on more than one occasion I had listened to the Jefferson Airplane perform on the small wooden stage. That was prior to the Airplane's appearance on the Ed Sullivan TV Show. After that show they became a national hit group and went *big*. The price of admission at the Unicorn went from fifty cents to five dollars just to listen to the same old group play its same old music. No one cared if the performance was good or bad because they were the *Airplane*!

The Unicorn was in the basement of an unused church, and it served a purpose in addition to the promoting of up-and-coming rock groups of the sixties. The management's first rule was to serve nonalcoholic drinks at outrageous prices, and the Unicorn was a gathering place for those of us who were under the legal drinking age (twenty-one). Between musical sets, students would get up on the small stage and speak about our country's involvement with the war in Vietnam, what stance we students should take toward draft opposition, and other important issues that were of interest to all of us at the time.

I never took an active part in these sessions other than to listen to what was being said. It was common to find all sorts of self-appointed representatives of issues, not only at places like the Unicorn Coffee House but, always, on the Boston Common and on all of the local college campuses.

Personally, I believed then that we, as a country, should be involved in stopping the war in Vietnam and that we, as students, should support the government's draft program. Those people who did not share these particular views of mine were, in my opinion, total assholes anyway. They served only to reinforce my narrow-minded opinions (as in "You can always tell a college student, but you can't tell him much").

I don't remember ever hearing any speaker who ever stood up and openly supported our government's position on Vietnam. At least none were present and preaching around the Boston area in 1968 as I rode that subway car toward the recruiting office.

There in the office marked UNITED STATES MARINE CORPS RECRUITER: ENTER, sat one squared-away Marine gunnery sergeant. There was no one else in his office. I walked in and introduced myself to him. He asked me to please take a seat, and we talked for no more than ten minutes about what I could expect from signing a four-year enlistment contract with the Marine Corps. He was honest, polite, and to the point. He said I was being stupid if I quit school, that I would be better off to go back and finish college. He suggested that I reconsider my hasty plans to enlist. He also told me that the likelihood of going straight to Vietnam, after boot camp, was extremely high. The words *cannon fodder* were brought into the conversation several times.

We struck a deal that was simple: I was to think over all the things that he had told me, then I was to talk it over with my parents and return to his office once I had made up my mind. I rode back to West Roxbury, disappointed in what options were available to me and angry at my own cowardice for not signing the enlistment contract as I had planned to do that morning.

I made up my mind that evening to return to Boston the very next day, sign whatever papers were necessary for my enlistment, and announce my plans to my family during our weekly Saturday night telephone conversation. When I entered the recruiting station the next day, the Marine Corps gunny's office was locked up tight. As I waited quietly in the hallway for him to arrive, I was approached by a Navy chief petty officer, the Navy's recruiter, whose office was only one door down the hall from the gunny's.

That chief, as I was to find out later, was the antithesis of the Marine gunny. He told me that life in the Navy was a much better affair than life in the Marine Corps. He explained the best way I could "put my two years of medical school knowledge to use in his Navy" as a hospital corpsman was the Navy's four-year enlistment program. The chief said that after I had served the Navy for three years, in grateful appreciation for my services to the fleet I would be eligible for what was called an "early out."

The frosting on the cake was the fact that in having completed almost two years of college, I would graduate from boot camp at the exalted grade level of E-2, rather than at the low, scum-sucking status of an E-1.

The chief had all the paperwork ready to go, and I signed each and every document that was put before me. Just as I was ready to leave his office, in walked the gunny. He was surprised to see me and even more surprised to learn that the United States Navy now had one new enlistee.

I was to return to the chief's office in two days for a trip to the induction center, and then after passing a small battery of dexterity tests and a physical examination, I would be sworn into the United States Naval Service.

As I was about to leave the building, the gunny invited me into his office. He shut the door and then proceeded to tell me what a first-class jerk I was for not waiting for him, and for getting involved with "that goddamned lying squid" in the first place.

The gunny was late coming to work because he had forgotten to pick up a *Boston Globe* newspaper article that he believed would interest me. Going back to get the paper had made him late. He handed me the clipping, and there in large bold print was the headline: NAVY HOSPITAL CORPSMEN AWARDED OVER 2,000 PURPLE HEARTS FOR WOUNDS RECEIVED IN VIETNAM.

After my all-day physical examination was completed and I was deemed healthy enough to serve in the enlisted ranks, I was taken back to the recruiting station for a short and rather informal swearing-in ceremony. There were handshakes and congratulations all around, and then a sudden quiet came over all of us. I was to report back a week later for transfer to the Naval Training Command Center at Great Lakes, Illinois. I was headed for boot camp.

Now the only remaining task was simply to explain to my parents—who happened to believe that I was still happily enrolled in college—that my position in life had changed, considerably.

Early on Saturday morning I hitchhiked from West Roxbury to Scituate and arrived at home just as my family was beginning to have breakfast. I had not been home in several weeks, and my mother and grandmother were very interested in my studies, my job at the funeral home, and what plans I had for the future.

I started to talk to them about school and my part-time job as the timing didn't seem just right to bring up the subject of my secret enlistment. Finally, my father asked, "What's new in Boston?" I could not hold off telling them any longer, and besides, that was why I'd just hitchhiked fifty miles.

"Well, on Thursday I joined the Navy," I said.

A thick silence hung over our kitchen table, and my mother, both sisters, and my grandmother all stopped eating. They appeared frozen; their eyes were riveted on my father, waiting for his reaction.

"Did you sign any papers?" he asked.

"Yes, I signed all of the papers that were put in front of me. I took the physical examination, and I was sworn into the Navy yesterday." Again, no one spoke a word.

"What about school?" he asked.

"I have decided to quit school, and I'll start again after I get out."

"When will that be?"

"I signed up for four years of service, but they said I can get out before that."

"Or you can be buried before that, too," he said.

Then came the questions from the rest of my family. I took each one in turn and satisfied their curiosity as to how and why I had arrived at doing the unthinkable. I received no hearty congratulations, no sincere encouragement, and no sympathy. They had collectively decided that there was an idiot in their midst, and since the deed was done, there was no use in discussing the matter further.

My sisters kept their distance from me for the rest of that day, and they avoided all conversation with me, lest my father learn that they had seen the rationale behind my reasoning, and they would then be guilty by association.

The next morning, prior to our driving to the Sunday communion service at the Episcopal Church, my father had his last discussion with me concerning my future in the service. I had waited for more than twenty-four hours before asking him his opinion as to what I had done. I wanted the dust to settle before I resurfaced this delicate issue again.

My father was an Army veteran of World War II and he had proudly served as a technical sergeant for more than four years in the Pacific theater with coast artillery and antiaircraft units. He was usually short on words and always direct in his approach to solving problems, especially if I was a part of the problem.

I had hoped that he would have given my actions some thought, comparing what I had done by enlisting to what had motivated him to enlist in 1941. Now came the moment I had been waiting for, and I asked him what he thought about my actions.

He said, "The way that I see it is that you will do one of two things. You will either nail two two-by-fours together with a rope at one end and a large boot on the other end, throw it over a tree limb and kick yourself in the ass, or you will make a career out of it." Then he walked away. There was no reason to argue, no reason to look for alternatives, and no reason for him to be pleased. The situation was accepted for what it was worth. Now the reality of what I had done began to settle in. I was on my own. I was eighteen years old. There would be no more college, no more nightmare-producing job at the funeral home, and no uncertainty over my future. I looked on this moment as a great opportunity and not as a serious mistake.

Certainly, the unknown was looming ahead, but hadn't other friends of mine enlisted, and survived? Hadn't my grandfather served in the trenches of France during World War I and made it home, even after being wounded twice and being left for dead? Didn't we have a family history of service to the country? What was the difference now?

Now it was my turn. It was my chance to prove myself, to do what I wanted to do, and not at the insistence or acceptance of my family. One weight seemed to have been lifted; another was about to take its place.

I returned to Boston for the following week, and after saying good-bye to my former employer and my friends from school, I went to West Roxbury and boxed up the few belongings that I had kept in the little studio apartment on the second floor. My last weekend, before leaving for boot camp, was spent at home with my family and friends in Scituate.

Yvonne Deschenes was a girlfriend of mine and she lived in the nearby mill town of Hope. She and I had attended high school together for four years. I had become very close to her and her family during that time, and I had kept in touch with them after I left Scituate to attend college. The Descheneses had always treated me as though I were a member of their family. I was always invited to every holiday dinner or party that was planned.

Knowing that this would be my last weekend at home and also being aware of how my family was reacting to my imminent and immediate departure, Yvonne and her parents decided to throw a going-away party in my honor. They contacted all of my friends and organized a terrific party on that Saturday night.

Her mother and father had prepared a great assortment of food and snacks and even decorated the downstairs family room for the party. There were about twenty of our former high school friends who had come to say good-bye and to wish me well.

Two close friends of mine, Charlie Hopkins and Pat Sullivan, happened to have been home on leave from Marine Corps boot camp. Yvonne was able to invite them, and they showed up at the party with several cases of beer.

They told all of us about their experiences at a place called Parris Island, South Carolina. Their stories about boot camp and their "high and tight" haircuts made them the center of attention. It seemed amazing to all of us that anyone could have possibly survived the ordeals that the two of them described in such vivid detail. But the difference in the way they looked—compared to what they looked like when they left Scituate several months earlier—was incredible.

Charlie and Pat had joined the Marines under a program called the "Buddy System." What this really meant was that if a potential enlistee could convince a friend to join the Marine Corps, the two of them would go to boot camp together and remain in the same series during their initial training. In reality, the Buddy System was a plan for mutual self-security during the misery that awaited everyone who went to Marine Corps boot camp. The Marine Corps needed bodies at the time, and this was only one of several deals that were available to enlistees then.

As their descriptions of basic training went on, and as we all drank more beer, the question was asked of Charlie and Pat as to what had happened to all of that hair that they had previously worn at shoulder length. Pat then volunteered to demonstrate how a Marine Corps–type haircut was performed on all recruits, using me as the example. Electric clippers were produced, and believing that I had nothing to lose except my hair, I got my hair cut. I was the perfect example of a high and tight in about forty-five seconds.

Pat and Charlie then congratulated themselves on the results while under the unsteadying influence of more than a few beers. They were really pleased to note that by cutting my hair, they had deprived "some stupid squid barber" of the opportunity to do the same thing to me when I arrived at boot camp. They said that the difference between a good haircut and a bad one was two days.

According to the two of them, an important part of Marine boot camp was being taught to dislike many things, and high on that list of despicable things disliked by every Marine was the U.S. Navy. I would find out all about this peculiar service rivalry in the months to come.

The party ended around 1:00 A.M. and sporting my new haircut, I drove back home. When I did wake up the next morning, the house was empty; my parents had taken grandmother with them to spend the day at the local golf course and country club where they were members. My sisters had left for the day, too.

When they did return, late in the afternoon, I was not at home. I had spent the day walking along the old roads on the reservoir property that I had traveled as a kid. For lack of use, they had long since become grown over with scrub brush.

I was certainly not too anxious to display my new look, but that was inevitable. The discovery would add insult to injury, for if the members of my family had thought me to be an idiot for enlisting, I quickly removed all doubt from their minds by looking the part, with no hair on my head.

Monday morning could not come soon enough for me, nor for them. I was driven, in silence, to the recruiting station in Boston. The great excitement that Monday was supposed to hold for me was lost in the sadness on the faces of my mother and grandmother all the way from Scituate to Boston. The saying of good-bye to them seemed, at best, superficial; I just wanted to get it over with and leave.

THE CALL

France, August first, 1914

Far and near, high and clear,
Hark to the call of War!
Over the gorse and the golden dells,
Ringing and swinging of clamorous bells,
Praying and saying of wild farewells:
War! War! War!

High and low, all must go:
Hark to the shout of War!
Leave to the women the harvest yield;
Gird ye, men, for the sinister field;
A sabre instead of a scythe to wield:
War! Red War!

Rich and poor, lord and boor,
Hark to the blast of War!
Tinker and tailor and millionaire,
Actor in triumph and priest in prayer,
Comrades now in the hell out there,
Sweep to the fire of War!

Prince and page, sot and sage,
Hark to the roar of War!
Poet, professor and circus clown,
Chimney-sweeper and fop o' the town,
Into the pot and be melted down:
Into the pot of War!

Women all, hear the call,
The pitiless call of War!
Look your last on your dearest ones,
Brothers and husbands, fathers, sons:

16

Swift they go to the ravenous guns,
  The gluttonous guns of War.

  Everywhere thrill the air
  The maniac bells of War.
There will be little of sleeping to-night;
There will be wailing and weeping to-night;
Death's red sickle is reaping to-night:
  War! War! War!

  Rhymes of a Red Cross Man
  (Robert Service)

─── BOOT CAMP ───

ABOUT TWENTY-FIVE OF US FROM THE BOSTON AREA had been sworn in together, and we were now gathered at the recruiting station for our transfer trip from Boston to boot camp. One of the older enlistees was selected by a chief petty officer to be in charge of our group, and he was given possession of a large manila envelope that contained our orders and travel documents. The Navy chief responsible for getting us to the airport had made it extremely clear that we were not to lose sight of this guy to absolutely ensure our collective departure and arrival at boot camp.

We rode in several chartered vans to Logan Airport, flew by commercial jet to O'Hare International Airport outside Chicago, and then boarded a blue U.S. Navy school bus that took us to the Naval Training Center at Great Lakes, Illinois.

Our group, now growing in size with new recruits, began in-processing by passing through several large, gray buildings in which we attended a series of televised lectures that started our basic transformation from the civilian world into that of the United States Navy.

The classes that we attended were mandatory. The subject of the first class was the Uniform Code of Military Justice. Here everyone's rights and privileges under military law were defined. The second class was a series of tests called the General Classification Test Battery. The Navy used the test results in selecting a particular career pattern for each recruit.

The next stop after these introductory administrative classes and tests was the barber shop, the first place where every man's link to the civilian world ended up on the floor. Each haircut took only thirty seconds, and the end product was universal. No one was an individual; we all looked the same. Even though I had received a

18

high and tight just two days earlier, I sat in the chair and had what few nubs remained, removed. No one escaped the barber's chair.

One of the next events during our in-processing was the issuing of uniforms and the assorted accoutrements that made up the clothing issue. We were led into a room that had three-foot squares painted on the floor. (From this point on, the floor ceased to be called the floor, it was now the "deck"; the walls were now "bulkheads," the ceiling was called the "overhead," and all stairs became "ladderwells.")

Instructed now to each stand inside one of these painted squares, we were told to strip down to our birthday suits. Standing there naked, we were shown how to get dressed by the numbers, putting on each piece of clothing, one piece at a time, as each piece was held up and described. No level of intelligence on our part was taken for granted.

Underwear, or "skivvies," were put on first, then blue dungaree trousers, belt, and a blue long-sleeve shirt. Socks, and a pair of black, half-cut boots called "boondockers," replaced shoes. A black watch cap was the finishing piece that went on top of each man's head. We looked ridiculous.

An "amnesty box" was passed before each one of us after we were dressed. It was the recruit's final opportunity to surrender dice, knives, razors, pornographic material, and anything else that could be considered contraband by the training staff.

Our civilian clothes were collected and we were told that the boxes would soon be mailed to our parents' homes. No trace remained of our civilian appearance just a few hours before. Once we were dressed as new seamen recruits, the ten-week Navy education and transformation process began. We were designated Company 389, 22d Battalion, 2d Regiment. Our company strength totaled eighty untrained and undisciplined recruits. The brigade commander was Lt. F. S. Sullivan, the regimental commander was Lt. R. A. Carlsen, and the battalion commander was WO-1 D. J. Knall.

Our company commander was MM1 Richard H. Clark. Machinist Mate First Class Clark was with us every day from well before reveille to after taps, and he was an exceptional individual. The Navy could not have found a better individual for the job. Modest and even-tempered, he tolerated no nonsense from us. He treated us with respect and earned our respect immediately.

Several weeks before his assignment as our company commander, Clark had been the recipient of the Silver Star Medal for his heroic actions while stationed on board the Navy's carrier USS

Forrestal. Clark had been a crew member on the flight deck when the ship was cruising Yankee Station, off the coast of Vietnam, a year earlier. A heat-seeking sidewinder missile accidentally went off from under the wing of a jet fighter that was positioned on the ship's flight deck. The accidental launch of the missile resulted in the catastrophic chain-reaction explosion of other aircraft, rockets, ordnance, and aviation fuel, that set the *Forrestal*'s flight deck, and many decks below, on fire.

Clark immediately organized a group of men to push five-hundred-pound bombs and loose missiles that were rolling around the deck over the side of the burning ship. His actions on that day undoubtedly saved countless lives, not to mention the saving of many Navy aircraft that were prepared to launch at the time of the tragic accident.

Like thousands of men who had undergone recruit training before us, we had now crossed over that imaginary line which separates a civilian from a serviceman. We began to learn what Navy life was all about.

The weeks of recruit training went by quickly. Each day was taken up with close-order drill, endless classes, and the studying for tests scheduled for the next day.

We practiced our close-order drill using '03 Springfield rifles. We wore puttees (better known as leggings) left over from World War I, and our daily uniform consisted of the blue dungarees, bell-bottom trousers, and shirt that we had first been issued when we had shed our civilian clothes.

Indoctrination into the Navy was more of a mental change than a physical process. Classes on naval customs and traditions, obedience to naval discipline, and Navy esprit de corps were all part of the initial process. We learned the importance of teamwork in joint tasks and the responsibility that each of us had toward his shipmates.

The purpose of shipboard damage control was to teach recruits how to fight fire on board ship, and how to defend against nuclear, biological, and chemical warfare. This, too, could only be accomplished by teamwork, but I learned a valuable lesson during the first phase of the damage-control class.

According to the damage-control petty officer instructor, that period of instruction was designed to "remove the unwarranted fear of fire," and, by so doing, enable all of us to develop confidence in our ability to "conquer fire." To do this we would have to "experience the fear of fire." I already knew that I was not particularly fond of being in a room or building that was on fire, let alone a ship's compartment, and I thought it would take much emphasizing on the part of the Navy to remove my fear.

A building called the smokehouse was used to demonstrate just how frightening conditions were during an actual shipboard fire. The smokehouse had a series of pipes running through it which emitted a thick, black, diesel smoke into a closed compartment.

We sat and watched as a generator pump began to fill the compartment with diesel smoke, and the exterior was set ablaze. We were broken down into groups of ten men each and formed into a column of twos, locked our arms together, holding on to the belt of the man directly in front, and so configured we marched like lemmings into the burning and smoke-filled compartment, under the direction of the damage-control instructors. The hatches were closed behind us.

Absolute panic took over. None of us had ever been locked inside a smoke-filled room. It was impossible to see, and our lungs quickly filled with thick, choking diesel smoke. The heat was tremendous.

We were supposed to cross the compartment to exit the other side and not lose control of our formation, but that plan collapsed immediately, and the situation became a matter of individual survival.

Some guys dropped to the floor to avoid the rising smoke, others ran or crawled toward the other side to locate the exit hatch, but the damage-control instructors would not open the hatch until we had reformed into our original configuration.

The time that we spent inside the smoke-filled compartment while we tried to regroup could not have exceeded sixty seconds, but that was all the time it took before there were pitiful screams for help, calls for God, and even one recruit crying for his mother.

It was anything but a comical situation, and it dramatically demonstrated just how quickly real panic and total confusion will take over any man no matter how well prepared he thinks he is. We felt like cowards in the presence of our shipmates, but that was because we had been the first group to be tested. The scene was repeated many times during the day until every recruit in Company 389 had been through the smokehouse.

As we left the damage-control training site, we were still coughing and puking. Our faces were blackened from the diesel smoke, and our uniforms were filthy and covered with soot. The "unwarranted fear of fire" had just been realized by every man. I don't believe that the experience had created a confidence level that would enable any one of us to "conquer fire," only to run like hell from it.

Seamanship classes brought us an entirely new language. Knot tying, ship recognition, and the principles of shipboard organization rounded out our training in seamanship. We began to talk the talk of the bluejacket.

Each week brought a personnel and a barracks inspection. We were schooled on the correct manner in which to stow our gear, how to properly make up a bunk, and how to wash and iron uniforms. The barracks were stripped bare, and the cleaning process, or "field day," started from scratch each and every week.

Swimming and individual survival at sea were considered important parts of our training curriculum. The Navy wanted to ensure that each recruit departed boot camp equipped with the methods of sea survival. Emphasis was placed on the fundamentals of swimming strokes, survival-at-sea procedures, and long flotation drills.

As we progressed with our training, a developing sense of teamwork built unit cohesion within Company 389. We spent much of our time learning the fundamentals of military drill: the sixteen-count manual of arms, marching, and physical drill using the '03 Springfield rifle. Here is where our efforts as a unit were directed toward precision and instantaneous obedience to orders.

Probably the most important subject that any of us learned during boot camp was how to live with other men in a military organization. The living conditions in the Navy differed greatly from anything that we had known in civilian life. Learning to live together in close quarters became a major mission of our recruit training.

Each recruit was given a choice of three different ratings, from among many, that he could request or "strike for." Since the operating philosophy was that the "needs of the Naval Service come first," there was no guarantee that we would get our first, second, or even third choice of rating.

I had requested only two different ratings; the first was hospital corpsman, the second was gunner's mate.

Machinist Mate First Class Clark had a formation in the squad bay, and as our names were called off, we learned what school, ship, or duty station we would go to immediately after graduation. The Navy, in its infinite wisdom, decided that it could certainly use more corpsmen than gunner's mates.

Somewhere between the time that I had taken the General Classification Test Battery, during in-processing, and just a week prior to my graduation from boot camp, it was determined that my test scores were of a general quality that would enable me to attend the Hospital Corps School located, conveniently, at Great Lakes. The school was a Navy "A" School, and would require eighteen weeks to complete before I would receive orders to my first real duty station.

Now that each man in Company 389 had received the word as to where he would go, our attention was turned to the final formal event, which was graduation parade. We practiced each morning and each afternoon for a week. The effort paid off, and this was our first chance to display newly learned abilities in military drill and bearing and to perform in our graduation parade.

The period that I remember as boot camp was only the beginning of an educational process. The experience certainly made a lasting impression on me. There were guys in my company who had never owned a pair of leather shoes until they joined the Navy. There were men who had never yet seen the ocean. There were guys you learned you could depend upon when things got difficult. The characters that surfaced within our company ranged from those types of men to barracks thieves. There was a cross section of virtually every ethnic background, religious preference, and every type of personal character, all within the eighty-man unit.

Despite each one of us always trying to hang on to our individuality, we learned that we could accomplish more as a group than as individuals. That was the value of boot camp, and it remains true to this day.

Company 389 graduated on the afternoon of 30 August 1968, and by nightfall we had all departed the Naval Training Center by taxi, plane, and bus, still innocent, but anxious to see what waited at our first duty station.

HOSPITAL CORPS
———— SCHOOL ————

THE NAVY'S HOSPITAL CORPS SCHOOL WAS LOCATED at the Naval Training Center, Great Lakes, Illinois, and the U.S. Naval Hospital was the training center for the formal school program that prepared new hospitalmen for duty with the Navy.

When those of us who had been selected for training as hospital corpsmen arrived at the school, we found that our living conditions had not changed from the open squad-bay style that we had just left behind at boot camp. The barracks were two-story wooden buildings that were steam heated. The floors were covered in black linoleum. All sixty beds were steel-frame, double-bunk beds, and the head (bathroom) had twelve evenly spaced mirrored sinks and an equal number of open-stall toilets. Vanity was apparently never a consideration for the nameless individual who designed the layout of heads for the U.S. Navy.

The Hospital Corps School's courses lasted eighteen weeks and were divided into four phases that included the study of human anatomy, hospital patient care, medications, individual first aid, and preventive medicine. The school administration arranged us into a company class that was built around three platoons of three squads with twelve men to a squad. Of course each squad was arranged alphabetically. It was there in the squad bay that we each learned how to coexist, just as we had done in boot camp.

In 1968, the United States Naval Service had strict rules concerning personal appearance, but those rules did allow for any sailor, no matter how junior in rank, to grow a mustache or beard if certain conditions were met. The individual sailor requesting permission to alter his appearance had to submit a chit (written request) which was either approved or rejected, depending upon the mood swings of the chain of command. If the request to grow a mustache or beard was approved, and most were, then the sailor was restricted to his base until his facial hair had reached an acceptable length and color that would require a new Armed Forces Identification Card to be manufactured. Until that time, no off-base liberty would be granted.

I had never attempted to grow a mustache before then, and by requesting to do so, I found a most convenient way to make some additional cash. For having attained the pay grade of E-2, hospitalman apprentice, I was receiving the worldly sum of forty-eight dollars every two weeks, whether I needed it or not. It didn't last too long. But there were a number of apprentice hospital corpsmen in our training company who were married or had girlfriends living outside the two-hundred-mile radius allowed for weekend liberty. Those truly lovesick individuals were more than willing to abide by the rules of the squad bay and pay cash to anyone who would stand in for them during their weekend duty. Once free of their duty within the squad bay, and having borrowed enough cash to get themselves outside the liberty limits, they would take advantage of their two days off.

Those of us who were trying to grow mustaches were restricted to the base, and knew that it would take anywhere from six to eight weeks before our new appearances would mature, so we stood as much extra duty as was possible. In addition to "buying duty," which was strictly forbidden, we would also lend money to our fellow sailors, thus ensuring that they had a great time while on liberty. The interest rates on these squad-bay loans was one hundred percent, payable on their following payday. If you loaned an individual one hundred dollars, he would agree to repay the lender two hundred dollars! Depending upon the reputation of the loanee and just how desperate he was to get off base, the rate was adjustable.

The true capitalists of the money-lending program were the young blond guys who tried but could never grow anything on their faces other than a half-assed mustache or beard. These fair-haired boys made small fortunes during the time they restricted themselves to the base. Interestingly, no one ever welshed on repaying one of the inflated loans as this was an accepted part of life in the squad bay.

Our life at Hospital Corps School was usually spent either in the classroom, studying, or on endless working parties. These working parties were usually work details designed to keep our squad bay clean, the outside area spotless, and the decks shipshape. If there was time for liberty after all of those barriers had been crossed, it didn't last too long. What was important at the time was to pass the weekly "phase test," to pass the weekly personnel inspection, and to pass the weekly barracks inspection.

Once we had successfully passed our classroom tests and had demonstrated a sense of practical application, we were sent to the Naval Hospital for two weeks of duty on one of the many wards. It was on the ward that, for the first time, we came face-to-face with the cruel realities of the war in Vietnam.

There were patients on those wards who had been in Vietnam less than seventy-two hours before we saw them. Most of those men were very seriously wounded, requiring them to be returned to the United States for recovery. Their overseas duty had ended, and our job had just begun. It was the policy of our government to send wounded servicemen to the military hospital that was geographically closest to their home of record. The first time that we were allowed to tour the wards of the hospital, it became obvious that the state of Illinois had sent plenty of her men off to the war in Vietnam.

Watching the new patients as they were reunited with their families certainly made for many emotional and, oftentimes, difficult moments, as mothers and fathers, sisters and wives, met with sons, brothers, and husbands for the first time since they had bid them farewell as they departed for the uncertainty of Vietnam. As apprentice hospital corpsmen, we were sent to the hospital to observe patient-care procedures more than to help. We had not graduated from corps school and were not recognized as real corpsmen. We had no real credibility, but whether we gave a little patient care or only watched, it did not take long to understand how significant was the role of the corpsman when it came to the success of the patient's total recovery.

There was no difference between those men lying in the beds on the ward and myself. I was the same age as most of them; we probably had experienced the same type of schooling, the same type of upbringing, and we had probably hoped to achieve the same types of personal goals, but there was a very real difference in what they had seen and what I had yet to witness. They had seen combat up front and close, and I had only seen its results.

As the eighteen weeks of my formal schooling came to a close, I felt confident in my newly learned abilities as a hospital corpsman. I hadn't set any scholastic record at Hospital Corps School, but I was ready to apply what I had learned to the people who would need it the most.

Upon graduation I received two sets of orders. First, I was ordered to report to the Navy's Field Medical Service School, located at Camp Lejeune, North Carolina, for additional schooling that would prepare me for duty with the Fleet Marine Force. Following that short four-week course, I was to report to the U.S. Naval Hospital at Newport, Rhode Island.

Initially, having joined the Navy to see the world, I was disappointed to learn that I was going back to Rhode Island. But I was soon to learn that duty close to home would last for only a short time.

FIELD MEDICAL SERVICE
———— SCHOOL ————

THE FIELD MEDICAL SERVICE SCHOOL (FMSS) WAS LO-
cated at Montford Point Marine Corps Base, Camp Lejeune, North
Carolina. It was administratively controlled by the U.S. Navy, but
it was operationally run by the United States Marine Corps. The
purpose of this school was to teach all Navy hospital corpsmen
how to function in a Marine Corps environment, and it was designed to introduce us to what life would be like when we were
assigned to the Fleet Marine Force (FMF) for combat duty.

I was to spend the next four weeks living in the field, learning
the small-unit tactics needed to survive under combat conditions,
and demonstrating techniques of emergency first aid that I had just
mastered during the eighteen-week course at Hospital Corps
School.

The day I arrived in North Carolina for Field Med School was
memorable. At least ten of us who had been in the same Hospital
Corps School class were on the same Allegheny Airlines flight.
Late on a Sunday afternoon in early January, we were approaching
the airport at New Bern, when the pilot's voice announced over
the intercom that we would have to circle the airport until wan-
dering cows had been escorted off of the runway. We were assured by the pilot that it was not an uncommon event for daily
flights into New Bern.

The plane landed without incident, and after collecting our
seabags, we hired one of the station wagons used as taxis to take
us to Montford Point. These taxicab owners had a great racket
going for themselves. They knew exactly what the incoming flight
schedule was for each day, and they would wait patiently by their
cabs until they had collected a group of six or seven Marines or
sailors before they would begin their trip to Camp Lejeune. We
each had to pay twenty dollars up front for the ten-mile journey to

Montford Point. This same rip-off was repeated day in and day out for all trips leaving Camp Lejeune to the airport. These local characters made thousands of dollars from the youthful ignorance of countless servicemen who had to pass through the portals of the New Bern airport. A lesson in reality, courtesy of a North Carolina taxi driver.

First impressions are the ones that last, and as I went through the age-old process of checking in that evening, it became immediately apparent that things were done much differently at this Marine Corps base than by the U.S. Navy.

The Navy petty officer third class who was on duty that night was busily spit-shining his boots when he was interrupted by our arrival. There was no telling how long he had been working on them, but they were made of black glass. The entire boot, not just the heel and toe, had been made to look like that. "These," he told us proudly, "are my field boots," and he put them on the countertop for us to inspect and admire. "Your boots will look like my boots when you fall out for the personnel inspection at 0630 tomorrow morning." It was already 2200 hours and taps was being played over the camp's speaker system. "Welcome to the FMF," was all he said as he handed us back our orders.

During our four weeks of training, we were configured like a Marine rifle company: four men in a fire team, three fire teams to a squad, three squads made up a platoon, three platoons were a company. Our actual strength for this training company was about sixty men.

We did have some hospital corpsmen in our class who had been in the Navy for years. These petty officers had finally received their orders to join a Marine unit in Vietnam, and now they had to attend and complete Field Medical Service School before going overseas. They were given responsibility for the rest of us, and initially, most of them were made fire-team leaders, squad leaders, and acting platoon sergeants.

Our first few days were administrative days; we moved into our respective barracks; we were given cold weather clothing, all of the individual equipment that was required, and then we were issued M-14 rifles.

Our barracks had been built during World War II. They were made of plywood and were not insulated; they were designed primarily for the humid weather of North Carolina. The barracks were heated by a unique system using elevated aluminum steam pipes that provided hot water to the entire camp. Each of the barracks was built above the ground, so they were extremely drafty, especially during the winter.

The equipment that we would use in the field was called "782 gear" because that was the number of the equipment custody card we signed for each item. We quickly shortened the term to "deuce gear." We were taught by the Marines on the school staff how to properly put the deuce gear together and how to wear it correctly and comfortably.

We wore the Marine Corps' green sateen utilities, and were given classes on how to iron the uniform, how to properly starch the cover, and to at least look like a Marine.

We carried our rifles with us everywhere we went. Wooden rifle racks were located in the middle of the squad bays where we locked the rifles when we were not required to carry them. (The rifle was placed in the rack, and a steel bar was placed through the trigger guard. This bar was then locked.)

We were immediately taught to disassemble and assemble the M-14. We learned how the rifle functioned, and how to keep it spotlessly clean and in proper working order. The smell of Hoppe's #9 bore cleaner filled our squad bay every day. We received the same type of classes on the .45 Colt automatic pistol, the T/O weapon for all hospital corpsmen who served with Marines. We were required to fire the pistol and we quickly learned how to use it, how to take it apart, clean it, and put it back together.

In the Navy's basic-training vocabulary, rifles were called "pieces," an old Navy term. The Marines did not adhere to any of this nonsense. A rifle was called a "rifle," not a "piece," and that lesson was reinforced with twenty push-ups by anyone who made the error of calling the Marine M-14 a "piece."

Nearly all of the Marines and the corpsmen on the staff of Field Med School were recent combat veterans, and they were greatly respected and feared by most of us. They had an unusual and often difficult job—taking Navy hospital corpsmen, reeducating us over to the Fleet Marine Force as school-trained medical technicians who could, hopefully, survive in a combat environment.

To undo what the Navy had done to us from the first day of our naval basic training, the Marines occasionally had to resort to unusual methods of instruction.

Since I was well over six feet tall, I was made the squad leader of the 1st Squad of the 1st Platoon of our training company. This was not because of any great leadership ability I might have displayed; it was based solely on my height. The Marines figured that if you were tall, you could be seen by the men assigned to your squad, so several of us tall corpsmen were given positions of responsibility. The Marines certainly did have unique methods of approaching and solving problems.

Shortly after being assigned as a squad leader, I was able to serve as a teaching aid to an individual named Staff Sergeant Bradley.

Staff Sergeant Bradley looked the part of the Marine staff non-commissioned officer. He was about five and a half feet tall, lean, had a shaved head, a bulldog's face, and he appeared to be constantly angry at the world.

Staff Sergeant Bradley had been given the task of preparing our training company for a rifle and personnel inspection in honor of a Marine Corps colonel named Bell. Colonel Bell was to inspect the Field Medical Service School, and a personnel inspection was made a part of his visit.

Bradley knew that we had never learned how to do the manual of arms with the M-14 rifle, let alone gone through inspection arms or performed close-order drill with one, and he declared to us that he was determined to present to Colonel Bell "one squared-away company of totally fucked-up Navy hospital corpsmen."

As we stood in formation for the very first time at the position of attention, Staff Sergeant Bradley demonstrated exactly how we would each bring the M-14 rifle from the position of order arms, to the proper position for inspection. He explained that when the inspecting officer stood before us, we would bring our rifle to the correct position and then wait for the officer to move to take the weapon from our grasp. When the inspecting officer moved we would "immediately let go of the goddamned rifle, and stand at the position of attention, while your rifle is being inspected."

Staff Sergeant Bradley then stated that he would demonstrate this intricate maneuver. He came to the position of attention in front of the 1st Squad leader, who happened to be me.

After going through all of the movements of inspection arms, which I had remembered from boot camp, I stood at attention with my rifle position at port arms, and waited for him to take the rifle from my grasp. Bradley moved, and I released the rifle. It smashed to the ground between us. "Pick it up," was all he said.

As I bent over to retrieve my rifle Bradley told me to assume the push-up position, and as I lay flat on the cold ground he stood on the small of my back and proceeded to tell the entire platoon that we were never to anticipate the inspecting officer's movement because it could lead to an embarrassing situation like the one we had all just witnessed. Staff Sergeant Bradley then returned to his position in front of the shocked platoon. I was told to recover, and he continued the period of instruction. No one ever dropped his rifle after that class.

Later that day, Staff Sergeant Bradley called me out of formation and said that he greatly appreciated my assistance during his class on close-order drill and then he thanked me for making all of the men aware of how easy it was to screw up during a rifle inspection. I *still* believe that this was his unusual way of offering an apology and, at the same time, not losing any face as a known disciplinarian.

When Colonel Bell did come to Montford Point on the following day, it was snowing heavily; the personnel and rifle inspections were canceled and we sat in the indoor theater and were treated to an amazing movie about the Army's success in rehabilitating soldiers who had lost their sight during World War II. The Army's Medical Department had taught them how to ski as part of their physical therapy program for the blind.

As our classes progressed, we spent more and more time in the field. We were given classes by the Marines on land navigation, basic communications, and demolitions and weapons demonstrations. The Navy side of the school taught us how to inspect a field mess for cleanliness, how to choose the proper location for latrines, and how to work properly in a company first-aid station in the field.

My fondest memories of Montford Point have always been centered around events that took place in the field. The Marines taught us a great deal about living in the bush, and we really enjoyed those classes because the practical application was usually much different than the classroom instruction. One of those memorable classes was presented to us by a Marine warrant officer. Marine warrant officers were called "gunners," and this veteran gunner gave us our first class on how to properly eat C rations and make proper use of all the items in the C-ration box. He sat on a red, wooden platform that was about four feet above the ground. We were told to sit and watch the demonstration. The gunner had with him a cardboard box banded with several strands of wire, and that box contained twelve individual meals, each in a separate cardboard box. He told us the differences between the meals. He produced a metal can opener from inside the C-ration case. The can opener was known by two names, "P-38" or "John Wayne." After opening several of the cans, he showed us how to cook the main meal by using a heat tab, and he demonstrated how to make a field expedient coffee cup, using the empty fruit can, a piece of wire from the banding material, and a stick for the handle of the cup.

We were shown how to repack the empty cardboard boxes with all of the empty cans, so that the trash could be disposed of easily.

The gunner had saved the best part of his class for last. He held up what he called an accessory pack, an envelope containing individual packets of salt, pepper, sugar, powdered coffee creamer, instant coffee, one book of matches, and, finally, four small sheets of toilet paper.

The gunner then posed a problem: how was it humanly possible for any individual to use a "cat hole," a straddle trench, or any other type of latrine, and be confident that he carried with him enough toilet paper to do the job, if given only these four pieces of toilet paper? The gunner said that countless months in the bush had given him the wisdom to solve this age-old problem.

He took the four pieces of paper and folded them in half twice. He then tore a small triangular piece from the corner tip of the paper, unfolded it, and held it up high so that we all could see the small hole he had created.

He shared his secret of victory as he explained that when used properly, we would "place the four sheets of paper over your middle finger, insert that finger into your butt, and then use the paper to clean off the soiled finger."

One hand in the audience shot up straight, and the fool asked, "Hey, Gunner—What about the little piece you tore off from the edge of paper?"

"Glad you asked, Doc. You use that to clean the shit out from under your fingernail!"

The gunner was one of the most popular instructors at Field Med School.

The Marines taught us the fundamentals of functioning as an important member of a Marine rifle platoon. Our time at Field Med School had begun with the classes that prepared us for individual actions. Now, as we progressed, we learned how Marines worked as a fire team, then as a squad, and finally as a platoon. We learned where to position ourselves in all of the different combat formations. We practiced the use of arm-and-hand signals, and learned how to protect ourselves against small-arms fire, artillery shellfire, aircraft fire, and the crushing action of enemy tanks.

During this time spent learning Marine tactics, we constantly practiced first-aid techniques, too. We used a rubber training aid called a moulage to simulate all the injuries that we could encounter in combat. We had simulated broken arms and legs, terrible head wounds, stomach wounds with exposed intestines, and simulations of white phosphorus burns. There were even moulages that squirted fake blood to simulate a severed artery.

When applied properly, the moulage looked real, and when we were in the field, someone would be designated to wear one of these devices. When we "engaged the enemy" with blank rifle fire, someone would scream "Corpsman up," and the designated corpsman would treat the injury as though it were real, even to the degree of getting emergency medical evacuation for the "injured man." Because we did it so frequently that it became routine, this quality of training was to pay off later when the call for help was for real.

The training was to culminate in a "company war," and during that three-day evolution we would be able to put to use all the field knowledge we had been taught during the past several weeks.

Three platoons from our training company were designated to operate as one unit and the fourth platoon became an aggressor unit. Both offensive and defensive tactics would be used. We had learned our lessons well, and one small incident made it apparent that some guys had learned too well.

During a combat patrol we had ambushed an enemy fire team. We had been taught that there were certain actions that took place once the firing had ceased, and part of these actions were the physical searching of the wounded and the dead for information such as maps, documents, photographs, and the like. A team of men was designated as the search-and-recovery team, and that team always included a corpsman.

We were taught by the Marines that the Vietcong and the North Vietnamese Army (NVA) regulars would "fight to the death, and then some."

What that meant was the enemy was known to booby-trap their own dead, and when seriously wounded, they would even place hand grenades under themselves in hopes of killing anyone foolish enough to move the body without first having checked for the booby trap. The way to combat this neat but evil little trick was to always use a covering team, which would aim at the suspected dead man while the search was being conducted, just in case he wasn't so accommodating. Then, if available, a rope or a length of wire would be placed around the body so that it could be dragged off the grenade without killing any of the search team. The last method used to search the dead was to physically pick up the body and then slam it back down onto the ground, giving the grenade spoon time to fly and then using the body to absorb the explosion.

In theory these actions sound easy enough to carry out, but what occurred on our patrol was closer to reality than the written lesson.

One of the corpsmen was designated to search the bodies of the four "dead enemy," and on the first three bodies, he had done exactly what he had been taught, finding no evidence of intelligence-type papers or booby traps.

The fourth "dead man" *was* booby-trapped, and as the corpsman began to search the body, he remembered to pick up the "dead enemy." As he did, the spoon from a green smoke grenade flew off and the "body" was immediately thrown down upon the grenade. Problem was, the "dead enemy" was not dead, and the smoke grenade immediately started to burn a hole through his flak jacket and into his chest. A fight broke out between them, one man trying to hold the other down on a white-hot smoke grenade. Perhaps training was taken too seriously by some of us.

After three days of combat patrolling, and three very cold nights waiting in the defensive positions that we had dug, we started to see that our training was paying off.

We quickly learned that the flak jacket was a cumbersome piece of gear. We were told that the grunts often threw away the fiberglass plates that were sewn into the jacket, making it lighter but knowing that they would lose the protection from the missing plates.

At Field Medical School I began to witness the bonding that took place between Marines and hospital corpsmen. Our Marine instructors saw the platoon corpsman as a person who fulfilled several roles. The corpsman was obviously a life link to the wounded Marines. He functioned not only as a Marine, but as a trained emergency first-aid man. He usually cross-trained Marines in his platoon as additional first-aid men.

The corpsman was also a father confessor. Marines would tell a corpsman things in confidence, and because of this unique relationship, the platoon commander or platoon sergeant knew that the "Doc" had his fingers on the pulse of the entire platoon. The position of importance that the corpsman held was never overlooked by the Marines.

Graduation from Field Med School was a short but formal affair. Our green sateen utilities had been packed and put away. Today we wore our Navy dress blues. We would all get the opportunity to wear the Marine uniform again, some much sooner than others.

We now had a military occupational specialty (MOS) of 8404. We were looked upon as school-trained emergency medical technicians who could now anticipate duty with the Fleet Marine Force.

I felt quite proud of the fact that I had graduated from the school. I now believed that when my time came, and I did join a Marine rifle company, I would be able to do the job that was required. There was no doubt in my mind that the Marines were a much more demanding group of men than the Navy, but given their mission, the Marines had to demand more from their men.

The day of graduation brought another snowstorm to Montford Point. The only way out of the area was by car. I had an airplane ticket for Providence, Rhode Island, but the airport was closed, so I teamed up with another Field Med School graduate, a guy named Pat Kelly, and the two of us made our plans to escape from the snowstorm in North Carolina.

Kelly and I had been in the same company at recruit training, the same squad at Hospital Corps School, and we were in the same platoon at Field Med School. Now we had orders to the same duty station, the naval hospital at Newport, Rhode Island. Remembering the scam of the taxicab drivers, we left Montford Point and hitchhiked toward the Raleigh/Durham airport. We heard that the airport was still operating and that we could fly to Providence from Raleigh for less.

Our first ride got us several miles away from Camp Lejeune, and the next car that stopped for us was an old, black '56 Cadillac that belonged to a black Baptist minister who was on his way to Raleigh. He had more than enough room in the trunk of his car for our two seabags, and we told him that we would pay for the gas as long as he could get us to the Raleigh airport by 3:00 P.M. He said that he could do just that as long as we could stop at his favorite restaurant for lunch.

Somewhere between Montford Point and Raleigh, and along our route, there was Tiny's Fish Camp, an all-you-can-eat catfish place that had long been the favorite of the old minister. The tenderness of the catfish, and the seasoning of the hush puppies, was all that the man could talk about. Aside from having such a strong yearning for catfish, he also mentioned that he had a talent for making wine. He told Kelly to pass the gallon jug of his home brew up to the front seat so that we all could sample his work.

After thanking the Lord for ''giving me the wisdom to make

such a holy sacrament,'' he took the first of many long pulls on the jug, and kept at it all the way to Tiny's Fish Camp. But as we pulled into the parking lot at Tiny's, the front door opened and out stepped one of North Carolina's "good ol' boys." The man must have weighed 350 pounds and he crammed every ounce of it into his old Ford pickup truck. We went into Tiny's as the Ford truck left the parking lot.

As the three of us took up a stool at the counter the cook said, "I hope you guys weren't plannin' on any catfish, 'cause the guy who just left here cleaned me out." After settling on some of Tiny's barbecued pork instead of the much-talked-about catfish and hush puppies, we were again on the road to Raleigh.

The minister was true to this word, and Kelly and I did arrive at the Raleigh airport in time to catch our flight to Providence. We laughed like hell as the big black Cadillac swerved away. The minister was completely shit-faced, but nonetheless happy for having been able to help us on our way to Newport.

NEWPORT NAVAL
——————— HOSPITAL ———————

THE FLIGHT THAT HAD TAKEN PAT KELLY AND ME away from North Carolina landed at the Rhode Island State Airport, in the town of Warwick, around 5:30 P.M. The storm that we had tried to outrun in the south had quickly moved up the eastern coast, and was now dumping snow all over southern New England.

We took a shuttle-service van to Providence, the Ocean State's capitol, and from Providence we rode by bus toward Newport, on the shores of Narragansett Bay.

The snow continued to accumulate as we traveled the forty miles from Providence south to Newport, and because of the steady increase of snow, our one-hour trip had become a three-hour crawl by the time the bus had arrived at the Newport station.

No cabs were moving due to the storm, but Kelly and I both knew where the naval hospital was, so still wearing our dress blue uniforms, we began the two-mile walk to the hospital at 10:00 P.M. The weight of our seabags, combined with the ice on the streets and the poor traction that leather-soled service shoes provided, made the walk almost impossible. When Kelly and I finally arrived, around midnight, we walked into the main hospital building and asked the corpsman seated behind the information/duty desk to point us in the direction of the barracks, then shouldered our seabags again and walked a short distance to an old, brick, three-story barracks that was used for permanent personnel.

The petty officer on duty in the barracks that night was known as the master at arms (MAA), and he quickly showed us the way to an empty, cold, and open squad bay, our home for the next five months.

The MAA told us to pick out any rack and wall locker that we wanted to use, and as we began to unpack our gear, he brought us each a set of fresh linen, a pillow, and two woolen blankets. We were told to "hit the rack, but be ready to shovel snow at 0600."

When 0600 arrived, Kelly and I were standing outside in a formation with a dozen other shivering corpsmen. The snowstorm had ended at some point during the night, leaving over two feet of snow on the ground, but the snow-shoveling detail lasted only an hour.

Reporting back to the master at arms, we were told to go and eat breakfast before officially reporting in for duty.

Kelly and I then managed to find the petty officer in charge of personnel assignments and went into his small office. We had brought our service records books (SRBs) with us, and we presented them to a corpsman second class (HM2) named White. White talked with each of us as he looked over our record books, and then he asked me what type of ward did I want to work on. I told him that it really made no particular difference to me, but if there was an opening on a surgical ward, I would gladly go there.

Kelly made the mistake of giving Hospital Corpsman Second Class White a smart-ass reply about wanting to work on any ward where there wasn't too much to do. White was not amused. He had had a tour of duty with the Marines in Vietnam, and had been wounded four times. He did not have the temperament to deal with a wise-guy hospitalman apprentice who was not serious about working on one of his wards. He immediately assigned Kelly to the sick officer's quarters (SOQ), telling him that this particular ward was the least desirable of the six hospital wards there and assignment to the SOQ might serve to quickly change Kelly's outlook on life.

White sent the two of us up the stairs and in the direction of Ward D, the dirty surgery ward. The SOQ ward was located one flight above Ward D. I said good-bye to Pat Kelly, and that was the last I would see of him for several weeks. Hospital Corpsman Second Class White wasn't kidding about duty on the SOQ.

Ward D's patients were recovering from infected ("dirty") surgery. There were twenty-six beds on the ward, which was practically full. I walked down the center of the ward to the nurse's station and introduced myself to Navy Lt.(jg) Sandra Wright, the senior nurse in charge of this ward. Lieutenant Wright introduced me to two other corpsmen assigned to the ward, and I was instructed, "stay close to Doc Harrison, and he will show you the ropes."

Life on Ward D was always a learning experience. The work day was divided into three shifts; A.M.s went from 0700 to 1500,

P.M.s from 1500 to 2100, and night duty was from 2100 to 0700. Each new ward corpsman began his life as a "ward coolie" on the A.M. shift, and that duty lasted for at least two weeks.

The work tempo on the ward was based strictly as to the time of day.

At 0700 the A.M. corpsmen crew arrived on the ward and listened to the ward report that was given to the incoming nurses and corpsmen by the outgoing night shift. Patient admissions that occurred during the previous night were reviewed, and the ward report was an oral explanation of what was to be accomplished on the ward during the A.M. shift by the nurses and corpsmen.

After the ward report was completed, the daily routine began. Breakfast trays were collected from the bedsides and moved to a cart destined for the kitchen; all the beds were stripped and the linen was changed. Ambulatory patients managed their own linen change; those who could not move had the linen changed by the ward corpsmen with help from ambulatory patients. Self-help was the rule.

Medications were then given out, and the ward was cleaned and made ready for the morning visit by the doctor. The individual needs of every patient were met, and corpsmen were educated by the nurses and doctors during the morning visits as to particular types of treatment required for the various injuries that were being treated.

Lunch was delivered at noon, and usually from 1300 to 1500 quiet hours were observed throughout the hospital. At 1500 the P.M. shift came onto the ward; the ward report was repeated for them, and the P.M. crew took over. The procedure was repeated for the night shift by the P.M. crew.

The P.M. shift on all wards lasted at least two weeks and at the end of that shift the corpsmen were given two days off. The nurses, however, were given four days off. The night shift was worked only by corpsmen who were dependable, because only one corpsman was assigned to each ward during the night shift, and one nurse usually covered two, or even three, wards during the same time. At the end of the night shift, which lasted three weeks, the corpsmen were given three days off, and the nurses received a gracious five days off.

Working three shifts with such long hours, there grew to be a very close relationship between the corpsmen, the nurses, and the patients on Ward D.

During my first several weeks of working on the A.M. shift I met HM2 Terry Daily, who worked for Lieutenant Commander

Junkin, our ward doctor and the resident hospital proctologist. The procto clinic was located at the entrance to the ward, and between appointments in the clinic, Terry would come onto the ward and tell me about his experiences with a Marine reconnaissance company where, as a recon team corpsman, he had been awarded the Silver Star Medal for heroism.

When he did take the time to talk with some of us new ward corpsmen about Vietnam—something most of the senior petty officers avoided—Terry was always honest and sincere. He was considered one of the best corpsmen at the hospital, and to this day I owe him a personal debt of thanks for the advice that he gave me and for steering me in the right direction.

One of the first real patient "characters" that I encountered on the ward was a Marine private, a fat, loudmouthed clown who tried to intimidate the new ward corpsmen. He could be counted on for starting some sort of trouble on a daily basis. He tried to sleep in after being told to get up. He refused to eat. He "borrowed" things from other patients while they were sleeping. Argumentative, he was considered a general pain in the ass to all who came in contact with him.

He had told those few people who cared to listen about his combat experiences in Vietnam, and listening to the guy, he had practically won the war by himself. His glorious self-image took a great turn for the worse when one of the ward's new corpsmen reviewed his medical record and announced to the dozen Marines on Ward D that the patient's infected leg wound did not actually come from an AK-47 round during his unit's assault on an enemy-held hill but was, in fact, a self-inflicted wound. The Marine private had been with a supply unit located near Da Nang, and when the unit had volunteered him for duty with a Marine rifle company, he decided not to go.

The sad part about the entire incident was that the coward had tried to shoot himself in the leg, but the bullet had glanced off a bone, changed direction, and then shattered his foot.

After the secret of the wound was exposed, the other Marines on the ward would have nothing to do with him. They said it wasn't so much the fact that the man was a known coward that alienated them, it was the simple fact that he couldn't even shoot himself in the leg without screwing up the job. He made the Marines on the ward look bad by his poor example.

Another Ward D Marine patient from Vietnam during that time was Lance Corporal Makalandra, who was from Woonsocket, Rhode Island. In Vietnam he had been a scout-dog handler during his tour. While on a patrol he had pushed open a booby-trapped bamboo gate, and the subsequent explosion had sent dozens of fragments into his lower body (his back had been protected by a flak jacket). Makalandra's prognosis for a full recovery was very good, and when he first arrived on the ward he said that all he wanted to do was return to Vietnam, and "get the little slant-eyed bastard who set up the booby trap."

Each morning when I arrived on the ward for A.M. duty, I would help Makalandra change his bed linen, and as the sheets were stripped from the bed, I heard the strange but unmistakable sound of metal hitting the linoleum floor. The shrapnel had worked itself out of this Marine's body during the night. We saved all of these pieces of metal, as well as those that I was able to remove with forceps, and within several days we had collected over fifty grenade fragments. He kept them in a jar.

The weeks of normal duty on the ward passed by quickly. I felt comfortable with the ward routine, and I was soon working on the P.M. shift with more responsibility and far less supervision. Instead of two nurses and three corpsmen on the ward for the A.M. shift, P.M.s had only one ward corpsman, and shared a nurse with several other wards.

It was not too long after my assignment to P.M.s that I was promoted to hospitalman (HN), pay grade E-3. The word "apprentice" was deleted from my rating, and I received an increase in pay of thirty-eight dollars per month. I was then the senior corpsman of Ward D, and I was responsible for teaching newly assigned corpsmen how to work on *my* ward.

The working relationship between the nurses and the corpsmen could not have been better. We were really a family, and there were never any personality problems that could not be quickly resolved.

The system for feeding all of the people that were assigned to the hospital was called "the mess," and the galley, or kitchen, was the center of that operation. The permanent personnel ate in one dining area, patients who were not assigned to a ward were allowed to eat in another area. Patients assigned to a ward selected their own meals from a menu, and food was delivered to the ward on a cart.

The chief cook for the hospital was a guy named Stan. Stan was also an avid fisherman, and whenever he managed to get some time off, he pursued the striped bass that were found in Narragansett Bay. His speciality was the baked, stuffed striped bass that was served each Friday to the hospital personnel. Stan also had some connections with the local Rhode Island lobstermen, and it was not uncommon to find baked lobster offered on the menu to all the hospital's patients.

When those of us who were assigned to the P.M. shift knew that lobster was to appear on the menu for the Friday noon meal, we would find out what patients on the ward didn't want their lobster, then offer to bring them whatever they wanted to eat from town in exchange for the lobster. It was surprising how many of the ward patients didn't care for lobster. By the time we began the Friday P.M. shift there were usually a half dozen lobsters saved from the noon meal and conveniently placed in the ward refrigerator.

We would take the lobster down to the proctology clinic, post a guard outside, heat up the steam autoclave (normally used for sterilizing surgical instruments), then return to the ward and enjoy a reheated lobster dinner. Our dissection of the lobsters was made easier by using the instruments in the suture-removal packs to extract the meat from the little red bodies.

During April the ward received a new patient, a Marine Corps staff sergeant who had been wounded in a firefight then injured when his medevac helicopter was shot down. The staff sergeant was visited by his girlfriend regularly, and one evening she brought him a pint of vodka to make his suffering a little more tolerable. At 2000 hours all visitors were asked to leave the ward, and the ward lights were turned off. As I sat at the desk located at the end of the darkened ward, I heard the unmistakable sound of a wheelchair as it squeaked toward me. There, in the faint light cast by the desk lamp, was the staff sergeant, quite talkative and quite inebriated. This was a new experience for me, as alcohol was not tolerated on the ward, and making the situation worse was the fact that Lieutenant Commander Hermann was the P.M. shift nurse. She had a well-known reputation for being difficult with the patients and was extremely demanding of the ward corpsmen. Miss Hermann, as she was called, was easily recognizable because she wore those ridiculous black horn-rimmed Navy glasses that made her look like every kid's nightmare vision of his worst elementary schoolteacher. I knew that if she showed up, found the staff sergeant half in the bag and in a wheelchair instead of in his traction bed, I would be in serious trouble.

All the staff sergeant wanted was for me to bring him some orange juice so that he could add his remaining vodka to it, and then he would return to his rack, medicated for sleep. I went and got the orange juice; he added vodka and then offered me a drink. I didn't refuse, and as I lowered the coffee cup from my face, there before me stood Lieutenant Commander Hermann, NC. I knew then that I was going to the brig.

Commander Hermann asked the staff sergeant what he was doing out of bed, and before he could answer, I asked her if she would like a cup of coffee, hoping to divert her attention. She asked me what I was drinking, and when I told her orange juice, she said that sounded better than coffee. As I headed toward the coffee mess room to get her a cup, the staff sergeant began telling her about how great it was to be back in the States. She sat down at the desk to listen to him and picked up the coffee cup loaded with orange juice and vodka and took a mouthful.

An unfamiliar look took over her face; she smiled. She got up from the chair, simply said "Good-bye" to the sergeant and me, and walked off the ward. Amazingly, she never mentioned the incident to anyone.

We had received two new patients on the ward during my second tour of the P.M. shift. The first patient was a petty officer I'll call Able Baker, who had broken his right ankle several weeks before. Able was on the mend until one evening when he decided to visit several of Newport's finer drinking establishments. At one of them, for some reason, an altercation took place in which one of the participants jumped on Able's already-broken ankle and refractured it. Already feeling no pain, he was admitted to the ward.

The same day that Baker was admitted to the ward, a Seabee petty officer I'll call John Doe arrived on Ward D. Doe had fractured his right arm while on an overseas assignment; the fracture had become infected, and that bought him a ticket to the naval hospital at Newport.

These two individuals soon became close friends, and Doe helped Baker around the hospital by pushing his wheelchair whenever the two of them were able to leave the ward.

One evening, during my third week on the night shift, I was surprised to learn that both Baker and Doe had failed to return to the ward before taps (2200 hours). At 0200 I was seated at the desk at the head of the ward, and I noticed the light from the elevator as it shined out into the hallway. Just as the doors closed, a dark colored laundry bag was pushed out into the hallway. Then, as I looked down the long corridor from the ward's desk to the elevators, I heard the sound of someone softly crying.

I took the flashlight from the desk and walked down the ward toward the abandoned laundry bag, and as I shined the light onto the bag, it began to move. It was Doe. He was covered in blood, and he was going into shock. I ran back to the nursing station, woke up one of the ambulatory patients, told him to telephone the SOQ ward, explain what had happened, and have the duty nurse get down to my ward. I sprinted back to Doe with an emergency medical bag and began to apply bandages to his lacerations. I asked Doe where Baker was, and he replied, "He's in the head, dying."

I ran to the head. There stood Able, up on his crutches, in a pool of his own blood, trying to urinate into a sink. He was oblivious to his own situation. His nose had been practically severed from his face, and he had deep multiple lacerations on his head and arms.

I placed him in one of the wheelchairs that had been left in the head. I replaced his nose where it should have been on his face, and then I began to bandage his head, face, and arms.

Baker now asked about Doe. I told him that Doe was all right, and that I was going to take the both of them down to the emergency room, two floors below.

I opened the door to the head, pushed Baker's wheelchair out into the hallway, and when the elevator arrived, I pushed in Baker and dragged in Doe. When the doors opened, I got the two of them out of the elevator, ran down the hall to the emergency room and got the ER corpsman to come and help me.

Both Doe and Baker were brought into the ER by the corpsman. I explained to the doctor what I had found and what I had done for them and I headed back to the ward.

When the charge nurse came onto Ward D from the SOQ, I was nowhere to be found. The patient who had made the telephone call to the SOQ's desk wasn't sure why I needed her, and he really couldn't give her any details. When I did show up on the ward, she began to read me the riot act, reminding me about leaving, unattended, the twenty-two patients who were dependent upon my presence at all times. I could not get a word in edgewise. It was at this time that one of the duty corpsmen from the ER came onto the ward and, in interrupting her, explained on my behalf what had happened to Doe and Baker.

When they had decided to leave the hospital, a mutual friend lent them a car. They then went barhopping on Jamestown Island, got drunk, and with Doe behind the wheel and racing back toward the hospital, they rolled the car coming off the Newport Bridge exit half a mile from the hospital. Doe pulled Baker from the wrecked vehicle, and they began their crawl back to the hospital, hoping to sneak back onto Ward D, unnoticed.

The corpsman from the ER was named Mike Barry, and he also explained to the charge nurse that if I had not stopped their bleeding and gotten them to the ER when I did, they might have died from the loss of blood and shock.

Somewhere close to 0500, Baker and Doe were returned to the ward. They had been X-rayed, sutured up in the ER, given some pain medication, bathed, and put into hospital pajamas.

When Dr. Junkin came onto the ward that morning, he peeled the sheets off of a sleeping Baker and Doe to take a look at the previous night's damage. Baker woke up and asked the doctor if they were going to be charged with unauthorized absence. The doctor just shook his head no, and said that they had already paid the price for their stupidity. It would now be several more weeks on the ward before they would be discharged.

It was reassuring to me that Doe and Baker had the presence of mind to try and return to the hospital after the accident. It was also a good feeling to know that they felt safe about coming back to the ward where they knew they would receive care, even in their drunken stupor.

The doctor who had been on duty in the ER when I brought in Doe and Baker came up to the ward to talk with me the next evening as I began the night's duties. He said that he was looking for some new corpsmen for emergency-room duty and asked if I would be interested in that type of an assignment.

Lieutenant Wheatley had a great reputation not only as a doctor but with all of the corpsmen in the emergency room at the hospital. He had done a tour of duty with the "Charlie Med" Battalion located in the northern part of South Vietnam. He spent a great deal of time teaching the emergency-room corpsmen those skills that would help them in treating trauma situations.

Mike Barry, an HM3, and a corpsman named Frank Hanhs, had spoken to Doctor Wheatley concerning my being assigned to the ER, and the incident the night before with Doe and Baker, which helped in the selection process. I was notified that I would be going to the emergency room for duty the following week. I then went to the hospital's administrative office and requested orders to Vietnam.

I had mixed emotions about leaving Ward D, but the patients I had seen over the past four months would be well cared for, and most of them would be discharged from the ward, only to be replaced by new names and faces. I did look forward to the new demands in the ER, and I hoped that I would be able to learn to work in that type of environment.

One of my last duties on the ward was to nominate to the ward nurses my replacement as senior ward corpsman. Four nurses worked the three shifts covering the ward: Sandra Wright, Jan Tallmadge, Nancy Lyon-Vaidon, and Sandy Busom. These nurses were all seated around a table in the solarium, prior to the ward report being given, and their conversation turned to travel.

Several of the nurses said that they had been to the Bahamas, one nurse said that she had been to Canada and Mexico. Each was trying to better the other with their story. It was at this moment that a ward corpsman named Ronnie La Mountain stated that he had gone around the world, and this news started the nurses talking about how wonderful it must have been to have done this, being so young and able to afford such an undertaking. La Mountain smiled, and said that he had gone around the world in Buffalo one night, and it had cost him thirty dollars. Those of us who knew what he was talking about laughed so hard at this stunning declaration that tears came to our eyes.

La Mountain became my immediate choice for senior corpsman. Anyone who could handle the job of senior corpsman and still have a sense of humor would be an asset to the ward staff. La Mountain got the job.

Duty in the emergency room was better than I could have imagined. The majority of people who came in were dependents seeking treatment for coughs, colds, influenza, and similar ailments, and many of them came into the ER after attending church services each Sunday. The church was conveniently located on the hospital grounds. Hospitalman Second Class Frank Hanhs was one of the senior corpsmen assigned to help run the emergency room. Occasionally, when the shift was slow and there was a little free time, he would tell us about some of his experiences in Vietnam. We would sit in the admissions office, fascinated, as he related the funny and sometimes sad stories about his tour with a Marine infantry platoon. His stories were always about someone other than himself, but following one of these sessions, another senior corpsman waited until Hanhs left the office and then told us a story about Frank.

"When Hanhs takes the time to share some of his war stories with you, I hope you pay attention. He is a real hero. He won't talk about himself, but I think you should know about him. He was awarded the Silver Star for what he did one night when his platoon made contact. During the firefight, one of the Marines in his platoon was badly wounded, almost having his leg blown off. There was no way that a medevac bird could land to take out any of the casualties because of the intensity of the enemy fire. Frank knew that this Marine would bleed to death if he didn't do something. He had already used up the plasma bottle that he carried with him. As a last resort, Frank positioned the wounded Marine below him on the ground, and by using a tourniquet, the plasma tubes, and gravity, he transfused his own blood into the Marine during the night. He saved the guy's life at the risk of his own. In the morning, the wounded Marine was still alive to be evacuated to a hospital ship. Think about that!''

It was Hanhs who also taught us the techniques of fine suturing. A board was wrapped in a towel and the towel and board were covered with a chamois skin. We would take a scalpel and cut the chamois at different points and then practice suturing the cuts. The finished product was then graded by Hanhs or one of the ER doctors, and this process was repeated often, so that the actual suturing of lacerations was routine. The only time that we were not allowed to suture was when it involved a serviceman's dependent with a facial laceration.

The use of drugs by U.S. Naval personnel had not yet become an everyday problem in the later part of the 1960s, but one episode in the Newport ER comes to mind. We had received a call from a dispatched ambulance driver that he was bringing in a dependent wife who was "experiencing some sort of violent behavior." When the ambulance arrived at the hospital, the lady was immediately brought into the ER, and she remained physically restrained in the stretcher while she was examined. She was hallucinating. Most of us had never witnessed anything like that before, and the staff did not know initially what was wrong or how to treat her condition.

As the hallucinations subsided, she was medicated and became sleepy. The doctor on duty began to question the woman's husband concerning her medical history. She had been healthy, had not been under any type of medical treatment, and her condition posed a great mystery as to how she could be in this dangerous situation. Finally, the husband confessed to the doctor that he had obtained some LSD from one of his friends and, though he was afraid to take the drug himself, he had slipped it into her drink to await her reaction to it before he dared try it himself. After hearing this admission, the senior corpsman in the ER asked the husband to accompany him to one of the unoccupied examination rooms, and there he quickly knocked the husband out cold with one good shot to the jaw.

One of the last memorable incidents that took place prior to my departure from the naval hospital was the party that was thrown to celebrate two great happenings in June. The hospital's spring softball team had experienced a winning season, and Doctor Wheatley was going on leave to honeymoon in the Bahamas. Here was an opportune time for the corpsmen to celebrate. The Old Narragansett Cafe was the place where the hospital's softball team always rendezvoused after each practice, team meeting, and game. It seemed only fitting for Doctor Wheatley, a team member, to have his bachelor bash coincide with the softball team's victory party.

On that particular Friday night the bar was packed and pitchers of ice-cold Narragansett beer lined the mahogany bar. Incredibly stupid speeches were made, poor fielding plays became great athletic achievements, and Doctor Wheatley's secret wedding plans became common knowledge. Those corpsmen who had been associated with the good doctor the longest knew that his tolerance for beer was low, but he was a first-to-arrive-and-last-to-go type of guy.

The softball team members, in what appeared to be the evening's last celebratory gesture, hoisted the unsuspecting Doctor Wheatley onto their shoulders and took him outside and across the street, and promptly threw him into the cold waters of Newport Harbor.

After the cheering and laughter subsided, several corpsmen lent him a hand and pulled him from the cold water and onto the dock. Doctor Wheatley was then unceremoniously stripped of his trousers and skivvies, only to have gentian-violet dye applied to one particular part of his anatomy, as a "gift" to the bride from the corpsmen in the ER. How the doctor explained his immediate case of "blue balls" to his bride remains his secret.

My orders for duty in Vietnam arrived at the hospital shortly after that event, and I made plans to leave Newport and return home to Scituate for a few days before flying due west.

Duty at the Newport Naval Hospital was one of the finer experiences of my life. The people whom I was privileged to serve with there left their mark as the finest naval personnel that I have ever met. I was confident that the skills I had acquired, on Ward D and while working in the emergency room, would serve me well at my next assignment. I left Newport hoping that I would be fortunate enough to return there after my next tour of duty.

When I went home to Scituate, it was really for one purpose, to walk the familiar, overgrown trails around the reservoir. I knew from having spoken with corpsmen who had returned from Vietnam that I stood an excellent chance of not returning, or at least a good chance of being wounded. I thought that I was mentally prepared, but I was young, and I was soon to discover that I had been foolish enough to believe myself.

My parents, accompanied by my two sisters and my grand-mother, drove me to the airport. It was one of those awkward moments that all sons experience when they face the grave un-certainty of a good-bye; no matter how old you are, you are still a kid in the eyes of your mother and father.

The one thing that I recall from that farewell was my mother's strict warning not to return home with an Oriental wife. Old ways die hard, and for some people who lived through the second World War, the Oriental was still the enemy.

- STAGING ON OKINAWA -

MY OVERSEAS ODYSSEY STARTED WITH A COMMER-
cial flight from Providence, through Chicago. Eventually I arrived, midafternoon, at Travis Air Force Base outside of San
Francisco. After checking in with the people who prepared the
flight manifest, I learned that my flight to Okinawa would not
leave until 0400.

I knew no one in the busy terminal, but that situation changed
when a Navy senior chief hospital corpsman introduced himself to
me and asked if I, too, were headed to Vietnam. He must have
seen people like me before.

The chief offered to buy me a beer so we left the main terminal
and walked to one of the enlisted ranks' bars, where the old chief
told me a number of stories about his tours of duty with different
Marine Corps units. Most of what he told me concerning his combat
experiences was encouraging, and whatever apprehension I may
have exhibited gave way to my being anxious to leave Travis Air
Force Base for Okinawa. I just wanted to get on with it.

The chief had managed to drink half a dozen double scotches
during our endless wait for departure, and soon he was mumbling
something about needing some food to soak up all of the cheap
booze he had just put into his empty stomach. We left the club and
went to the all-night cafeteria hoping to solve the chief's problem.

The only food that appealed to the chief was a very large slice of
blueberry pie, and after he had bought and paid for his pie and my
coffee, we sat down at a table not far from the marshaling area.

The chief had more than a little trouble in bringing his fork to
his face, and he was soon wearing more of the pie than he had
eaten.

Frustrated at his inability to maintain his military bearing, he
picked up the stainless-steel napkin dispenser and proceeded to

use both sides of this device to wipe the blueberry pie stain from his face. His solution to the problem drew the immediate attention of a pair of the Air Force security police officers, and the chief was immediately escorted, under some protest, out of the cafeteria and toward the receiving end of an Air Force blue paddy wagon. It vanished into the night. Good-bye, Chief.

Without the dubious benefit of the chief's company, I went outside and found an unoccupied bench and tried to get some sleep, but the continuous roar of jet engines taxiing on the runway made the attempt impossible. I was only able to close my eyes between takeoffs and landings until 0330, when our flight number was called out over a loud speaker, requesting all embarking personnel to move to the ready circle and await the final preparations for boarding. Nearly two hundred men, representing all the branches of the services, were assigned to the same flight.

We flew on a commercial jet that had been chartered by the Military Aircraft Command (MAC) from Travis Air Force Base north to Anchorage, Alaska. When we landed, we were instructed to move from the aircraft to a holding area inside of the main terminal. We were a captive audience for the capitalists of Alaska.

The single open snack bar will always be remembered by every serviceman who passed through the Anchorage, Alaska airport. There a cup of coffee cost $1.00; a hot dog cost $2.00; a small hamburger was $3.50; a cup of orange juice was $2.00. Those individuals who were headed overseas for their second tour, and had experienced this same situation before, had that smug, I-told-you-so look written on their faces. It was that look the informed use on the ignorant.

Once refueled, our plane left Anchorage for the air base at Sasebo, Japan, ten hours away. We stayed at Sasebo for less than two hours, then proceeded south to the island of Okinawa, with about half of our original number of passengers.

Kadena Air Force Base was the flight's final destination, and I then went by bus from Kadena north to the Marine Corps base at Camp Hansen, located on the eastern Pacific shore, halfway up the island.

Camp Hansen was the principal receiving area for Marines and corpsmen who were awaiting flights to the Republic of Vietnam. I was processed into the camp and was assigned to live in one of the open squad bays with a dozen other hospital corpsmen. We were told that we would be there, in staging, for four or five days before another flight was scheduled to leave for the Air Force base at Da Nang.

While we were at Camp Hansen, we were assigned to help the permanent medical personnel with the screening of health records so that each Marine would enter Vietnam with an updated medical record. That meant that all departing Marines and corpsmen would have their immunization records updated as well.

One of the best rumors then being circulated concerned an injection that was known as the "GG shot." GG stood for gamma globulin, and all Marines and corpsmen received that injection prior to leaving Okinawa for duty in Vietnam. The rumor had it that the GG shot, though painful to receive, was designed to speed up blood-clotting time, and once we had the shot, we were in no immediate danger of bleeding to death if we were unfortunate enough to be wounded.

For a squad bay rumor this was a good one, and it was not dispelled because no one wanted to bleed to death. The GG shot was a large, ten cc injection that was normally delivered to the cheek of one's butt, and if the sciatic nerve is hit with the misdirected needle, then the recipient of the injection will, unfortunately, have to limp around the area for several days. In reality, the GG shot was meant to treat infectious viral blood diseases, like hepatitis, and it had absolutely nothing to do with blood-clotting times. The only humorous outcome of this necessary procedure was to witness the dozens of Marines, and a few unlucky corpsmen, walking around Camp Hansen looking as though they were impersonating Chester from the television series "Gunsmoke." To them, the ordeal of the dreaded GG shot was not funny.

Those of us who were in staging were required to meet three times each day, at musters, during which important information was passed to all transient personnel explaining the plan of the day, and detailing who would be assigned to the various working parties during the periods between formations. The musters were designed only to take up waiting time and account for our whereabouts.

All transient hospital corpsmen were sent to the dispensary for our work periods, and we were not required to do the menial tasks that the junior Marines were assigned, like picking up paper and cleaning up the filthy squad bays.

At our first morning formation, we were given the scoop about liberty—there was none. Those people who had attained the pay grade of E-6, or above, were granted off-base liberty, and those personnel of lesser grade were confined to the limits of Camp Hansen. Personnel in the pay grades of E-4 and E-5 were invited to use the "45 Club"; and the rest of us could visit the enlisted

club, commonly known as the animal pit, which opened its doors
at 1800 hours. The enlisted club was the scene of numerous fist-
fights and real barroom brawls. The reasons for the fights were as
varied as the Marines who were involved, but they were an every-
night occurrence. One Marine would accuse another of staring at
him, and the fight was on. One Marine would insult another by
telling him that because he had graduated from boot camp in San
Diego, he was considered to be a "pussy," or a "Hollywood
Marine," as only Marines who had graduated from boot camp at
Parris Island were "real Marines." The animal pit was a cross
section of Marine humanity that would have been a psychologist's
dream come true.

On my third night in the animal pit I was seated in a booth with
another corpsman and three Marines. Their conversation turned to
the importance of one Marine taking care of another during combat. Even though none of the three Marines had ever seen any
combat, they believed that they should make a binding pact, right
then and there, agreeing to one never leaving the other on the field
of battle.

The exact wording of this important oath could not be readily
agreed to, so several more rounds of beer were required before any
of the three was close to acceptance. The other "Doc" and I were
invited to witness the contract and sign our names to the pledge,
making it "legal."

A paper towel was brought from the head, and their oath of
mutual allegiance was written out and then signed by all three
Marines, and witnessed by the other corpsman and myself. As the
three stood to shake hands and congratulate one another, the small-
est Marine, a private, sucker punched the largest one, also a
private, knocking him out cold. He then turned and announced to
all, "I've known that asshole since boot camp, and I don't believe
that he would cover me if I were hit." Everyone around us understood his concern, and the fallen Marine was put back in our
booth as drinking resumed. Marines take care of their own.

Only four things could be consumed in the animal pit: beer,
soda, stale popcorn, and cigarettes. The beer, soda, and cigarettes
cost only a quarter; the stale popcorn was free. The place was a
dump, but many a lasting friendship had its origin in the animal
pit. For some reason, probably known only to the Joint Chiefs of
Staff, hard liquor was never made available at a servicemen's club
to anyone in pay grades of E-3 or below although it is they who
have always made up the majority of the ground fighting forces.
Of course, the animal pit really didn't need hard liquor as the

amount of beer that was consumed nightly certainly filled any void that may have been left by the absence of hard stuff.

Four endless days passed on the island of Okinawa until my name was finally called out at the 1630 formation, verifying my existence, and informing me of my flight number and the time of my departure for Da Nang. Now, with less than twelve hours remaining, there were a few things of great importance that I had to remedy.

I had flown from Providence, Rhode Island, to Okinawa in my Navy dress blue uniform. That woolen uniform would not be necessary in Vietnam. The green sateen utility uniform was the working uniform for Marines. I was now able to box up my dress blue uniform and send it back home. I had been issued three sets of utilities at Field Medical Service School, and I was ready to put that uniform on.

One of the things that I had learned from the older Marines while waiting to depart for Vietnam was that the appearance of one's boots was particularly important. It was routine to shine boots each evening so that they would look sharp at the next morning's inspection, but now, the shined boot was the unwelcomed mark of the FNG (fuckin' new guy), a NIC (new in country), or newbie. It was necessary to remove that look from my boots, lest I be accused by anyone of what was obvious. By 1900 I had two smartly ironed sets of utilities and I had obtained from a dumpster one pair of scuffed, well-used combat boots, ready to wear on the next day's flight. At least I looked ready.

I walked down to the animal pit with several other corpsmen, as this would be our last opportunity to get drunk together, and we, too, sat in a booth and discussed our chance for individual survival after landing in Vietnam. Our chance to discuss the possibilities was short lived because a Marine ran into the club and announced that there was some guy up on top of the water tower getting ready to jump. This news cleared out the club, and we watched as the camp's officer of the day and the duty noncommissioned officer tried to talk some sense into the Marine perched on the railing of the camp's forty-foot-high water tower.

He told the officer of the day, in no uncertain terms, that he was not going to Vietnam. When given the order by the duty NCO to climb down, or go to the brig, the Marine yelled back, "Fuck you, Gunny." A great cheer went up from the patrons of the animal pit. Then the Marine jumped.

During the summer months, Okinawa receives more than its share of rain, and daily thunderstorms are a matter of course around Camp Hansen. Because of this rainfall the ground beneath the water tower was saturated and spongy. The impact of the Marine was absorbed by the wet ground, and his injuries were minimal: a broken right arm was all he received for his idiotic effort. The patrons of the animal pit were injured in a far worse manner, however, when the officer of the day ordered the club immediately closed, hoping to curtail the number of alcohol-fueled jumpers. I don't believe he enjoyed the cheer, either.

The Marine who jumped had not been in the animal pit, but that story cut no ice with the OD. That is the only reason that two hundred and fifty enlisted Marines, and three corpsmen, were not hung over as we slowly boarded MAC flight 289 from Kadena to Da Nang at 0400.

The flight into Da Nang was unusual for only one reason: no one talked during the two hours we were airborne. On most military flights, going to or from a training exercise, there is always lots of loud conversation. But this flight was bringing all of us to the reality of war. This was no training exercise, it was the real thing. Once we were on the ground we would be out of our own element and at the mercy of the unknown, and this was cause for some very serious soul-searching. The harsh reality of what was about to happen made us each keep our mouths shut, as we were sharing our innermost thoughts only with God.

As we approached Da Nang, the pilot announced that there was the very real possibility of the aircraft receiving ground fire, and that we might be caught in a mortar or rocket attack. The aircraft's emergency exit doors were again pointed out. We were also told that Air Force ground guides would immediately lead us from the aircraft toward a safe area, and from there we would go to our administrative check-in points for further assignment.

The jet slowed for its approach, and we strained to peer out of the small windows for our first glimpse of Vietnam. Fortunately, there was no ground fire, and there was no mortar or rocket attack, but the anxiety attacks that we experienced will never be forgotten.

As I stood in the doorway of the aircraft I drew my first breath of Vietnamese air. It was humid, hot, and stale, and reeked of aircraft kerosene. The humidity was stifling, and there was no time to waste looking around. We were all on the move, led by one of the ground guides and headed toward a holding area where we would be processed to our new units.

Welcome to Vietnam; you have arrived.

- REPORTING FOR DUTY -

ALL PERSONNEL REPORTING IN FOR DUTY WERE DI-
rected into a huge hangarlike building. At the far end was a long
counter, and hung high above the counter were three giant red
signs with yellow lettering, spaced equally apart. They read: 1ST
MARINE DIVISION HERE, 3D MARINE DIVISION HERE, and ALL
OTHER PERSONNEL HERE. I stood in the long line of 3d-Marine-
Division-Here people.

Checking in was designed to be a simple matter of having your
orders stamped indicating that you had arrived no later than the
date that you were expected. The unit to which each man was
assigned provided some sort of transportation that took him from
his point of arrival to his final destination.

That system worked extremely well with incoming Marines but
it was not always the case with incoming hospital corpsmen. My
orders directed me to report to the 3d Marine Division's Division
Surgeon's Office. The division surgeon was the senior naval medical officer assigned to the staff of the division commanding general, and his administrative section was to assign me to a specific
unit, based upon the needs of the Marine Corps.

I progressed slowly forward, finally arriving at the counter
where the order-writing clerks were standing. When the clerk
stamped my orders, I asked about my next step in checking in. He
told me to report to the division surgeon's office at Dong Ha. The
enlisted-personnel officer there would assign me to a particular
unit.

I had been in Vietnam for less than one hour, had no idea of
who, what, or where a Dong Ha was, only knowing that Dong Ha
was the solution to my problem. I asked a Marine staff sergeant
for some help. He said that Dong Ha was a town fifty miles north
of Da Nang. He also said that he knew of only two ways to get

57

there, walk or fly. Luckily for me, he was also headed for Dong Ha. I grabbed my seabag from the mountain of stacked luggage, and I was Dong Ha bound, staying close to the helpful and knowledgeable Marine NCO.

The staff sergeant was beginning his second tour in Vietnam; he knew that we would have to get a "TWA" hop from Da Nang to the airstrip at Dong Ha, where the 3d Marine Division's command post was located. From there I would be able to find the mysterious office of the division surgeon.

We started walking from the main terminal down a dirt road toward "Teenie Weenie Airlines." The distance from the main terminal to TWA was about a mile, and when the staff sergeant stopped a passing Marine Corps truck, our ride to TWA was assured.

Teenie Weenie Airlines was a Marine C-130 organization that made routine flights to northern I Corps. Inside we were told that it was certainly possible to get to Dong Ha; all we needed was an aircraft.

At this time a Marine Corps colonel came into the small terminal building and told the Marine on duty that he, too, needed to get to Dong Ha. The colonel wore gold aviator's wings on his uniform. He asked the Marine behind the desk when the next available bird was to leave. The Marine on duty pointed out the window and said, "That is the only flight headed north today, sir." The plane was in motion, taxiing into position for takeoff. The colonel told the duty NCO to contact the aircraft by radio, have it return to the terminal, and pick up him and anyone else headed to Dong Ha. We watched out the window as the radio call went from the duty NCO's desk to the cockpit of the moving C-130, and immediately the plane began to slow down and change direction. It was headed back toward us. The unquestionable authority of a colonel in the Marine Corps was quietly demonstrated to one staff sergeant and one hospital corpsman.

The three of us were given hearing protectors called "Mickey Mouse ears" and told that when the C-130 returned it would drop its rear ramp and we were to run aboard carrying all of our gear.

Once we were on board and seated, the plane resumed its effort to fly north, and we were now headed for Dong Ha. For the first time I was able to look out a window and see the country of Vietnam. Great hills ringed the coastal city of Da Nang, and the land below was in different hues of green from the dense vegetation. As we headed north along the coast, the topography began to flatten out, and rice paddies identical to the ones I had seen on the island of Okinawa were everywhere. The land was also covered with perfect circles full of water, the result of past aerial bombings and artillery fire. These countless old craters gave South Vietnam a green lunar complexion, and I wondered what had been down there to warrant that much bombing. Could anyone on the ground have survived?

The C-130 crew chief came back to where we were seated and told us that we would land in just a few minutes. We got off the same way that we got on: the ramp came down, the aircraft slowed to a crawl, and we carried off all of our gear, leaving the mouse ears on the seat.

The colonel quickly led the way off, and we followed him to a small plywood building and thanked him for helping us get to Dong Ha. He wished us luck, then quickly departed in a waiting jeep. The staff sergeant told me that Dong Ha airstrip was the end of the line for him; he also wished me well and walked out of the shack.

I asked the lone Marine inside if he could point me in the direction of the division surgeon's office, and amazingly he happened to know that the office was located three miles south of where I stood. The only transportation made available to me was the single pair of used and abused combat boots that I had found in the dumpster in Okinawa.

As I started down the dirt road, I couldn't help but think just how vulnerable I was: alone and walking down an unnamed road, no equipment, no weapon, no water, no compass, helmet, or flak jacket, and no sense not to go. I was a sniper's dream come true, but why would he want to waste a round on me?

After fifteen minutes of walking south, I heard the unmistakable rumble of a tank headed my way. The tank commander had the driver stop when they came alongside, and he asked me where I was headed. When I explained to him that I was looking for the division surgeon's office, he told me to throw my gear aboard and hop on. I spent my last dusty mile and a half riding to the division surgeon's office high on the back of a Marine Corps M-60 tank.

I looked like Pigpen when I jumped down by the red sign lettered DIVISION SURGEON'S OFFICE. I thanked the tankers for their great hospitality and walked up the trail toward a series of green plywood hootches, office spaces of the division surgeon.

Throwing my seabag down, I used my cover to beat five pounds of dust and dirt off of my utilities before I made my grand entrance into the enlisted-personnel officer's hootch. To say that I was unexpected is an understatement.

The Navy chief who was designated as the enlisted-personnel officer offered me a chair and asked me how I had gotten here from Da Nang. After I finished relating my story the chief's face broadened into a huge smile. He said that for a guy who had only been in country for three hours, I certainly knew my way around. The conversation grew a lot more serious when he asked me where I wanted to go for duty.

I told the chief that I had heard the often repeated stories about duty with the grunts from the corpsmen and Marine patients at Newport. "The grunts carry everything they own on their backs." "The grunts never move." "The grunts make too much noise when they do move." "The grunts were a quick ticket to Arlington National Cemetery." "If you want to survive your tour go anywhere, but don't go with the grunts." The chief laughed and said that I could substitute any type of unit for the word *grunt;* those same quotes had all been reused endlessly. Then he gave me some good advice. "Norton, if you believe nothing that you hear, and only believe half of what you see, you'll do all right."

The chief explained the needs of the Marine Corps, and he showed me a personnel board that listed all of the corpsmen, the units they were assigned to, and what units were short of hospital corpsmen. The display indicated that the division's reconnaissance battalion was short two corpsmen and I asked the chief about the possibility of that type of duty. He said that those vacancies had just been filled by two corpsmen who had transferred over from the infantry units. Then he told me of only one other possibility.

There was one Marine Corps unit called 3d Force Reconnaissance Company, and that unit was in need of a hospital corpsman, but there were certain prerequisite skills required for that type of duty. First, 3d Force Recon Company was a volunteer-only company. They wanted a corpsman who could swim, who had field sense, and who could work independently. Usually this duty was reserved for a petty officer second class, with an 8404 rating, who was also a qualified parachutist and scuba diver. I had the rating but lacked the required experience level, formal training, and rank. I volunteered. I told the chief that 3d Force Recon was where I wanted to go. I told him about my background: I knew how to swim; I knew I had the field sense that would be required for independent duty.

I explained that I had worked for months on the wards at Newport and spent weeks working in the emergency room, and I told the chief about Hospitalman Second Class Daily's parting advice to me. Finally, I reminded him that I was the only corpsman checking in. Who else was there? The chief understood. He said that if I wanted to go to 3d Force Recon Company that bad then he would take me to a place called Quang Tri, and I could report for duty at 3d Force Recon the following morning.

The chief hung a well-worn sign on the door of his hootch that read GONE TO QUANG TRI, strapped on a .45 colt automatic pistol that he carried in a shoulder holster, and slid in behind the wheel of his jeep. We were headed for Quang Tri, home of the division's 3d Reconnaissance Battalion, and 3d Force Recon.

The jeep ride from Dong Ha to Quang Tri was a short one, but the chief told me that he was due to leave Vietnam within the week, and as he drove he talked in general terms about those things that would help me through this tour. I knew his advice and concern were genuine, and I paid attention to everything that was said.

As we approached the battalion command post, I could not help but notice several white ball-like objects that sat atop the fence posts leading into the battalion's compound. At first glance I thought that they were football helmets that had been forgotten and left out on the posts, but as we drew closer I saw what they were, six human skulls.

The chief waited for me to comment on what I had just seen, and when I said nothing, he explained that they were not souvenirs from Vietcong bodies, but that an old South Vietnamese cemetery had been laid open by a recent bombing mission and the skeletal remains were brought back by one of the battalion's recon teams that happened to stumble across the site. He said that the skull and crossbones were a symbol of the reconnaissance battalion and the skulls seemed to keep uninvited Vietnamese from coming into the battalion area. They probably kept a lot of other people from visiting 3d Recon Battalion as well.

When we stopped at the battalion's aid station, I was greeted by two corpsmen whom I had worked with at the naval hospital in Newport. Jim Jersley and Doc Logan had left Newport several months before I did, and here they were assigned to the battalion aid station. The chief from the division surgeon's office introduced me to the battalion's senior chief and explained to him that I would be going over to 3d Force Recon Company for duty. The senior chief then turned me loose with Jersley and Logan and told me to spend the night at their hootch before walking over to 3d

Force in the morning. I thanked the chief from the division surgeon's office, both for the advice he had provided and for the ride. He wished me luck and headed back toward Dong Ha and, eventually, home.

As I was shown around the inside of the battalion's area, I was introduced to many new faces, all acquaintances of the two corpsmen. Most of the Marines that we met were headed toward the enlisted club, and we followed. The club's walls had been decorated with murals painted by some of the battalion's resident artists, depicting the various scenes of bloody combat, but the centerpiece, situated behind the bar, was a giant exaggerated caricature of a Recon Marine. He held his rifle in his left hand, and in his right hand a bug-eyed enemy soldier was grasped tightly by the neck. Beside the painting was a beautiful example of calligraphy that read; "Yea though I walk through the Valley of the shadow of Death, I shall fear no evil . . . because I am the meanest motherfucker in the Valley."

As we sat in the club talking about how wonderful life had been for us at Newport, Marines would stop by our table and remind Jersley and Logan that it was Sunday. I assumed that these reminders were in reference to some church service that was to occur later that night. When I asked why so many Marines kept mentioning Sunday, I was told that Sunday nights were the prime time for enemy rocket attacks. They were dead serious.

The club manager gained everyone's attention when he began to bang a steel bar against an empty shell casing that hung from the ceiling. "The club will close in fifteen minutes; don't forget it's Sunday, and observe light discipline rules. Last call!" With that announcement, everyone drifted away from the club. We walked back to the battalion aid station and waited for the afternoon's long shadows to fade into nightfall. I was given a Unit-1 first-aid bag that contained a various array of bandages, battle dressings, tape, instruments, iodine, and other medical supplies that would be needed to treat injuries. With a helmet and flak jacket on, I headed toward a huge sandbagged bunker.

On Sunday nights when the North Vietnamese fired their rockets into Quang Tri, they aimed them at any source of light, believing that where there was light there were people. More often than not they were correct. Poor light discipline had caused more than a few units in Quang Tri Province to be on the receiving end of enemy incoming B-40 rockets, so the Marines had learned to take every precaution that would ensure their survival: stay close to a bunker, have the corpsmen ready, and shut off the lights. They were a way of life.

We sat on top of the command post bunker, and I asked a thousand more questions. When was the last time you were rocketed? Last Sunday. Was anyone killed? No, but four Marines were wounded. Why can't they stop the North Vietnamese from firing the rockets, if they know where and when they would shoot?

The gooks set up their rockets on the sloping sides of rice paddy walls and hooked them up to a timed firing device. The gooks were simply not there when the rockets went off. They hid deep underground in cave networks and were two clicks (kilometers) away when their rockets fired. How are you going to kill someone smart enough to fire his rockets into your backyard and still be two clicks away at the same time?

Jersley and Logan had a little more than passing personal interest in Sunday nights. The word had been passed that the 3d Marine Division was soon leaving Vietnam. They wanted to be among those who left the country walking upright. Obviously, I would not be able to leave with them, so they talked about their experiences with 3d Recon Battalion, hoping that I would benefit from what they said before beginning my tour with 3d Force Recon.

At 1930 the first rocket slammed into the ground three hundred meters short of our bunker. Suddenly the cry "incoming" was being repeated by dozens of men who were running for the safety of the bunkers. We were inside and safe as our bunker filled with Marines. In the distance a siren was wailing the incoming warning, and the earth shook as four more rockets crashed close by. The four concussions caused loose sand and dirt to fall over us, and the bunker was filled with a cloud of dark brown, choking dust. There were no lights inside other than the flashlights that a few of the Marines brought with them. There was only silence.

We had waited inside the bunker for five minutes when the shouts of "all clear" began to be heard. No one inside the bunker had needed any first aid; there had been no report of Marines being wounded. Someone later said that the rockets had landed in or near the 3d Force Recon Company area only five hundred yards away.

My first night in Vietnam, and I had witnessed an enemy rocket attack. No one killed, no one injured, and no real damage done in the battalion area for two reasons—the limited number of enemy rockets fired, and the well-rehearsed Sunday night incoming drill.

The next several hours were spent waiting at the battalion aid station as the Marines made sure that everyone was accounted for and that no last-minute casualties were discovered. None were.

I tried to sleep in one of the unused racks in Jersley's hootch, but sleep did not come easily: I lay awake and thought about what had happened earlier and assumed that it would happen again at any time.

Most everyone around me had been calm during the incoming. They were prepared, knew where to go for immediate protection, had an alarm system, and a well-rehearsed plan for personnel accountability. It was reassuring to know that these simple actions worked and that everyone, including a corpsman on his first day in country, would be protected by the plan. The men were quite cool under fire.

I awoke at 0530 to the sounds of a cadence being called out as a platoon of Marines ran past the hootch. They all wore camouflage shorts with T-shirts, jungle boots, and large green floppy hats called "bush covers." They carried twenty-foot-long logs on their shoulders. They were headed out of the battalion's compound and down the road in the direction of where the rockets had landed.

Most of the corpsmen in the hootch were dressed and ready to walk over to the mess hall for breakfast. The mess hall was a plywood building with a dozen picnic tables that seated three men per side. The breakfast was typical of any Marine chow hall, and after scrambled eggs, toast, and coffee, I walked over to the aid station to talk with the senior chief corpsman, getting my final instructions before going over to 3d Force Recon Company. The chief said that he really didn't know much about the way the 3d Force operated. They were new, kept to themselves, and did not associate with the Marines from 3d Recon Battalion. "Force is different," was the consensus.

I was told to throw my bag in the back of the admin jeep, which was used exclusively for administrative trips around the Quang Tri area, and I would be dropped off at the company aid station in the 3d Force Recon Company's compound.

The guys I had known from Newport wished me luck; instead of shaking hands, they all gave me the "thumbs-up." That was the way it was done they said, and to shouts of "get some," I was driven out of the 3d Recon Battalion's area.

To avoid any confusion, clarification as to the "official" difference between a Force Reconnaissance Company and a Reconnaissance Battalion is given below:

The Force Reconnaissance Company

A. *Mission.* The primary mission of a Marine force reconnaissance company is to conduct pre-assault and distant post-assault reconnaissance in support of the landing force.

B. *Organization.* The company is composed of a company headquarters, a supply and service platoon, and four reconnaissance platoons. Each reconnaissance platoon contains three reconnaissance teams of six men each for a total of twelve teams in the company. The company is organized to provide the landing-force commander with individual teams and requires support personnel to execute specific missions. All members of the reconnaissance platoons are trained as surface swimmers, inflatable boat handlers, and parachutists. A limited number of men are trained as underwater swimmers (scuba).

(1) *Company Headquarters.* The company headquarters contains a headquarters section (S-1), an operations section (S-3), and a communications section (Comm). The operations section contains both an operations officer and an intelligence officer (S-2), with appropriate enlisted assistants. Although the company is concerned primarily with the collection and reporting of raw information, which is processed into intelligence by the receiving headquarters, the organic intelligence personnel have the capability of limited intelligence production to serve the needs of the company commander. In addition, intelligence personnel are used to brief and debrief patrols and to prepare formal patrol reports. The communication section, operating under the supervision of the company communications officer (Comm O), has the capability to enter and guard the force command nets, control nets, and intelligence nets when the company operates as a subordinate element of the landing force. Each reconnaissance team contains one radiotelegraph operator in addition to communicators in the company headquarters. Communications support for the reconnaissance teams is provided by the communications section of the company headquarters.

(2) *Supply and Service Platoon.* The supply and service platoon is organized to provide limited logistical support to the company in garrison and in rear areas in the field. The platoon consists of a platoon headquarters, a supply section, a mess section, a parachute maintenance and repair section (paraloft), a medical section, a motor transportation section, and an am-

phibious equipment maintenance section which is referred to by members of the company as the scuba locker.

(3) *Reconnaissance Platoons*. The nature of employment of the company is such that normally each team acts independently of all other teams in the conduct of a specific mission. Patrols are briefed, landed into their operating area by various means and methods, and recovered separately; consequently, coordination among patrols is rarely required. On the other hand, coordination becomes increasingly more important and much more difficult whenever a number of patrols are landed or recovered by a single means or are operating in the same area.

C. *Employment*.

(1) The force reconnaissance company (or elements thereof) is employed to collect information of military significance for the force commander and, when necessary, to provide terminal guidance for assault helicopters. The company has no offensive capability and is not employed as a tactical unit; that is, the company is not assigned tactical missions to be executed by the company as a whole, nor is it assigned tactical missions, objectives, or tactical areas of responsibility. The company performs its assigned mission by furnishing small scout teams and by using supporting personnel for the performance of specific reconnaissance, surveillance, or guidance tasks.

(2) Information-collection missions are assigned to acquire information otherwise unobtainable or to verify data collected from other sources. The collection effort is not in the form of a direct service to subordinate elements of the landing force. Raw information is provided to the force commander, whose staff uses the information in the production of intelligence. The company does not evaluate or process into intelligence the information collected by its own elements.

(3) In addition to collecting information about the enemy, the force reconnaissance company possesses the capability to perform the following tasks:

(a) Engage the enemy by supporting arms when so directed or authorized by higher headquarters.

(b) Implant, monitor, and retrieve sensors.

(c) Capture selected prisoners.

(d) Conduct specialized terrain reconnaissance, including beach, route/road, and helicopter landing/drop zones.

(e) Conduct initial terminal guidance operations.

(f) Conduct special missions requiring the use of entry
capabilities unique to a force reconnaissance company.

(4) Each reconnaissance team performs its assigned tasks
through stealth. The teams are introduced clandestinely into
inland or coastal landing areas and observe or physically recon-
noiter the area or object of interest. Patrols report directly to the
landing force commander or to his representative using a relay
station, if necessary. In addition to reporting directly from the
field, after recovery, patrols also report by message and written
supplementary reports which are accompanied by physical or
photographic exhibits that were acquired on the mission.

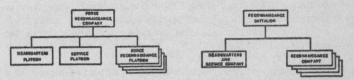

Force Reconnaissance Company (1969)   Reconnaissance Battalion (1969)

The Reconnaissance Battalion

A. *Mission.* The primary mission of the reconnaissance battalion, for a Marine division, is to conduct reconnaissance and observation in support of the Marine division or its elements.

B. *Organization.* The reconnaissance battalion is an organic
unit of the Marine division and is composed of a headquarters and
service company and four reconnaissance companies. All reconnaissance Marines are trained as surface swimmers and inflatable
boat handlers. A limited number are trained as underwater swimmers (scuba).

C. *Employment.*

(1) The reconnaissance battalion (or elements thereof) is
employed to gain intelligence information in support of the
Marine division or subordinate task organizations. It is not
equipped for decisive or sustained combat and must accomplish
its mission through stealth, maneuver, and accurate, rapid reporting. It is not capable of screening or counterintelligence
missions. The battalion is dependent upon the extensive use of
helicopters and light motor vehicles to provide mobility.

(2) Maximum effectiveness is achieved by employing the
reconnaissance battalion as a unit under division control. This

method of employment provides for maximum efficiency and exploits to the fullest extent the mobility and extensive communications of the battalion. Unit employment makes maximum use of the battalion staff in the detailed planning required of reconnaissance operations and utilizes the battalion logistics and maintenance system with greatest effectiveness. When operating under division control, the battalion commander will receive orders for a mission from the division commander and will render his report directly to the division commander.

(3) One or more of the companies of the battalion may be attached to be in support of subordinate units of the division or wing. When the mission or the area of operations presents a reconnaissance requirement beyond the organic capability of the infantry battalion to perform, battalion landing teams organized for a special task and operating independently of the division may be supported by a company or smaller-size units of the reconnaissance battalion.

(4) During amphibious operations, all or part of the battalion may be introduced ashore prior to H-hour, at H-hour, or during the landing of nonscheduled units, as the situation dictates.

(5) In addition to collection information on the enemy, a division reconnaissance battalion possesses the capability to perform the following tasks:

(a) Engage the enemy by supporting arms when so directed or authorized by the division commander.

(b) Implant, monitor, and retrieve sensors.

(c) Capture selected prisoners.

(d) Conduct specialized terrain reconnaissance, including beach, road/route, and HLZ/DZ reconnaissance missions.

(e) Conduct initial terminal guidance operations.

(f) Perform special missions.

3D FORCE RECON
——— COMPANY ———

THE ONLY CORPSMAN WORKING IN THE COMPANY AID station the morning I reported in for duty was a corpsman called Doc Solis. Doc Solis was considered "short"; he had less than a week remaining with 3d Force Recon before returning to the States. This was his second tour of duty in Vietnam. He was close to thirty-five, pleasant, soft-spoken, and tried to make me feel welcome to the company as he read over my orders and reviewed my service record book.

"The company area was hit by four incoming rockets last night, and people around here are still recovering from what happened. We had a dozen recon Marines wounded and one corpsman was hurt pretty bad. Have a seat, and we'll talk." He went on, explaining that he had been expecting a corpsman second class to check in from the division surgeon's office to replace one of his "short-time" corpsmen, and he was only a little surprised to see a hospitalman (E-3) walk through his door. Then he began his personal welcome-aboard speech.

"You'll find that 3d Force is a very special company. It's a no-nonsense company and not like anything you've ever seen in the Navy. I don't know what those shitheads over at battalion recon might have told you about Force Recon, but you can forget everything they said and just listen to me. I'm here, and they're not. There are only five corpsmen in this entire company of 130 Marines now, including yourself. If it's decided that we keep you, you'll be assigned to one of the four platoons as the platoon corpsman, and you will be expected to do the same job as any Marine of the same rank in your platoon. The only obvious difference is that you will be the medical expert when you become a member of one of the recon teams. You will eat, sleep, train, shit, shower, and shave with your platoon in garrison, and you will have to hump your ass off with your team in the bush. All they expect from you is your best effort. These Marines think that they are special. They are very well trained, very close knit, and they don't like outsiders. If you want their respect, you will have to earn it. If you don't have any questions, then welcome aboard.''

Doc Solis stayed with me and told me more about his own observations of the company as I once more checked in. My medical and dental records would now be kept with everyone else's at the aid station; my shot card was up-to-date; I needed no new immunizations. My next stop was at the company administrative office, the S-1 shop.

A first lieutenant named Wayne Morris was the officer in charge of the administration section for the company. He was also the company's adjutant. It was immediately apparent that the Marines that worked for him were not the typical office ''weenies'' that military administrative sections seem to breed. I was soon to learn that the company's policy was that even the administrative-type Marines would spend at least half of their twelve-month tour in the bush before they would be considered for any soft office job. No ''office pukes'' were allowed to breed around here. One paid one's dues for the rare privilege of comfort.

After presenting my service record book to the administrative section chief, a sergeant named Schemmel began to make me a set of dog tags. ''Lieutenant Morris is over at Charlie Med and he will want to see you when he gets back to the area. I'll send for you when he returns.'' As Sergeant Schemmel handed the new tags to me he said, ''Wrap some electric tape around these, Doc, so that they don't make any noise. No one in the bush wants to ever give their position away.'' I was told by Schemmel that I was now assigned as a member of the company's third platoon and once I had completed all of the required stops, I would then report to my platoon sergeant first and then the platoon leader. Doc Solis would stay with me through checking in.

From the S-1 shop we walked over to the company supply hootch, where I was to draw my necessary 782 gear: one pair of new combat boots, two sets of green, rip-stop utilities, one medium-size gas mask and pouch, one sheathed K-bar knife, one nine-foot length of nylon rope, a cartridge belt, suspenders, four canteens, one canteen cup, a lensatic compass, two steel snap links, a green bush cover, several bottles of insect repellent, a handful of camouflage paint sticks, one poncho liner, one ruck-sack, one day/night flare, a little brown bottle of water purification tablets, a strobe light, a flak jacket, one helmet with helmet liner, one sleeping bag, one poncho, one wool blanket, and a dirty, mildewed, smelly old pillow.

Most of this equipment I was quite familiar with from Field Med School, but some of the specialized equipment—strobe lights, night vision devices, and electronics gear—I had never used before. I signed the custody card for receipt of all that, and then the supply clerk told me that I would get the rest of my gear later. What more gear could there possibly be?

Next stop was the company's armory. I had imagined that the armory would be a high security area surrounded by barbwire but was surprised when I walked into one dimly lit, green, and sandbagged plywood hootch. The armorer on duty was busy doing an inventory when Solis and I approached him. He saw by my uniform that I was a corpsman and without saying a single word, drew a .45 Colt from a pistol chest, picked up some cleaning gear, and then handed me an M-16 rifle, bayonet, and sling. "Welcome to 3d Force, Doc. Initial this card next to all the Xs. Keep these weapons good and clean and bring 'em back here only if they don't work. Make sure you test-fire 'em today. See ya in a year."

Loaded down with more clothing, equipment, and weapons than two people could normally carry, Solis and I headed for the platoon's living area to meet SSgt. D. P. Williams, the third platoon sergeant. Solis said that Staff Sergeant Williams was new to the company, had done his first tour in Vietnam as a grunt, and was now the senior enlisted Marine in the third platoon. He explained more about 3d Force as we walked on.

"In 3d Force a recon platoon usually consists of a lieutenant platoon leader, your platoon sergeant who runs the platoon, and three teams of eight men each with one corpsman per platoon. The recon team leaders are usually corporals; some teams are run by sergeants. Last night's incoming changed all of that. We will reorganize the company today, get new people in here, and rebuild. Luckily for us we have two teams out on the DMZ right now. Lucky for them, and unfortunate for us. That's why your hootch looks deserted."

Staff Sergeant Williams was waiting outside on the steps as Doc Solis and I approached. Introductions being completed, Solis then departed. Williams immediately welcomed me to the platoon and told me to come in and sit down in his small living area at the far end of the hootch.

"Last night we took four rounds of incoming rockets in and around the company area. We lost one corpsman named Doc

Silver. He was medevaced over to Charlie Med Battalion last night. Did you know him?'' I told the staff sergeant that I did not know the wounded corpsman and that I had spent my very first night in country on the other side of the wire at 3d Recon Battalion and had only seen the first rocket impact and heard the other rockets from the safety offered by one of their bunkers.

''We had about a dozen men wounded when the second and third rockets landed down by the company supply area. The first one made a direct hit on the 'white house.' That's what we called the officer's shitter. When the big cheer went up from those guys who saw that first rocket hit the outhouse, the guys inside ran outside to see what was up; that's when the second and third rockets came in and caused all the casualties. The last rocket hit just outside of the wire and nailed one of the company's jeeps, blew it all to hell, but you can see it later.'' He then stood up and said, ''Now take a look at this.'' He pointed to a kitchen-size, white refrigerator that had a huge jagged hole right in the center of the door. ''A piece of shrapnel from one of those damned B-40 rockets made that hole. It came right through the wall of the hootch. I have to figure out a way to patch it up, but the refrigerator still works. Just take a real hard look and remember how wicked that shrapnel can be.

''The third platoon leader is Lieutenant Hensley. When he comes back from Con Thien, he'll want to talk with you. I'll let you know when that will happen. For now, make up your rack at the end of the hootch, get your gear cleaned up, and write a letter home to let 'em know that you got here okay. Once all that's done, you can go and meet the rest of the docs at sick bay. That should take you a couple of hours. When you get back from sick bay, we'll go to the pit and test-fire your .45 and M-16.''

Staff Sergeant Williams went on to tell me about the daily routine: physical training (PT) each and every day at 0600 (that was for everyone), morning chow, followed by platoon formation, morning training classes, noon chow, afternoon formation, afternoon training classes, afternoon PT, then we were on our own, remaining always in the company area until lights out at 2000 hours.

He explained that the entire company area was no larger than the two acres of land containing our twenty hootches, all of which were identical—green plywood, single-story buildings, built two feet above the ground for protection. Each one housed twelve Marines. The roofs were made of heavy corrugated metal, and several sets of sandbags were draped over each roof to keep the sheet metal from blowing away during the heavy winds of the monsoon season.

The company area was surrounded by triple bands of razor-sharp concertina wire. There was one gate into the compound, and one gate leading out. There were no paved roads, only dirt roads that turned to mud when the heavy rains came.

The company area was divided into several sections. The four platoon living areas comprised one section; the company command post, communications bunker, training office, admin office, and company commander's and first sergeant's hootch were in the second section. Supply, the company armory, the small motor T section, and the sick bay made up the third section. The scuba-gear locker and the parachute loft was the fourth. That was the physical world of one self-contained Force Recon Company, in Quang Tri Province, South Vietnam.

Having finished the jobs that the platoon sergeant had given to me, I walked over to sick bay, hoping to meet the other company corpsmen. Hospital Corpsman First Class Solis had gathered all of them together, and I met Hospitalman Third Class Bennette from the first platoon; Hospital Corpsman Third Class Parrish, assigned to the second platoon, and Hospital Corpsman Second Class Montgomery, with the fourth platoon. Doc Parrish had come to 3d Force from a tour with the Marine air wing; he was getting short. Doc Bennette had been in Vietnam for nine months, and Doc Montgomery had been with 3d Force for only one month. Solis's replacement was due to arrive in several weeks.

Solis wanted to know how everything had gone after my initial meeting with Staff Sergeant Williams. I explained to him what I had accomplished and asked him to explain to me how my duty at sick bay differed from duty within the platoon. It was simple: if anyone from third platoon was sick in garrison, I was to bring him to sick bay for treatment immediately. I was not to use any medications from my Unit-1 bag while I was in the rear. I was to use the sick bay's medical supplies and save the Unit-1 bag's supplies for the field.

Since there were five of us now in the company area, Solis decided to post a duty roster and assign one corpsman to sleep at sick bay each night in case of emergency. That plan also protected the medical supplies on hand from disappearing when no one was around.

My assignment to 3d Force Recon Company was to be independent duty. My life was centered around the medical needs of the Marines in the third platoon while we were in the company area, and I was about to learn what would be required of me, mentally and physically, as a member of a recon team.

Hospital Corpsman First Class Solis broke up our friendly little meeting with his announcement that company PT would begin in fifteen minutes. There was just enough time to change into PT shorts and combat boots. We would do calisthenics as a company, and go for a five-mile run in platoon formation. Company PT took place twice a day. No one could be absent, "skate," this event.

It seemed incredible to me that even though we were living in a combat zone and capable of being on the receiving end of incoming enemy rocket or mortar rounds, we would run in platoon formation each day, out of our company area, past 3d Recon Battalion, and down the road toward Dong Ha and back.

The company PT session was not an easy event, and any personal lack of attention to detail added to the difficulty. Once the company was formed up and ready to begin, one of the company gunnery sergeants yelled, "dog tag check," and grabbed hold of the tags that hung around his neck, holding them in front of his face. Those few unfortunate individuals who had lost or forgotten to wear their dog tags were told to get down and pump out ten fast push-ups for their failure. Repeat offenders were rare. The same type of corrective motivation was used on those people who failed to bring certain items to company PT: no bush cover, ten push-ups; no T-shirt, ten push-ups; not jump qualified, ten push-ups; the same applied for nonscuba qualified Marines. The push-ups were done in the spirit of fun; punishment was never vindictive as it conveniently served to build everyone's upper body strength.

The first set of standard exercises that we went through was known as "the daily seven." The company gunnery sergeant would first demonstrate the particular exercise so that we all could see it, and then he would shout out the number of repetitions that he expected us to do. We would begin our loud song of cadence in unison as the exercise was being done, "One, two three, one. One, two three, two. One, two, three, three . . ." until we had reached the desired number of repetitions of jumping jacks, toe-touchers, push-ups, side-straddle hops, bend and reach, etc., to cover the daily seven.

Once the movement of the particular exercise stopped, every man froze in position. If anyone moved after the exercise was finished his movement cost him ten additional push-ups, all done on the honor system: no one ever had to be told to "pay" his ten push-ups for not paying attention to what was going on.

Following the daily seven was the company run. These runs

were always led by the commanding officer and company first sergeant, with the company gunnery sergeant running beside the formation and calling different cadences and songs as we ran. The distances were usually between four and five miles along the dirt roads of Quang Tri. Our PT sessions usually lasted for at least an hour, sometimes longer. (Occasionally there were some organized games like football, boxing, or baseball between the platoons that would begin after the run was over.)

I was expected to participate in these PT sessions just like any other member of the company. There was no quarter given to any corpsman simply because he was "not a Marine." We were all expected to keep up with the Marines and do exactly what they did, whether that meant daily PT, long runs, or our other daily training. There is no doubt that my first few sessions of company PT with 3d Force Recon were more than difficult. They were a bitch and they were meant to be that way. My initial state of physical readiness, or lack of it, made me immediately aware of what was expected of me, and I was soon exercising two to three times a day to enhance my stamina whenever I was in the company area.

When the company finally returned to the area from the run, each platoon was dismissed and we returned to the day's planned activities. After showering and getting back into new utilities, I reported to Sergeant Williams with my .45 Colt and M-16 rifle. I knocked on the door to his cubicle, and he growled out, "Enter."

"You told me to report to you after PT so that I could test-fire these weapons in the firing pit."

Williams had not forgotten. "Let's do it."

We carried several magazines for each of the weapons. Sergeant Williams had brought along his .45 and M-16. As we walked over to the test-firing pit, he asked me if I had ever done any real shooting, and I told him that I had hunted as a kid and had shot a lot of trap and skeet. He wanted to know if I had any reservations about the possibility of having to shoot gooks. I told him that I had never shot at another man, but if his question was whether or not I could do it, I felt that I could. He said that he needed to know "before you went to the bush." We test-fired the .45s without any problem, and the M-16s were next.

I had shot the M-14 rifle at Field Med School and had liked it. The new M-16 was a much lighter rifle, not only in weight but in the bullet-caliber weight, too. Marines familiar with the complexities of hunting rifles argued that the M-14 had a much better knockdown capability because of its heavy .30 caliber bullet. The M-16 fired a lighter, .223 caliber bullet, one that in the civilian world was normally used for long-range varmint or target shooting.

The M-14 came in two designs: one, the M-14E2, had a selector switch that made it a fully automatic rifle; the second design was without the selector switch, and that limited the rifle to the semi-automatic mode. All M-16s, however, were manufactured with a selector switch, and a simple flip of the finger would allow for all twenty rounds to be fired in less than a few seconds.

Staff Sergeant Williams fired first. The M-16 spit out the brass casings as fast as he pulled the trigger. He then set the selector on automatic and the remaining ten rounds emptied from the rifle in a second. Williams said, "You try it," and I got down into the pit, loaded the rifle, and fired one magazine of twenty rounds, one shot at a time. I put in a fresh magazine, put the selector on automatic, and pulled the trigger. The rifle's muzzle climbed several inches as all twenty rounds poured from the gun. A wisp of white smoke rose from the barrel, and our test-firing was almost over. My T/O weapon as a corpsman was the .45 Colt automatic pistol, which was also the sidearm of a Marine staff sergeant. Williams handed me his pistol and said, "Doc, try this." I checked to see if it was loaded, which pleased him to know that I was safety conscious with his loaded weapon. I aimed it at a four-by-four block of wood laying in the bottom of the firing pit and fired seven rounds into it. There were no misses.

"For a new corpsman you seem to know what you're doing with a rifle and a pistol. Where did you learn to shoot?"

"I learned to shoot in the woods, Staff Sergeant." That reply suddenly caused a big smile to appear on his face.

"Yeah, me, too."

My short answer caused us to talk for a long time about our hunting and marksmanship experiences, and as we finished picking up the spent brass cartridges, Staff Sergeant Williams said, "Well, Doc, I know now that I won't have to worry about you when it comes to real trigger time." I took his comment as a compliment, and we returned to the platoon area to clean our weapons. I was told that I would report to the third platoon leader, First Lieutenant Hensley, after my weapons were once again inspected.

The lieutenant used the staff sergeant's little office to begin his initial interview. He asked me questions about my hometown and background and asked what I had done at my last duty station. He then explained exactly what he wanted me to do as the platoon's corpsman.

Lieutenant Hensley explained that 3d Force was rebuilding, that there were vacancies thanks to the previous night's incoming, that the company had a new commanding officer and a new training officer, and that the company first sergeant was due to leave soon. The 3d Marine Division was leaving northern I Corps, which meant that 3d Recon Battalion was leaving, too, but 3d Force was staying on to cover the DMZ. He also said that two of the teams from our third platoon were due to return from a mission on the demilitarized zone (DMZ) within two days, and that the third team of the platoon was due to go out on a mission in three days. Because Doc Silver had been medevaced, I would be going out with the third platoon's recon team. As I was dismissed, Sergeant Williams said that I had to report back to First Lieutenant Morris with my check-in card to finish processing. "Welcome to the third platoon."

As I left the S-1 office, Doc Solis was standing outside with a group of Marines. He waved for me to come and join them. I listened as they talked about the problems and plans for the reorganization of the company's platoons. Solis then introduced me to Captain Hisler, the company executive officer; then First Lieutenant Morris; First Lieutenant Coffman, the operations officer; and First Sergeant Henderson.

Lieutenant Morris asked, "When did you join us, Doc?"

I answered, "This morning, sir," and they all smiled.

The first sergeant said, "Why hell, the doc's so new he's still shittin' stateside chow." That comment brought a great laugh from all of them, and they could see that I was on the outside of their joke. At that moment another officer approached the group. The group came to attention, saluted, and said, "Good afternoon, sir."

Major Alex Lee was the commanding officer of 3d Force Recon. The major returned the greeting, looked at me, and spoke to Doc Solis. "And who is this?"

Solis spoke with the major for a few moments and then said loudly, "His name is Norton, sir. He arrived in country yesterday, spent last night at 3d Recon Battalion, and checked aboard today."

Major Lee walked the few steps over to where I stood, looked me up and down and said, "Go shave that mustache off of your face, lose ten pounds, and then you may come and talk to me." With that as his welcome-aboard spiel, he turned his attention to the officers in the group, and Doc Solis and I left for the security of sick bay.

My experience with Marine officers was extremely limited, having met only a few of them while I was a student at Field Med School. I had nothing to compare them to other than the naval medical officers that I had served with at the hospital in Newport. Solis tried to reassure me as we headed back to sick bay. "I think that the new CO likes you. If he hadn't, he would have ripped that mustache off your lips and handed it back to you. He isn't a big fan of hair on his Marines, and that includes his corpsmen. Don't worry, the older Marines in the company say that he has a good reputation. He certainly has made some changes for the better, and he's only been here for a few days. I would shave that caterpillar off first chance I got if I were you."

Hoping to write another letter home before evening chow call, I left Doc Solis standing in front of sick bay and went back to my hootch. A Marine was seated on the steps of the hootch, and he was busy cleaning a pile of 782 gear with a scrub brush. "You must be the new doc." Offering his hand, he said, "My name is Corporal Swederski. Sergeant Williams told me to teach you how to put your pack together the right way, so go and get your gear. You'll be going out with Sergeant Chapman's team on the DMZ the day after tomorrow, and I'll teach you as much as I can before you leave. Normally, you'd go to recondo school for two weeks before you went to the bush, but things have gotten screwed up after last night, and we still have to keep two teams out on the Z no matter what has happened back here in the rear." Vincent Swederski had been with 3d Force for six months and was a wizard when it came to knowing how to stow 782 equipment properly and how to wear all of the gear without producing noise. Vince had received his reconnaissance training as a member of 5th Force Recon at Camp Lejeune, North Carolina, prior to this tour, and he was one of the platoon's three assistant team leaders.

"The idea is to carry only the gear that you really need, know where it is and how to get to it in the dark without making any noise. The gooks on the DMZ move a lot at night, looking for us, and all they need is an excuse to throw a bunch of Chicom grenades at any sound they hear. All it takes is for one hungry newbie to go ripping through his pack looking for a C-ration can in the middle of the night, and eight team members will die 'cause of his screwup."

In the next two days I would depend upon Cpl. Vincent Swederski's common sense and field knowledge as though my life depended on it. It did.

The next morning I went to sick bay, clean shaven. My mission was to put together the Unit-1 bag that I would carry with me on the patrol missions. Eight men (including the corpsman) were assigned to a recon team and it was necessary to carry enough emergency medical supplies to support their needs for seven days in the bush. Based on their past experiences, the other company corpsmen contributed their advice. "Take a bottle of serum albumin. It's a blood volume expander, and it's smaller and lighter than the standard IV bottle of Ringer's D5W [5% dextrose and water]. Take Benadryl capsules too; your people will come down with rashes from the heat. Don't forget salt tablets, malaria pills, and lots of tape." It wasn't long before I had assembled more medical gear than could possibly fit into the small, waterproof Unit-1 bag.

Doc Solis came to my rescue. "If your team makes contact and you have a wounded man, your job is to keep him alive long enough for him to get picked up by a medevac chopper. There's no telling how long that might be, but you are not out there to set up a field hospital. Your emergency first-aid knowledge will keep the men alive until a doctor goes to work on 'em. They will look out for you, and you'll look out for them."

I returned to the hootch with my freshly packed Unit-1. It had taken less than an hour to get those items that I knew I would need from sick bay supply and to pack them all inside of the Unit-1 so that I could find things in the dark, just as Swederski had taught me with the gear in my pack.

The Unit-1 was only one part of the equipment system that Corporal Swederski helped me put together. His guidance was based on not reinventing the wheel, and "there is a place for everything, and it must be easy to get to." He started from the beginning. "Throw away all of your underwear 'cause you won't need any of it. White isn't natural in the bush, so keep your white T-shirts for rags. Always wear two pairs of socks, too. When we go to the bush, we use tape around our trouser legs to keep leeches and insects from crawling up. You won't ever take your boots off in the bush. Don't shave the day before you go out. Your beard will hold the cammie paint better, and the insect repellent that you mix the paint with won't sting your face if you haven't used a razor. Wash out two sets of utilities and let them air-dry outside. The local "mama-san" who runs the laundry uses too much soap when she uses any. When she dries the utilities, she does it over burning buffalo shit, and they stink. The gooks have good noses, so we won't help their cause any."

By the time Corporal Swederski was finished with me, he had

assembled a comfortable and practical fighting uniform and rig. Now it was time to put it all together and see how it fit.

The first piece of equipment that was strapped around my waist and secured to my left leg was the gas mask, complete with eyeglass inserts. At the bottom of the gas mask pouch was a small snapped pocket where I kept a bottle of insect repellent and one camouflage cammie stick.

The belt suspender harness was put on next. This consisted of the standard web belt and suspenders, with the additional equipment attached to the harness with fastening hooks. In the center of the web belt was placed a small first-aid pack, containing two battle dressings, some small Band-Aids, and iodine. Two canteens were placed tight against each side of the first-aid pack. Swederski explained that only in the movies were your canteens hung on the hips (if you had to hit the deck and roll, that would have been not only painful but impossible to accomplish). Four M-16 magazine pouches were positioned on the right and left sides of the front of the web belt with enough space left between them to accommodate hand grenades that were secured to each magazine pouch.

Attached to the web belt was a pair of thinly padded, web shoulder suspenders. On the front right side of the belt suspender pad was a nine-foot length of nylon rappelling line attached to a steel snap link. A lensatic compass pouch was secured to the pad beneath the nylon line. It was purposely placed there upside down to allow it to drop down quietly. On the left side of the suspender pad was a K-bar knife. It, too, was taped in place upside down. The leather strap that held the knife in the sheath had to be relocated next to the hilt of the knife. If this adjustment wasn't done, fingers were cut by the exposed blade. One day/night signal flare was usually taped to the sheath of the knife for immediately availability.

Following the placement of the gas mask, web belt, and suspenders, the rucksack was placed on my back with the shoulder straps positioned and adjusted for a correct and comfortable weight displacement. Corporal Swederski showed me that "quick releases" were made at each connecting point of the pack; once the tabs were pulled, all of the equipment would drop onto the ground in seconds. We tried the quick releases, and they worked perfectly.

My rucksack was an old U.S. Army frame pack that had been adapted and bastardized for better use by the Marines. The steel frame was tossed aside by most of the Marines: it hung up on vegetation and, more dangerous, the frame could cause the unwanted and unnatural sound of metal banging in the jungle. According to one knowledgeable corporal, that sound could prove to be terminal.

Four large pockets were sewn on the outside of the main pack. Based on each individual's needs, items that were routinely used were kept in the four pockets. The main compartment usually held one extra set of utilities, food, a sleeping shirt, extra socks, a poncho liner, rain gear, binoculars, a flashlight, and extra ammunition. Additional items such as maps, notebook, pencils, signaling mirror, pencil-flare gun, coded "shackle sheets," and cleaning equipment were spread out among different pockets on the utility uniform. (The term "shackle sheet" describes the device that each recon team carried with them to encrypt messages. As an example: a double column of capital letters ran down the right side of the page and another double column of letters was printed across the top of the page. Beneath each column of letters were double sets of numbers. There was no sequence to them. When map coordinate numbers were radioed from one position to another, the sender "shackled" his numerical information before sending out his position. Each team had the same shackle sheets and could figure out the code easily. Each shackle sheet was only good for a twenty-four-hour period and was then either changed or destroyed.) We never wore helmets in the bush, and we did not wear flak jackets. We never carried sleeping bags. They were considered defensive pieces of equipment, and their weight only added to our burden. Fully loaded with weapons, ammo, food, water, and all equipment, a recon team member's average load was no less than sixty pounds. That weight could rise significantly when items such as extra claymore mines, M-60 machine-gun ammo, Starlight scopes, and radio batteries were spread-loaded throughout the entire team.

The second day had been longer than I expected. My Unit-1 was ready; my gear had been packed and unpacked until I knew exactly where everything was located. My pistol and rifle had been cleaned and thoroughly inspected by Corporal Swederski. The next phase of my hasty education was personal conduct during a patrol.

"The sole purpose of a reconnaissance team is to SEE what is happening in a specific area and to accurately REPORT everything that you have seen." This was the first entry that I wrote in my patrol report notebook. Corporal Swederski had been tasked by Staff Sergeant Williams to teach me enough about the basics of patrolling so that I would not be a liability. Swederski had said that the company operations officer, First Lieutenant Coffman, had met with the company platoon commanders and they were then redistributing Marines from within the four platoons to cover the loss of company personnel and still be able to field the required number of manned and fully operational recon teams. That also meant that Corporal Swederski had less than one day to instruct me in how to be a member of the new recon team that was being built in the third platoon.

My lessons were short, and many were a recapitulation of what I had been taught at Field Med School. Hand-and-arm signals were the only method of communication that was used in the bush; absolutely *no* talking was allowed. Methods of movement were demonstrated. Changes to this would be made based on terrain, available cover, weather, and the daylight conditions. After several hours of Corporal Swederski's cram course, I was told to report to Sergeant Williams. "Your name's on the kill sheet," he said. "It means that you're going out on the next patrol."

My "formal" schooling was over. The new team would be made up of eight men: Sergeant Chapman was the team leader, Sergeant Peterson was the assistant team leader, Lance Corporal Kilcrease was the primary radio operator, Lance Corporal Kegler was the point man, Lance Corporal Perry was the secondary radio operator; the team's riflemen were Lance Corporal Silva, Private First Class Furhman, and me. We would leave the next morning by truck for Con Thien. From there we would walk out to recon a twelve-kilometer area of the DMZ. Our team's code name was Isthmus.

— FIRST MISSION: DMZ —

AT 0700 ALL THE MEMBERS OF ISTHMUS WERE TO BE seated in the company's S-2/S-3 hootch for our final briefing session. The operations officer, First Lieutenant Bucky Coffman, was prepared to give us the latest detailed information concerning where we were going, what our objective was, the proposed route, the number of days required to move into the DMZ, cross the Ben Hai River (*Song*), recon the area, and return, undetected, to the camp at Con Thien.

The assistant team leader, Sergeant Peterson, had closely supervised our rehearsals of "immediate-action drills" for hours the day before, and it was during the IA drills that information was given to us that detailed just how Isthmus would function as a team. Our "order of march" explained exactly the physical position that each of us would maintain during the entire patrol. The "friendly situation" indicated who, if anyone, from another friendly U.S. unit, was near our assigned area, what they were doing there, and what their radio frequency and call sign were in the event that we needed to contact them. The "enemy situation" explained the last reported sightings of any enemy activity in our AO (area of operation).

The geographical characteristics of the DMZ, and specifically our AO, were explained by use of a large and detailed sand-table model. Any special equipment that might be required was obtained, checked out, and carried along. A schedule was posted by Sergeant Peterson that detailed, hour-by-hour, the time to test-fire our weapons, pack our food and gear, test our communications gear, and then present ourselves for our team leader's detailed, final equipment inspection, which was designed to ensure that the first rule of Roger's Rangers (Revolution-era) was strictly adhered to: "Never forget nothin'. " The assistant team leader gave the

83

command for us to fall in for inspection, and we did so according to the order of march. Sergeant Chapman inspected each of us.

He was responsible as the team leader, and he assumed his role with authority and seriousness. Nothing was left to chance. That was made obvious during the inspection of the team. As Sergeant Chapman stood in front of each man, he instructed that Marine to jump up and down several times and then shake his body. That was a noise check. Loose equipment was secured by dull black electrical tape, anything that was shiny was covered over or cammied up, anything that made a distinguishable sound was muffled, and any ordinance or special equipment was physically displayed to see that it met with Sergeant Chapman's complete satisfaction.

This system and minute attention to detail simply ensured that each man in the team was totally prepared and that the sergeant's orders had been carried out to the letter. Each one of us knew who carried what, and where it was kept.

The personal physical condition of each member of the team was my responsibility, and I was required to know if any member of the team had a cough, a cold, an allergy, or suffered from any other mental or physical ailment that could interfere with the conduct of our mission. This responsibility was detailed enough to include knowing who in the team wore glasses and ensuring that each man who did carried with him not only his corrective lenses for his gas mask but an additional pair of glasses for the bush. Each man's blood type was made known to the entire team in case of a requirement for an emergency blood transfusion. This information was written in each member's notebook. I also informed each man as to exactly where I carried my box of six morphine injectable Syrettes.

This system of sharing all of our common information was nothing more than good field sense. If any one man was injured or killed, whether it was during daylight or in the black of night, we each knew exactly *who* carried *what* specific equipment and exactly *where* it was kept on each member of our team.

It was now 0650, and we walked away from our platoon area over to the S-3 briefing hootch.

Sergeant Chapman had us drop our packs, rifles, and rigs outside of the hootch, and we were standing at attention inside the small briefing room when Lieutenant Coffman walked in.

"Break out your maps, your notebooks, and your pens, and copy down these freaks" (radio frequencies). He continued on through a checklist of information that included the radio frequencies and call signs for Marine helicopter and fixed-wing aircraft and our artillery support. Then he briefed a modified version of what is known to all Marines as "SMEAC," the five-paragraph order (Situation, Mission, Execution, Administration, Command and signal). We took notes.

The first paragraph described three current situations: enemy forces, friendly forces, and any attachments or detachments to the unit. The second paragraph stated the exact mission. The third paragraph was a detailed execution, or description of the operation. The fourth paragraph stated the logistical requirements, and the fifth paragraph listed the command (location of each person) and what signals would be used during the mission.

Some of the information of the standard five-paragraph order did not apply to the conduct of our mission, but the format was familiar and immediately understood by every Marine in our team.

Questions were held until the operations officer was finished with his briefing, and at that time any specific questions that we had were addressed. No one's question was considered dumb, and Lieutenant Coffman made it a point prior to leaving to say that "the only stupid question was the one that wasn't asked."

Satisfied that we were as ready as possible, Sergeant Chapman gave the word to move outside and throw our gear into the back of the "six-by" truck that would take us to Con Thien. This was called, appropriately, a rough ride.

The six-by driver was accompanied by a Marine A driver (assistant driver), who rode shotgun in the cab. The rest of us sat on wooden bench seats that ran down both sides in the back of the big diesel truck. The bed of the truck was covered with a single layer of sandbags, which were to protect us from the blast effect of mines.

It was no secret within the company when one of the recon teams was scheduled to leave the area for a mission, and this day was no exception. A team departure had become a somber social event. Major Lee, Captain Hisler, First Lieutenants Coffman, Morris, and Hensley were there to say good-bye and good hunting. The company first sergeant and Staff Sergeant Williams were there too, as handshakes were exchanged and last words of encouragement were shouted out to us when the big green truck came alive. The roar of the engine and the huge cloud of thick black diesel smoke signaled our departure from the small compound, and to shouts of "Get some," we lumbered past 3d Recon Battalion and headed north to the Army camp at Con Thien, fifteen miles away.

We sat quietly as the truck headed up the dusty two-lane road, and for the first time in five days I was away from the tiny company area; even though I was in the company of nine other Marines, I was alone in my thoughts of what was about to happen. As the truck moved along, I was given my first real view of northern I Corps. The country of South Vietnam had been divided into military areas of responsibility called corps. The northernmost corps was depicted on our maps with the Roman numeral one (I), and it was commonly referred to as "Eye corps," not "one-corps." The Marines had been given responsibility for northern I Corps, and the northern boundary of I Corps was the famous demilitarized zone. The land to the north was flat and devoid of all trees. To the west the land began to grow steep, and the foliage was much denser. To the east was the South China Sea, and it was easy to see the white sand dunes of the coast not more than a few miles away.

The highway was busy with military and civilian traffic, but there were no civilian automobiles to be seen: mopeds, small Honda motorcycles, and brightly painted civilian trucks covered with chrome made up the nonmilitary traffic. Occasionally we passed wooden carts that were pulled along by several women. Some carts were moved by a pair of water buffalo, usually herded by a kid with a stick. The majority of the civilian traffic was headed south.

We left the limits of Quang Tri and were headed north along Route 9 when we came to a roadside guard shack that was manned by one South Vietnamese soldier and one U.S. Army military policeman. A barbwire-and-pole barrier across the road required us to stop. The MP asked our driver for the trip ticket that authorized us to travel on Route 9 and to enter the camp at Con Thien. We were told that we would have to wait until five vehicles joined us to make a convoy into Con Thien; that would prevent us from being ambushed as a single vehicle. It wasn't long before the other vehicles came along, and we met the requirement to become a convoy.

One of the five vehicles that joined our small group was an Army invention called a "quad-duster," a six-by truck with four .50 caliber heavy machine guns coaxially mounted in its bed. It had hydraulics that enabled all of the guns to train and fire as one. With a rate of 400 to 500 rounds per minute per gun, and with an effective range of over 2000 yards, it was a force to be considered carefully by any opposing ambush unit. The Army gunner who sat between the machine guns said that he could use the gun system to "cut down bushes like a hot knife going through butter." It was reassuring to have such a devastating piece of artillery moving along with us, and I believed that the mere presence of the quad-duster prevented any ambush from happening as we traveled the remaining five miles toward Con Thien.

We arrived at the large Army outpost around noontime, unloaded our gear, and said good-bye to our two truck drivers, who immediately headed back to the company area at Quang Tri. Sergeant Chapman then lead our team toward a manned observation tower that looked out across the wide-open territory of the DMZ. I had read about that very place in *Time* magazine and in *Newsweek*, and I had seen pictures of it in the pages of *Life*. Now I stood on a very small hilltop next to a wooden, forty-foot observation tower, commonly referred to as an OP, and I looked into the great enemy land of North Vietnam.

Our plan was to spend the night at Con Thien and wait for the return of one of the other two teams that were on reconnaissance missions somewhere out on the DMZ. Once they had been extracted, we would begin our movement north from Con Thien and into the Z.

There was a wooden trapdoor at the base of the tower, and Lance Corporal Kilcrease, our primary radio operator, wanted to show me what was beneath the door. He banged on the door with the butt of his rifle and shouted, "Comin' down." He pulled up on a huge steel ring and raised the trapdoor high enough to expose a wooden ladder that was the only way down into the subterranean communications bunker.

"Kilcrease, you skinny little redneck, are you back here again?" The Marines who lived there were communications technicians and operated a radio-relay site. Our reconnaissance teams that operated inside the DMZ radioed all information back to that relay site, and from there the information was relayed to the company area in Quang Tri. Kilcrease had gone to communications school with several of the Marines who were assigned to the outpost, and he introduced me to them.

Judging from our climb down, their underground comm bunker was at least thirty feet below the surface. It was two stories tall. The working areas were very small and crowded with different types of radios. The Marines manning them wore headsets that helped to keep them from being distracted by our conversation.

I asked one of the sergeants who knew Kilcrease to tell me about the OP. He said that the entire place had been built by Seabees several years before, and it was considered to be the safest place in Con Thien. The men who manned the radios came from one of the Marine communications battalions, and they looked at their assignment on the border of the DMZ as skate (easy) duty.

One of the corporals went on to say that no one ever bothered them there, there were few visits from "the flagpole," the Army chow was always better than C rations, and the bonus for being on the Z was that they all got to watch the nightly firefights and artillery duels between the Army's big 155-millimeter howitzers and the North Vietnamese Army's guns. He said that the only drawback to living underground was in constantly losing track of the time of day. "If I didn't have to change the date-time groups on my daily message reports, I'd never know what day it is."

The men in the comm bunker worked on rotating shifts, and that made their molelike existence easier to take. It was only when visitors like us appeared that their normal routine was broken. "Our first indication of a visitor is the damned blinding light that fills up the ladderwell, followed by all that loose dust and dirt dropping in on us. Other than that we're glad to see ya."

As the sergeant showed Kilcrease and me some of the latest improvements in the bunker, I couldn't help but notice that attached to each piece of communications gear were several red grenades that were held in place by chains. They were thermite grenades which could generate heat of over four thousand degrees in a matter of seconds. Their purpose was to melt down the radios in the event that the camp at Con Thien was ever overrun, thus denying the NVA access to our radios and frequencies. The bunker was considered a primary NVA target.

A ventilation system kept fresh air circulating through the different levels of the comm bunker, but nothing could take the place of the real thing. We went topside to have a cigarette and to leave the world of the comm moles to those who were not as claustrophobic as us.

When Sergeant Chapman returned to the OP, he told us that we would eat evening chow at the Army's field mess, spend the night at Con Thien, and then go out through the wire just before sunrise. The Army's unusual hospitality was really appreciated by us for two reasons—we would not have to use the food that we had packed for our mission, and the Army's food would be served hot. Open cooking fires were obviously not permitted on the line, but the field mess was protected by its dug-in location on the reverse slope of a nearby hill.

After we had eaten, we returned to where we had staged our

packs and broke out the gear that we needed for a comfortable night's sleep. There was enough daylight left to have one last smoke before covering up in our poncho liners. We had not been assigned to any defensive watches, and eight hours of uninterrupted sleep was considered a rarity, but someone in the north had decided that this was not to be.

The sound of a mortar round leaving the tube is unmistakable, and when half a dozen rounds have been dropped down the tube, it was only a matter of seconds before one of two things happened: either the darkness of night would be turned to daylight by bursting illumination shells or the heavy crunch of high explosive rounds landing on the deck would alert everyone to the possibility of a ground attack.

The stillness of the pitch black night was broken by the quick popping sound of six 81-millimeter mortar "illum" rounds breaking open, and this sound was quickly followed by the *woop-woop-woop* sound that the empty shell canisters made as they fell back to earth from several thousand feet above. Every man in the team was wide awake, and we looked out toward the ground that the illumination rounds had made visible. We knew that the mortar illum spread was only good for less than a minute and now more outgoing mortar rounds could be heard as they were fired skyward in the camp's attempt to keep the area well lighted.

Kilcrease had been given the conduct-of-fire radio frequency earlier by his pals in the bunker, and he was able to monitor the radio transmissions and tell us why the illum rounds had been fired.

"They say there are sappers in the wire." This news caused more than a little concern because a sapper probe was usually the prelude to a general ground assault. We took out several pairs of 7×50 binoculars and focused in on the illuminated area.

Sappers were highly skilled and fanatical North Vietnamese infantrymen who were in the bad habit of strapping high explosives to their bodies, sneaking up to the limits of defensive perimeters, and then hurling themselves into the barbwire. When the explosives detonated, the sappers blew themselves into a million pieces, and in the process of dying for their cause, they managed to open large gaps in the wire that allowed the NVA assault forces to pour into the area.

As another spread of illum rounds took the place of the first, an Army machine-gun position opened fire far to our left. We watched as the tracer rounds arched and bounced out across a small hill nearly three hundred yards to the north.

There was no incoming fire, there were no explosions in the wire, and there was no great NVA human-wave assault. When the illum rounds burned themselves out, we were left with only silence.

Kilcrease had kept the radio handset to his ear during the episode, and he said that one of the listening posts (LPs) had reported that they still had gooks in the wire. An Army M-60 tank tried to assist that LP by aiming its giant xenon spotlight in the direction of the reported movement. The spotlight produced a beam of light rated at several million candlepower. The LP had come up on the tank's radio frequency and directed the tank to move its light into the area where they had heard the movement. That did the trick.

Two unarmed, diaper-clad NVA sappers were caught in the center of the tank's light beam. There was only one thing they could do. *Run!* The U.S. soldiers who were manning the perimeter lines were as surprised to see the two NVA standing there as the sappers were to have been revealed to the world. The momentary delay saved them. The two sappers then began their spring out of the lighted area as rifle fire began to pick up in volume, and small plumes of dust from the impacting rounds kicked up where they had stood only seconds before.

Instead of running back toward the north they ran east, probably channeled in that direction by the wire. Still no one had hit them, and they continued their incredible spring, staying just ahead of the limits of the searching light beam. The machine-gun position that had opened up earlier again tried to pick them up, and the traversing rounds stayed only a few feet behind them. As the riflemen from the far left side lost sight of their two racing targets, they stopped shooting and only stared. This decrease in fire repeated itself down the perimeter line as the fleeing sappers ran parallel to the line.

Being on the hill afforded us a much better position to observe the scene that was unfolding, and during the last few minutes we had been joined by a number of soldiers who wanted to see what was going on. They began to cheer for the sappers, and to the whispered shouts of "Go, Go, Go" from the group of onlookers, the two escaped into the night. They had turned disadvantage to advantage, used the terrain to hide themselves while on the run, and had kept two feet ahead of machine-gun fire.

The tank that had tried to illuminate the area turned off its searchlight, started up its engine, and rumbled off to a new position. There was no more activity that night, but sleep did not come easy.

* * *

Sergeant Chapman was talking with an Army sergeant when Sergeant Peterson assembled the team. He pointed to the soldier and said, "He's our guide. He knows the way out through the wire and through the minefield. Let's go."

With that as our last verbal order, we began our movement away from Con Thien and onto the DMZ. Sunrise was several hours away when we moved out.

The terrain that we started to walk across was deceiving. From the elevation offered by the observation tower back at Con Thien, the DMZ appeared to be very flat and seemed to offer little in the way of concealment, but in actuality the terrain consisted of small rolling hills covered with dense brush that made it a perfect hiding place.

As the Army engineer led on, we began to move in a zigzag pattern that took us past many rows of triple barbwire and tangle-foot, multiple strands of barbwire strung close to the surface of the ground. It resembled a wire spider's web. The pattern of wire was so tight that it was virtually impossible to walk through. It was designed to make the enemy go around it, to channel them into killing zones covered by those weapons that were organic to the defensive infantry unit—mortars, machine guns, and rifle fire. As we moved away from Con Thien, we were looking back at the Army camp and seeing it from the North Vietnamese viewpoint.

The open terrain caused us to move slowly, and our interval between team members was no less than forty or fifty feet.

The signal to halt was passed down from the team leader, and the hand-and-arm signal for "minefield" came next. Passing through that area made it necessary to close up the gap between team members, as we tried to walk in the footprints of the man ahead. The mined area was not very broad, and as we came to the end of the minefield, the Army engineer waited for us to pass by, then signaled good luck with the familiar thumbs-up.

By noontime we had moved at least two kilometers north, and the signal to freeze came down the line, a clenched right fist held close to the chest. Once given, each man would immediately kneel down and face toward his area of responsibility. We had practiced these hand-and-arm signals for hours before we left Quang Tri. Each signal was recognized immediately.

Normally the point man's attention was to his direct front covering 180 degrees. The next team member in the line of march would direct his eyes and rifle to his immediate right, the man behind him to the left, and so on, right, left, right, left, down to the last team member. He had the responsibility of protecting the rear of the recon team. The last team member in the order of march was known as tail-end charlie; he walked backwards most of the time.

The freeze signal had been called by our point man, Lance Corporal Kegler. We were about to cross a large open area and Kegler wanted to get some guidance from the team leader as to where he was to go once he had crossed the open ground.

Lance Corporal Perry was directly behind me, followed by Sergeant Peterson and then Private First Class Furhman. There was a reason for this order of march. If our team sighted a numerically superior enemy force headed in our direction, it was far easier to signal a freeze, signal the reason why, change our direction 180 degrees, and then move away undetected with an experienced point man, assistant team leader, and secondary radio operator instantly in the lead, without having to turn the entire team around.

During the extended stop, I was watching to my left and noticed a thin green stalk of bamboo that kept waving back and forth. The bamboo wasn't more than a hundred yards away, and it attracted my attention for two reasons. Rarely does nature make things that are perfectly straight and green; they stand out. Secondly, the bamboo stalk was swaying to the left and right, but there was no wind.

I caught Perry's eye and motioned for him to look left and hoped that he saw the same movement. He did. Perry motioned to Sergeant Peterson, who moved up past Perry and over to where I was kneeling. He put his head next to mine so that I could continue to watch the movement and still be able to whisper, telling him exactly what I was looking at. Peterson picked up on the movement and moved forward to tell Sergeant Chapman what he had seen. I kept watching the spot, as did Perry, and then the bamboo stalk suddenly disappeared. When Peterson returned with Sergeant Chapman, I told the team leader what I had seen. He took out his binoculars and studied the area. "Someone's moving this way," he said.

Sergeant Chapman signaled for Sergeant Peterson, Perry, and Furhman to move up to where I was kneeling, and we began to form a hasty ambush position. I still couldn't make out any movement headed our way, but I did not have my binoculars out. Sergeant Chapman did.

His plan was quickly set in motion, and we prepared to ambush whoever was headed our way. Sergeant Chapman moved forward to put himself back in the center of the team.

I took out my binocs and focused them back to where I had seen the initial movement, but at first glance, there was nothing moving. But now to the right of the scrub brush, I could see that same piece of bamboo as it was silhouetted against the blue sky. It was moving toward our position.

The binoculars helped to solve the first part of the mystery. The moving bamboo stalk was a whip radio antenna, and that radio was attached to the pack on the back of one small individual headed toward us. But the scrub brush was at a height that made it impossible to get a good sighting of who the individual was and to know how many other people were with him.

The whip antenna continued to approach, and judging from its speed and direction, "they" would not only have to pass in front of us but they would have to cross the open area where Lance Corporal Kegler had stopped.

There were five of them and they were bunched up. It would make our hasty ambush easier because our firing would be concentrated in one small area. There was no time to set up one of the claymore mines that we carried just for ambushes and Sergeant Peterson was set in place with his M-14 on automatic. We were ready and waiting.

I took another look through the binoculars and began to scan the area beginning with where I had first seen the radio antenna. I could see the form of one man moving slowly toward the group of five. The bushes still made it impossible to get a clear view of him, but just ahead of him was an open area of about ten feet that he would pass by, and I would get my first view of the enemy.

He stopped at the edge of the clearing and waited for a few seconds before he started his movement forward. He was black! I motioned to Perry, but he was glued to his rifle and waiting for the five men to walk into the kill zone. There was no hand-and-arm signal to relay what I was watching, so I moved up to Sergeant Chapman and told him what I had seen. "Their tail-end charlie is black, don't shoot."

It was an Army six-man patrol, and they had no idea that we were passing through their area. We had no way of contacting them and Sergeant Chapman didn't want to take the chance of trying to signal them as their first instinct would probably be to shoot at us. They passed by us and continued toward Con Thien, never realizing just how close they had come to being ambushed. We waited for at least fifteen minutes before Sergeant Chapman signaled the team to move out and we continued on our mission north.

The heat and humidity had steadily increased, and during our second stop of the afternoon, Private First Class Furhman moved up to me and asked if I had anything that would stop him from itching. He said that he had prickly heat.

I carried two bottles of calamine lotion and one 35mm film canister full of Benadryl capsules, which would act to stop his itching but also make him sleepy. Not the best physical condition for our tail-end charlie. I gave Furhman the Benadryl and told Sergeant Peterson that he would have to keep an eye on Furhman to see if he was getting tired. Hopefully, the Benadryl capsules would relieve his constant scratching and help to reduce his constant movement.

By late in the afternoon we had moved about four clicks northwest of Con Thien, and Sergeant Chapman called for a halt. We were allowed to eat, one at a time; those of us who smoked were allowed to have one last cigarette before it became too dark. Once we all had eaten, we made our final plans to move into our harbor site, the place where the team would sleep, but there was a certain method to entering the site.

First, the tail-end charlie had to make absolutely certain that no one had followed the team from our last resting place. He would remain behind as the team moved toward the site, and he insured our safety from any possible enemy attack from the rear. The team leader then had the point man locate a very dense area of brush, and the team would begin a slow buttonhook movement into this area. Anyone who might have followed us would certainly be heard as they followed the buttonhook trail and moved around the outside of the team.

Once the team was in place, all eight men occupied an area no greater than eight feet in diameter.

With the team in the harbor site, the team leader designated two men to set up two of the defensive devices that were carried by each recon team. The first piece of equipment that was brought out of the harbor site was known as a "Pee-sid," PSID being the acronym for Personnel Seismic Intrusion Device.

The PSID could detect the movement of enemy men and their vehicles based upon the movement caused by vibrations. The PSID package consisted of five pieces of equipment, four battery operated transmitters and one receiver. The transmitters had a five-point sensitivity setting and each transmitter emitted its own coded signal. The sensitivity setting was based on the type of movement that we were likely to encounter and the density of the ground in which the transmitters were employed.

The second piece of equipment used with the PSID transmitter was the claymore antipersonnel mine. The claymore was not as technical as the PSID, but when used as part of the PSID system, it was worth its weight in gold.

The two team members would leave the harbor site and set up the first PSID in a northerly direction. The PSID transmitter probe was pushed into the ground and the transmitter was covered over with leaves and grass.

That first PSID would emit a single beeping sound audible only through the receiver. Next to that PSID transmitter a claymore mine was set up so that if it was detonated its blast would destroy the PSID. The second PSID would be set in the ground to the east, and the signal for that transmitter would cause it to beep three times. It, too, was covered by a claymore mine. The PSIDs covered the four points of the compass, and their individual signals revealed the direction of any movement. They protected and surrounded the recon team, and their existence would be undetected to the enemy because, once buried, the transmitter antennas looked like a single green blade of grass.

The men from the team who planted the PSIDs would then return to the harbor site and set up the PSID receiver next to the four claymore detonation devices, called hell boxes.

The schedule for radio watch was determined by the team leader, and radio watch consisted of three separate duties. First, we had to remain awake and alert and listening for a period of one hour. Secondly, we had to listen to the PRC-77 radio handset for radio transmissions coming in to the team. Last, but not least, we had to listen for the sound of any of the four PSIDs that might be activated by enemy movement.

The scenario for contact in the harbor site would happen this way: If an NVA patrol happened to enter the area near our team's harbor site and their approach direction was from the north toward the south, the northern PSID would begin to emit a single *beep* each time an NVA soldier's foot hit the ground.

Once the first enemy soldier of the patrol had crossed through the sensitivity zone of the first PSID and moved into the sensitivity zone of the southern PSID, it sent a *beep beep beep*. The recon team member on radio watch would have already awakened the team leader and explained what was happening. He would quietly awaken the team and then he would blow the claymores that covered the north and south sides of the harbor site, hopefully killing the members of the enemy patrol. His action would give the team time to get out of the immediate area amid all the confusion. The ritual of moving into our harbor site was repeated every night, as was the emplacement of the PSIDs and claymore mines. The security of the team depended on the PSIDs and on our ability to use them.

The exact position of our team was radioed back from Con Thien to Quang Tri by our primary radio operator, and our daily route and the position of our last radio transmission was plotted on the map of the DMZ that hung on the wall of the operations office. In that way all of the routes and exact positions of the operating teams were known to the company.

The mission of Isthmus was to move north onto the DMZ from Con Thien, cross the Ben Hai River, and recon a nine-kilometer grid that was suspected of being the launching place of 300-millimeter enemy missiles into the area of Cam Lo.

The S-2 (intelligence) officer who had been present during our premission briefing mentioned the fact that there was the possibility of us encountering Caucasian advisors if we sighted the suspected launching area. He said that the 300-millimeter rockets were "sophisticated Russian missiles that the average gook would need help in firing." We wondered what type of Caucasian would be helping the NVA fire missiles.

Our first night out on the DMZ was quiet. Sergeant Peterson had come over to where I sat and asked me if I had any questions about what had happened so far, and I told him that I had none, other than to ask about the condition of Furhman's itching. We went over the time that I would be on radio watch, where the hell boxes were located, and who was to relieve me from the watch. Sergeant Peterson also explained that it was the habit of the NVA to patrol the DMZ at night. He said that he had seen NVA patrols before, and they usually gave themselves away early because they used flashlights! At first I thought that he was pulling my leg, but Sergeant Chapman confirmed his statement and added that the real difficulty of spotting any NVA patrol was in distinguishing between flashlights and the hundreds of fireflies that lived on the Z.

It was Kegler who woke me up by placing his hand over my mouth and whispering, "It's 2300 and you got the watch." I knew from my brief training at Quang Tri that there would be a radio check every fifteen minutes from the relay at Con Thien, but I would not get to speak into the radio handset. The system for receiving any radio message traffic at night was designed around silence.

"Isthmus, Isthmus, Isthmus, this is Zulu Bravo, radio check. Over. The time on deck is 2315. If you are Alpha Sierra (all secure) at this time, give me one. Over.'' The "one" meant that I was to depress the rubber button on the radio handset one time. This would break the constant static hiss of the radio and that break would let the relay site know that someone was awake and the team was all secure. The PRC-77 was never turned off.

My first time on radio watch passed by slowly. The urge to sleep was not strong as I had fallen asleep quickly after we moved into the harbor site. All I could do was listen for some unfamiliar sound and wait to hear from the radio-relay team every fifteen minutes. There was no moon to look at, there was no noise, and there were no fireflies. At 2355 I woke Furhman and made sure that he was awake and ready to take the handset after I received the 2400 time check from Con Thien.

First light brought out clouds of insects, and as each of us finished eating in turn, we applied new cammie to our faces. The camouflage paint was inside a small green metal push tube with a cap on each end. Half of the tube contained a light green shade of thick greasepaint; the other side held a darker green version.

The application of cammie was a ritual. First, a small signal mirror was placed on the knee and a bottle of insect repellent was opened. The repellent was squirted into the palm of the left hand, and the exposed cammie paint was dipped into the repellent to break it down and make application to the face easy. Dark green paint went to the bony surfaces, and the light green shade broke up the contours of the face. Each man had his own particular pattern. The last rule about camouflage was that we didn't shave in the bush. Shaving was considered a waste of valuable water, and a thick beard helped to hold the cammie in place.

Once the PSIDs and claymore mines had been retrieved and repacked, we got the signal to saddle up, and we began our slow movement, always in the same order, toward the Ben Hai River.

Furhman had spent most of the night suffering from the effects of prickly heat, and it was obvious that he was not getting any better. The application of insect repellent only seemed to make matters worse, and by 1100 he had managed to scratch his arms and neck bloody raw. We stopped for a short break, and Sergeant Chapman signaled for me to move up next to him.

"What's wrong with Furhman? I thought that the pills you gave him yesterday would control that shit. If he keeps on scratching himself, he'll be a hunk of meat by tonight, and we still have eight more days to go. If you can't fix him, then I plan to call in a medevac bird and get his ass out of here.''

I told Sergeant Chapman that I could give Furhman Benadryl all day long, but it wouldn't help. With his arms and neck raw and bleeding, he had become a liability to the team. It was not Furhman's fault, the heat and humidity affected people in different ways. Furhman's solution was to scratch what itched, but the team leader's concern was that his constant movement could be the one thing that would catch the watchful eye of an NVA soldier.

Kilcrease called back to Con Thien and made the request for a routine medical evacuation. He was told to "wait out" until approval for the request was granted or denied.

We had moved nearly five clicks north of Con Thien, and our position on the map was just short of the red line that defined the southern boundary of the demilitarized zone.

One hour later the word came—"The medevac will be at your position in twenty minutes." Sergeant Chapman told us to break down Furhman's gear, take what we needed, and have him tagged and ready to go, ASAP. I took out a medevac card, filled in all of the information that described what was wrong with him, and we waited. The area where we had stopped was fairly flat and open, and the terrain would not present any problem for a CH-46 to land.

We took his claymore mine, his canned fruit, candy, and four hand grenades, and redistributed Furhman's water before the CH-46 and two escorts, Huey gunships, came into view.

The medevac was no problem. Furhman was ambulatory and could get himself on board without the help of anyone else.

Sergeant Chapman talked the pilot in without the use of signal mirror or smoke grenades. Furhman, colored pink by several coats of calamine lotion, got on board, and the CH-46 was gone in less than a minute. The routine medical evacuation of Private First Class Furhman could not have gone any smoother. Isthmus provided cover for the CH-46 when it landed, Fuhrman disappeared into the back of the bird, and the medevac bird with its escort gunships was up and headed south that fast. We knew that Furhman would be in the hands of some doctor at Charlie Med Battalion within half an hour, and once there maybe they could figure out how to cure Fuhrman's rash. While the routine medevac solved one Marine's problem, its appearance, landing, and departure created a greater one for the team.

A Marine CH-46 helicopter did not land on the southern edge of the DMZ without reason, and it was necessary for us to move away as quickly as possible from where the medevac bird had landed. The length of the DMZ was occupied by many different NVA units, and their interest in the CH-46 would certainly be cause for patrols to check out the reason for the landing.

We turned west and had moved another two clicks by late in the afternoon. Our route had taken us past several old village sites that were marked "destroyed" on our maps. There was nothing left of the villages except for the outline of a few buildings. Whatever had happened to destroy them had happened a long time ago.

The second night started out as uneventful as the first. Kilcrease had received a weather update from Con Thien that said a heavy thunderstorm was headed our way from the west and we should be getting wet sometime after 2200. We could hear the rumbling of the storm as it moved eastward, and we prepared for foul weather as best we could.

There are few acts of nature that compare with a great thunderstorm, and the anxiety level of each man in Isthmus was raised as the storm grew closer. The first concern of Sergeant Chapman was centered around the radio: our ability to receive and send information during the storm would be reduced, and a nine-foot whip antenna attached to a radio made for an attractive lightning rod that no one wanted to get close to. The second, and probably greater concern of the team, was that the sound of wind, thunder, and heavy rain would completely mask the sound of approaching enemy boots.

The rain storm lasted all night. Morning brought only steel gray skies and continued rain. The temperature had dropped from the high, humid, nineties to the low seventies with a cold and constant wind. Our ponchos had offered little in the way of protection during the night, and before leaving the harbor site, we took them off and put them into our packs. The temptation to wear the hooded poncho was great, but Sergeant Chapman knew that wearing it would reduce our field of vision and cover our ears, the two senses that our survivability was based upon.

We reached the Ben Hai River early in the morning, but what had been a slowly moving stream the day before, with help from the previous night's storm had now become a rapidly moving river. But the river had to be crossed, and there was only one way to do it. We paralleled the course until we found a narrow section of fast-moving water. Each man unhooked his Swiss-seat section of rope and passed it forward toward our point man. Seven lengths of nylon line were now one and were attached to Kegler's web belt. He removed his pack and slowly sank into the river and then crossed to the other side.

The speed of the river made it impossible for us to cross unaided with the amount of gear that we normally carried. Once Kegler was across, Sergeant Chapman followed so that Kegler could provide security for the rest of the team. In midstream Chapman lost his rifle. The force of the current had made him lose his grip, and one M-14 rifle had instantly become the property of the Ben Hai.

Sergeant Chapman did not give up his rifle easily. He continued across to the opposite side of the river and took the nylon line from Kegler. He tied the rope to his belt, judged where he had been when he lost his rifle, factored in the speed of the river's flow, and went under. On his third try at submerging and feeling his way downstream, he came up with his weapon!

We managed to cross the river without losing any other equipment, then headed northwest for another five hundred meters before stopping. As we moved away from the river, the terrain changed back to the low rolling hills and ground saturated from the recent heavy rains. Our rate of movement had slowed because of the mud, and the signal to stop and rest finally came down the line.

Sergeants Chapman and Peterson had taken out their maps and were in the process of writing out a sitrep (situation report) when Kegler came back to where they were seated. "I hear something up ahead. I'll take one man with me, get a little closer, and see what's up." Sergeant Peterson dropped his pack and moved forward with Kegler.

Sergeant Chapman finished writing the sitrep and had Kilcrease radio our progress to Con Thien. The rest of the team went to 100-percent alert and waited for the return of Kegler and Peterson.

Sergeant Chapman had watched them move slowly forward and gave the signal for the rest of us to move up. The next signal came down the line, this time in the form of a clenched fist held close to the face, then the index finger moved to the ear meaning "freeze and listen." With the exception of Kegler, Chapman, and Peterson, the rest of the team had no idea of what it was we were straining to hear. It was better that way, no preconceptions.

It was a bird—no, wait—it wasn't a bird, but it was a familiar sound. It was a chicken. No, it was more than one; it was a bunch of chickens, and what started out as the sound of a single bird could now be heard by all of us as a bunch of chickens squawking and clucking less than a hundred yards away. We moved to a better position but still could see nothing. Now we heard voices.

There were at least two voices talking back and forth in the high singsong that was Vietnamese. None of us spoke the language fluently, and we had absolutely no idea what was being said. We could only envision and imagine that these two individuals were somehow involved in moving chickens around in cages or crates. We couldn't see them because of the vegetation. They had no idea that we were practically in their hip pocket, and we had no way of knowing how many of them there were.

We pulled back for better cover and to give the situation some thought, making sure that our team's security was up and ready. Sergeant Chapman decided to call in a fire mission.

Sergeants Chapman and Peterson knew our exact location, and Chapman told Kilcrease to contact the 8-inch howitzer battery that was positioned back at Con Thien, then he got ready to write down his fire mission. Sergeant Peterson had Lance Corporal Perry turn on his radio, and Perry's radio became the team's primary radio with Con Thien, and this ensured that the people back in the company area would know what was about to happen.

The 8-inch howitzer battery at Con Thien had a range fan that covered our area of operation, and though we were more than four miles north of their position, they were more than capable of accurately firing their guns in direct support of our team.

As Kilcrease radioed back the information necessary for the fire mission, he was asked "What is the nature of your target? Over." He couldn't lie and say it was "gooks in the open" or "enemy platoon dug in," so he told them what he knew was the truth—"We've got twenty to thirty NVA/VC chickens out here. Over."

There was silence over the radio, then the question, "What did you say? Over." He repeated the description of the target. Howitzers asked "How do you know that they are NVA/VC chickens? Over."

Kilcrease looked down at his handset with a look of disbelief at their stupidity. "Because they sound like this, *baak bak bak baaak*. Now fire the goddamned mission. Over." We were located behind the crest of a ridge line that overlooked a narrow draw, and the small rise would give Sergeant Chapman the advantage and ability to adjust his call for fire immediately after the first rounds had landed. The message, "Shot out," came over the radio, meaning that the first round was on its way from Con Thien.

The elapsed time of flight of the artillery round, from the moment "shot out" was spoken to the next word, "splash," (the moment of impact), was less than twenty seconds, twenty seconds to take cover and to hope like hell that Sergeant Chapman had correctly plotted the location of the gooks and the chickens in the draw. We heard the first 8-inch shell as it came from behind us and detonated above the trees about three hundred yards to our front. "Drop one hundred, left one hundred. Over." Again we covered up, waited for the words "shot out," knowing that the VT (variable time) fused shell would now explode one hundred yards closer and above our heads covering the area to our front with white-hot pieces of shrapnel. Again came the sound of a single 8-inch shell as it raced past us and exploded right above the draw.

"Fire for effect, over." Three 8-inch howitzers had the order to shoot three rounds each, all nine rounds converging on the same place as fast as the gun crews could manage to fire them out. The result was awesome.

As the first volley of artillery rounds came in and exploded at treetop level, great black rings of smoke appeared with flashes of white and orange fire shooting downward from their center. Tall trees were ripped apart and blown down by the force of the explosions, and a mixture of earth and vegetation rained down around us. Chunks of shrapnel could be heard as they whizzed through the air and landed nearby. The fire-for-effect was over.

There had been no secondary explosions, no NVA emerged from the safety of their draw, and there were no more sounds from the chickens. The air was thick with the smell of smoke and cordite, and we looked over the edge of our hill to study the draw with binoculars. The entire length of the draw was still smoking, and the ground was turned over as though a giant spade had been applied to it.

"They want us to go in and take a look," Kilcrease said. We waited another ten minutes before we began movement toward the back of the draw. Sergeant Chapman wasn't foolish enough to lead us into the mouth of the draw and give the gooks the opportunity to hit us from above.

Kegler started down into the draw and moved slowly, following the folds of the terrain. When we got down to level ground, we began to pass by the area directly below the spot where the 8-inch shells had hit. Whoever and whatever had been in the draw half an hour earlier was gone. There was evidence of some small bamboo hootches that had been lashed together, and there appeared to be some fresh boot prints left in the mud, but the only real evidence that we found were chicken feathers scattered around the sides of the draw.

That was our team's first fire mission on the DMZ, and all we had to show for it was chicken feathers. The thought of how this unusual fire mission would be explained in the debrief was on Sergeant Chapman's mind.

We moved through the draw, and we were beneath the rim of the hills that had protected us during the fire mission. Kegler was trying to find a route that would bring us back out of the low area and once again give us the advantage of elevation, but terrain dictated how we moved. We were alert to the possibility of seeing whoever had been in the draw, but we didn't want to run into them on low ground.

The area began to open up, and that meant that we would increase the distance between ourselves. It was only possible for me to see Kilcrease, and as I watched him turn and move around a small finger of brush, I saw his hand go up and signal "freeze." Again, our well-rehearsed actions caused each team member to turn and face in the direction of his responsibility.

We had come to a trail that appeared to have been used heavily and recently. Sandal tracks marked the edges of the trail, and the patterns made from boots were not ours. Whoever had made the imprints had carried heavy packs, as the marks were sunk low into the ground, and the rain proved the tracks to be fresh.

The tracks showed the direction of movement was to the west, and we crossed the trail, not intending to walk on it. One of the first rules that we were taught was that a reconnaissance team "will never, ever, ever, walk on a trail. If you didn't make the trail, and you don't know who did, or how many had, then keep off of it. It is an open invitation to disaster to walk on an enemy trail."

Kegler led us across the trail, and we moved to set up and watch who was using it. As we crossed over the trail and began to move away from the low ground, Kilcrease motioned to me to come up next to him. He wanted some help in taking off his pack and getting to the whip antenna that was on his radio, replacing it with a smaller tape antenna which was shorter and more flexible than the whip. It didn't take but a moment to do this, and while he dug into his pack for the tape antenna, I looked back across the trail and stared at the opening of a small cave that had been dug into the side of the hill.

There had been no reason to look back as we moved forward and to our right, and that is why no one had happened to see the cave as we filed by. I whispered to Kilcrease, "What does that look like to you?" He stood up slowly and could see that I was looking back over his shoulder. He turned to study what had caught my attention. "It's a damn bunker; signal to Perry and move out of here, I'll tell Sergeant Chapman what we've found."

Sergeant Chapman signaled to Kegler to stop, and Kilcrease told the team leader about seeing what looked like the opening to a small bunker. The 7×50 binoculars came out, and Chapman and Peterson observed the opening for about five minutes. Judging from the color of the earth outside the entrance, it looked as though the hole had been recently excavated. The winds of the thunderstorm had blown down the fresh camouflage, revealing the opening to us. If the camouflage hadn't been replaced, then we reasoned that no one had been back to check on the bunker's condition or whoever had built it could still be inside.

Not wanting to take the chance of moving into an occupied enemy bunker complex, Sergeant Chapman had Peterson move up to a position from where he could fire CS gas into the opening of the bunker with his grenade launcher.

The M-79 grenade launcher was called a blooper, and one was normally carried by each recon team. Its versatility and three-hundred-meter range made it very desirable. The blooper man usually carried a mixed bag of four types of 40-millimeter ammunition—mostly high explosive (HE), buckshot, tactical CS (gas), and an illumination shell (white star parachute round) made up the bag. The CS rounds that Peterson carried with him had a range of three hundred meters and would detonate on impact, emitting CS gas for approximately twenty-five seconds.

Our plan was simple: shoot three rounds of CS at the entrance of the bunker and wait to see what happens. The *bloop* sound that the M-79 made, giving it its name, was slight in comparison to that made by rifle fire. What little wind was blowing would move the gas in the direction of the bunker and down into the draw. While Sergeant Peterson got the gas rounds ready, we broke out our gas masks in the event that the wind changed and blew the CS back to us.

Wearing a gas mask for any length of time is not a pleasant experience. But wearing a gas mask with correctable lenses and with the likelihood of having to do so in a firefight is no fun at all. As Sergeant Peterson fired the three rounds of CS in quick succession at the entrance of the bunker, we collectively hoped that no one was home. The small gas clouds disappeared; there was no sound of coughing, no movement, and no returned fire.

Kilcrease had been in contact with the radio-relay site and had told them what was going on while it was happening. The word now came down for us to move in and take a look at what was inside the bunker.

We stuffed our masks back into their carrying cases and moved forward, approaching the bunker from its side. It had been built recently and was reinforced with logs. It was Kegler's job to look inside and see what was there. As he moved to the front of the bunker he was covered by Sergeant Chapman and Kilcrease while the rest of us provided them security. Kegler moved inside with a flashlight and reappeared in a few seconds. It was empty. But once the three of them had moved close enough to inspect it, they realized that this was only one of at least a dozen other small bunkers that had been built between the two hills.

The NVA had done a beautiful job planning their bunker complex. The small openings had been built facing one another, and no artillery or mortar rounds would ever have enough angle to hit them.

We had to look in every one of them, using the same covering technique as we had done with the first. The only problem was that as we progressed down the line of bunkers we walked deeper into the draw and deeper into a very bad position. The higher ground was on both sides of us, and if we made contact, it would probably come from above.

"Look at all this shit," said Sergeant Chapman, and he shined his flashlight into the third bunker. The light beam exposed several stacks of antitank mines and at least two dozen wooden boxes that contained new Soviet 82-millimeter mortar rounds wrapped in oiled paper.

The searching of the bunkers continued, and within half an hour we had counted over forty mines and at least two hundred 82-millimeter mortar rounds. There was no possible way for us to move the ammunition or to destroy all of their hidden stockpile. That was not why we were there.

Kilcrease told Sergeant Chapman that the word from the rear was for us to take out some samples and copy down the ammunition identification lettering and lot numbers for the intell people. Sergeant Chapman had already requested that a platoon of engineers be flown out to the bunker complex so they could blow up the bunkers with C-4. That request came back as a "no go," and after a few minutes of bitching by Perry and Kegler, two of the twenty-pound mines and two 82-millimeter mortar rounds were attached to their packs.

It was getting late, and Sergeant Chapman did not want to spend any more time at the bunkers. He knew that the people who had built them had been scared off by our earlier fire mission and that they would return to check on their precious cache. He was right.

We had moved away from the bunkers, and Kegler had just started to cross another open area, when Kilcrease turned back toward me and suddenly pushed me down. He swung back toward Sergeant Chapman, sighted in, and opened up with his M-16, firing a full magazine of tracers at six kneeling NVA soldiers who had been watching Kegler as he crossed the open area. Kilcrease yelled, "Contact left, six gooks, one hundred yards," and he yanked out another magazine to replace his empty one. The twenty hot brass casings from his M-16 had bounced all over me as I tried to get to my feet and see what Kilcrease's firing had done.

For whatever reason, the instinct for me to shoot was immediate, and I sighted in on one of the NVA soldiers as he ran toward the top of their hill. I fired three shots but saw no telling results. Sergeant Peterson fired several rounds of HE from the M-79, and they impacted just to the left of where the NVA soldiers had been. Within these few seconds the entire team was firing in the same direction as Kilcrease's first magazine of tracers, but the six gooks were gone. There was no way to know if we had hit or killed any of them.

Once contact had been made with the NVA, many things happened in a very short period of time, and many questions needed answers. Some, if not all, of the enemy soldiers had survived our firing and now knew how many of us there were. All we really knew was that we had seen six of them. Were there only these six, or were they the point element of an NVA company on the other side of that hill?

Sergeant Chapman's first move was to get the team headed away from the NVA and moving toward the higher ground located about two hundred meters to our right. We wouldn't have to retrace our route, and the move would continue to take us away from the bunker complex. As we ran toward the higher ground, the elephant grass that we passed through became taller and dense. This slowed us down and caused us to bunch up again.

We had not taken any return fire from the NVA, but Chapman said that it would only be a matter of time before they would be on our trail. He wanted to make their attempt at following us as difficult as possible. He halted the team and told us that we would move straight ahead for approximately fifty meters, then each of us would turn to our left forty-five degrees and move forward another fifty meters, turn back to the right forty-five degrees, and then continue on until we got the signal to stop.

Anyone who was following our trail through the elephant grass would be following a single trail that suddenly became seven trails, all angling off to the left. The problem they faced was what trail would they follow and how many men made the seven trails. Their dilemma would give us time to set up a defense.

We had moved very quickly through the grass and did the

forty-five degree movements just as Sergeant Chapman had planned. When we were given the signal to halt, Sergeant Peterson went to his pack and took out one claymore mine, its wire, and hell box. He took Perry back to where the last forty-five degree turn had been made and set up the claymore mine.

If anyone was trailing our movement they would be heard approaching through the grass, and at the right moment Sergeant Peterson would detonate the mine and send three hundred steel ball bearings out to greet our uninvited guests. In the meantime, Sergeant Chapman had Kegler move forward to look for the best place to form a defensive fighting position in case the claymore didn't stop our pursuers.

Sergeant Peterson had hidden the claymore mine well, in a spot that was just past our single trail junction. He had aimed the device for maximum efficiency by tilting it back, not wanting to lose the blast effect to the dense elephant grass. Ten minutes had passed by since he and Perry had moved to their position, and then they began to hear the brush snapping as the first of the NVA pushed forward.

The sound of the claymore mine going off was the signal for us to move up to where Kegler was waiting, and Peterson and Perry joined us there.

Trying to catch his breath Peterson said, "There were at least six of them when we blew the claymore, and those are only what we saw. There's probably more 'cause the gooks wouldn't follow us unless they outnumber us."

Kegler had brought us to a huge bomb crater, and Sergeant Chapman had the seven of us form up into a 360-degree defense. Then he said, "Break out three grenades each. Put three CS grenades over here by me. Take out your gas masks and drop your packs. Kilcrease, get some air cover out here ASAP and call in this sitrep. We'll find out what it looks like from the air before we move out of here."

The first good news of the afternoon that we received was that an OV-10 Bronco would be over our position in less than ten minutes. We had not been probed by the NVA since the claymore had been fired, and the sun was beginning to set. Sergeant Chapman had called in the sitrep and told the people in the rear what had happened. Then we heard the shouts of the NVA off to our left. Still unsure of where we had gone, they had fanned out and started to shout to one another in an effort to draw our fire and reveal our position.

The timing of the arrival of the OV-10 was perfect. "Isthmus,

Isthmus, this is Cowpoke two seven, give me a mark on my first pass. Over.'' The pilot of the two-seat OV-10 had been given our position as he and his observer flew out to find us. Now they needed a visual sighting of our position before he would open fire on the approaching NVA.

Sergeant Chapman told Peterson to take out his strobe light. Peterson placed the strobe into the breech of his M-79 grenade launcher. From the safety of the center of the crater, Sergeant Peterson aimed the blinking M-79 at the Bronco and signaled our pos up to the circling OV-10.

"Isthmus, Isthmus, this is Cowpoke two seven. Be advised that you have two groups of gooners approaching your pos, one from the north and one from the west. It looks from here like there's about twenty of 'em. I'll make my first pass at the gooks to your north moving east to west. Over.''

Sergeant Chapman gave us the word that the Bronco was coming in hot, and we were to get down below the rim of our bomb crater while the OV-10 made the first pass with his miniguns. Sergeant Chapman came back on the radio to the pilot and told him that we would throw one white phosphorous grenade to mark our position, giving the pilot a good visual marker to fire around, in addition to keeping the NVA from moving closer to us.

As the OV-10 came in low on his first pass, the sound of AK-47s could be heard as the NVA fired up at the Bronco. The OV-10 was a more immediate danger to them than we were, and they were visible to him. The Bronco pulled up from his first pass and radioed to Kilcrease that his first run had looked good but he wanted to try a pass at the gooks who he had seen moving on our western side, too. The strafing runs by the OV-10 brought his 7.62 minigun fire to within fifty feet of the crater. As the impacting rounds ricocheted around us the sound of AK-47s could still be heard each time the OV-10 pulled up and away.

Cowpoke two seven had been on station for at least half an hour and had made at least a dozen passes, firing his machine guns and 40-millimeter grenade launcher with each pass. As darkness began to settle in, he came up on our primary radio one more time. "Isthmus, Isthmus, Cowpoke two seven. Be advised that I'm low on fuel and I'm returning to base. I'll be replaced by another OV-10 on this freq in about two zero mikes. Over.''

The twenty-minute wait for the return of another OV-10 was not the best news to hear, but we all knew that overhead protection couldn't stay with us forever, and as the silhouette of the departing Bronco became smaller, the shouts of the NVA began again.

Sergeant Chapman pulled Peterson and Kegler down to the center of the crater. "If the gooks still don't know where we are, then our pos is good. If they start to move in close, we'll break their probe with a grenade volley and move to that bomb crater over to our right. Just pass the word and be prepared to move."

For ten minutes we had sat motionless, waiting and straining to hear the sounds that would give away the presence of the NVA. There were no sounds other than the night sounds of the constantly buzzing insects. Then voices started again. There was movement out to our twelve o'clock position of the crater, and Sergeant Chapman signaled for Perry and me to move to the small pile of grenades that he had placed next to his pack. He handed us three fragmentation grenades and whispered that on his count to three we would each throw one grenade in a high arc out toward the sound of the movement.

The high pitch of the throw ate up the detonation time of the grenades, and the first volley exploded before hitting the ground. Immediately came screams of pain from out in front of the crater; the hot pieces of steel had found soft areas of flesh to rip through. We followed our first volley with another, and after hearing the heavy *crunch* of detonation, there was no other sound from the NVA.

The team was close enough so that Sergeant Chapman didn't have to yell. He said, "After this throw we move." Our third toss of grenades went to the right of the first two, and Kegler led the way out and over the rim of our bomb crater. He sprinted to the new position, and the rest of the team moved in quickly, taking up the same positions that we had held in the old crater. Sergeant Chapman was on the radio and talking to the incoming OV-10 as soon as he was inside the crater. He said that on the pilot's signal we would shoot up the strobe light from the center of the crater to mark our pos.

We had heard no sound of movement as we waited for the arrival of the OV-10, and again we stacked up grenades in preparation for another probe. We tried to make as little noise as possible in removing our packs and setting them down in the center of the crater. As we lined the rim and waited, we suddenly heard a series of loud electronic noises. *"Zizzzzzzzzz, click, click, Zizzzzzzzzzz click, click."* The sound was coming from one of the packs, and it was loud enough to give us away. Sergeant Peterson moved quickly to the center of the crater, and two fast jabs with the butt of his M-79 silenced what had been Lance Corporal Perry's new camera, stuck in the automatic film-advance mode.

No words were exchanged, and Sergeant Peterson moved back to his position on the crater rim.

The OV-10 arrived overhead and immediately picked up our signaling strobe. We had not heard any movement and radioed this to the Bronco. The pilot said that he was coming down for a closer look. Knowing that his approach would draw fire from the NVA, we tried to position ourselves to see how far away they were.

The Bronco made his first pass and drew no fire; on his second attempt at bringing his aircraft closer, he drew intense ground fire from their new position, less than two hundred yards away. Each of us had been told to load up at least three magazines of tracer ammunition before we had left the company area, and now we had a reason to use them. As the Bronco pulled up and banked over to make a firing run on the concentration of NVA soldiers, Sergeant Chapman radioed to the pilot that two of us would fire a stream of tracers in the direction of the NVA. The pilot would use our firing to mark his target for his copilot to fire on. This mutual air-ground support worked out well for the OV-10, but it also tipped our hand to the NVA, showing them where we were. We fired at the NVA area only once, and as the Bronco flew over us in his second and third passes, he took no more ground fire. The pilot came up on the radio and told Sergeant Peterson that he was headed back to his base, and by the time the Bronco's engines were a distant hum, it was midnight.

Kilcrease had taken the third turn on radio watch when he was told to get Sergeant Chapman on the radio. The people in the rear had decided that our position was not good and that we would be extracted early in the morning. After getting all of the particulars passed to him, Sergeant Chapman passed the word. We would have to move to the southeast and cross the Ben Hai River before a pickup by CH-46 helicopter could be made. It would be at least 0800 before we would arrive at the river, and there was an area on the map that showed a possible landing zone just two hundred yards away from the southern side. We would leave the safety of the bomb crater just before first light.

As a departing gift to the searching NVA, Sergeant Peterson decided to booby-trap the best approach to the crater. He took Perry and me outside the crater just before we left. At the base of the crater he rigged two of Furhman's extra grenades. Instead of using wire, he pulled out a length of dental floss and used it to tie off the grenades. Passing the white line across his cammie stick gave it the look of a white and green vine.

Ten minutes after we had left the crater we heard the two

grenades detonate, almost in unison. We picked up our pace and moved toward the river. Kilcrease had changed his radio freq to receive the incoming CH-46, and by the time we came to the river's edge, he had received their call saying that they would be at our prearranged position in less than ten minutes.

As we approached the northern bank of the Ben Hai River, it was obvious that it would take longer than ten minutes for seven of us to safely cross to the other side. Our crossing position gave us at least fifty feet of fast-moving, chest-high water, and the pressure of pursuing NVA only added to our problem.

Kegler crossed first and did not disappear below the surface, which was a concern to each of us. He moved forward, checked out the other side, and returned to signal for Sergeant Chapman to follow. Within several minutes Chapman and Kilcrease had crossed over, and Sergeant Chapman contacted the approaching helicopters and told them to give us an additional ten minutes before making their final approach before our extract.

Six of us waited for Sergeant Peterson to enter the water and begin his move to the southern side. He would be the most vulnerable because there was no one to cover his move from the northern side. When he had less than fifteen feet of water to wade through, two AK-47s opened up from downstream on the northern side.

The bullets shot small geysers of water skyward as they walked upstream toward Sergeant Peterson. Perry had yelled at him to go under and then he began to return fire in the direction of the AKs. Sergeant Peterson had let the current take him past the point where we had planned to grab him, and when his head broke the surface, he had only to move three or four feet to shore. He was safe and wasted no time in getting over the bank.

Kilcrease was already on the radio and telling the approaching "brown package" that we were under fire from an unknown size unit located on the northern side of the river. The escort Hueys started a firing pass down the river as we ran for the open area that was about three hundred meters to our front.

The "brown package" was a term that was used to denote the size of the approaching helicopter force. A "pink package" was one small observation helicopter, "red" was one observation bird and two escort gunships, usually Cobras. A "green package" was usually two CH-46s with escorts, and our "brown package" was the largest size, consisting of two CH-46s, two Cobra gunships, and two Hueys. Considering where we were, the people in the rear wanted to ensure that we had all the help we could use.

As Kegler moved to the edge of the proposed LZ (landing

zone), he signaled to Chapman and Kilcrease to move up. The lead CH-46 asked Sergeant Chapman if there was anything in the LZ that could add to the problem of his approach and when told "negative," he radioed back that he would make one pass over the area before setting down.

Sergeant Chapman had put the team into a 360-degree position that would provide some security for the CH-46, and as we had not received any more fire since Sergeant Peterson emerged from the river, we had no way of knowing in which direction the NVA would move.

We had practiced how we would handle boarding the extract bird from a hot LZ when we were in Quang Tri, never realizing how soon practice would become reality. As the CH-46 set its tail down for a fast landing, Sergeant Chapman pointed to each one of us, and we ran from our spot on the ground and into the ass end of the waiting CH-46. The last two Marines to run aboard were Kilcrease and Sergeant Chapman, connected to one another by the long black cord of the radio handset running from Kilcrease's rucksack to Sergeant Chapman's ear.

We stood up inside the CH-46, and each took up a position by one of the four windows. The large window openings that were located on either side of the helicopter and behind the cockpit each had a .50 caliber machine gun manned by a crewman. The small porthole-type windows located toward the rear of the CH-46 had had the Plexiglas coverings removed. Our rifles now protruded from each side of the still-grounded helicopter.

The big .50 caliber gun on the right side of the bird opened up first. The gunner shouted that he saw "gooks in the tree line," and fired again, this time with a very long burst. As the helicopter engines strained and picked up their rpms, the tail rotor was suddenly hit with a force that shook us hard enough to put us back down on the ground.

The pilot, copilot, and crew chief ran out of the back of the CH-46, leaving only one gun manned and us inside. The CH-46 was now filling with black smoke. The sound of rounds impacting on the Plexiglas of the cockpit could be heard, and the spider web of shattered glass was all we needed to see to convince us to get the hell out of the damaged CH-46. Perry and Peterson had the forethought to help the gunner pull the bolts out of the two .50 caliber machine guns, freeing them from their mounts. As we ran from the smoking CH-46, we put its position between us, the tree line, and a second CH-46 that was landing to extract us and the crew of the first bird.

The NVA who had been tailing us had managed to cross the river and then fire an RPG-7 (a rocket-propelled grenade) through the tail section of our CH-46. Unflyable, the crew had decided to bail out but had forgotten to mention their planned departure to the seven of us occupying space in the rear of the smoking CH-46.

When we boarded the second CH-46, we were met by Major Lee, who had convinced the crew of the second bird that it would be in the best interest of their longevity to keep the bird on the ground until all members of Isthmus were safely aboard. As our CH-46 lifted up and out of the LZ, we watched the gunships make firing runs on the now-smoking tree line.

Major Lee wore a helmet that allowed him to talk directly to the pilot of the CH-46. He said that we were to keep our eyes on the downed CH-46 as we gained greater altitude. From below and to our left we watched a flash of silver move past us, and then the CH-46 disappeared in a long ball of orange fire and black smoke. Two F-4 Phantom jets had just dropped four canisters of napalm on the smoking CH-46, rendering it a small lump of melted wires and burnt metal.

Team Isthmus had been out on the DMZ for only four days before being notified of our emergency extraction. Minus Private First Class Furhman, we had suffered no casualties, had broken contact with the enemy four times, and had barely managed to get away from them this time.

As we flew back to Quang Tri, Lance Corporal Kilcrease sat beside Sergeant Chapman and me. Sergeant Chapman was staring down toward the floor of the helicopter when Kilcrease tapped him on the shoulder. He asked Chapman what he was thinking about, and Chapman answered back that he was still thinking about how he was going to explain at the debriefing his calling in a fire mission on twenty to thirty NVA/VC chickens.

MONSOON

UPON OUR RETURN TO THE COMPANY AREA FROM OUR mission on the DMZ, we found that the reorganization process within the company had provided our platoon with six new people. We were losing some valuable team members, too.

Sergeant Chapman began his check-out process as did Sergeant Peterson. Their tours of duty were coming to a successful conclusion, and my first reconnaissance mission with them turned out to be their last team mission with the company. Lance Corporal Perry was sent down south to Da Nang for a few days prior to his leaving Vietnam for a well-deserved five-day R & R in Hong Kong.

The departure of two experienced team leaders like Sergeants Chapman and Peterson would be a considerable loss to the platoon and to the company because their experience and knowledge were difficult to replace. They were respected by all of us.

Under the direction of the company commander and the training officer and the guidance of First Lieutenant Hensley, Staff Sergeant Williams began his reorganization of the third platoon.

We were told that our reconnaissance teams would continue to operate in and above the demilitarized zone. They would be made up of eight men per team. The third platoon would now have enough men to build two eight-men teams, and each man's assignment to a team would be permanent. Officers were not permanently assigned to any of the reconnaissance teams in 3d Force.

The first team in our platoon was comprised of Staff Sergeant Williams, Corporals Bishop and Jenovich, Lance Corporals Kegler, Keaveney, Silva, Private First Class Furhman, and me.

I had, unknowingly complied with Major Lee's order to lose ten pounds, as upon returning from my first reconnaissance mission on the DMZ, I found myself twelve pounds lighter than when I had left.

There is something mysterious about carrying sixty-five pounds of equipment in daily temperatures that exceed one hundred degrees and with a humidity always above eighty percent that makes stateside fat just seem to melt away. What is left quickly becomes good solid muscle.

Like many other men who arrived in Vietnam from the States, wearing the results of too much good living, I found myself more than physically fit within a few weeks thanks to a well-organized company PT program in the rear combined with hours upon hours of humping the hills.

The second team in our platoon was made up of Sergeant Garcia, Corporals Swederski, Moss, and Snowden, Lance Corporals Perry and Breen, and Privates First Class Rowley and Villa, a radioman from the company's communications platoon.

We were given a new seven-day training schedule that was designed to improve our capabilities to operate independently. Every day of training was built around a period of classroom instruction, followed by demonstrated application. Our training started at the individual level and progressed slowly to the team level.

We began each day in the rear with a two-hour period of calisthenics, which included a three- to four-mile run to get our blood flowing, and then the daily classes began. Our classroom patrolling tactics were usually taught by one of the senior NCOs from the S-3 (operations) shop, assisted by several of the recon team leaders from the other platoons. The watchful eyes of Major Lee, Captain Hisler, and First Lieutenant Coffman monitored our progress.

After the patrolling classes ended, daily rehearsal of immediate-action drills began. We practiced these drills throughout the company area. The S-3 office would task one or two Marines to take their M-16s, along with several magazines of blank cartridges, and hide themselves within the company compound. As each team practiced moving around the small area, it would be ambushed and then demonstrate its ability to react to the direction of the attack. The sound of several blanks being fired, followed by the yell of "ambush left" or "ambush right" or "ambush rear," was a daily occurrence. We practiced our drills while carrying our weapons and wearing all of our equipment. We trained just the way that we would patrol.

The team corpsman was expected to teach classes to the team members on emergency first aid, and the particular type of first-aid instruction would depend upon the mission, terrain, and weather. Hourly classes on treatment for heat exhaustion, heatstroke, fractures, and emergency trauma were commonplace.

"Contact right! Kegler, you're shot in the gut, and your right arm is broken. The corpsman is dead. Okay, Keaveney—what do you do to take care of Kegler? Show me how you'd do it."

The team radio operator was tasked to teach classes to all of us on how to preset three different frequencies on the PRC-77 radio. The team leader would teach and review hand-and-arm signals. Each team had its own variations of the signals. The teaching point was made that "any arm-or-hand signal was a good one as long as it was commonly understood by all members of the team."

Since the primary mission of a reconnaissance team was to provide timely and correct information about a particular area and the enemy forces within that area, the use of reporting formats was always considered to be an essential part of the patrolling classes. The SALUTE report was the standard format for an information message that described the Size, Area, Location, Unit, Time, and Equipment information from an enemy sighting. A spot report was another standard format used by our teams to describe enemy activity in a particular area. All team members were taught how to write accurate reports quickly and how to use the radio to transmit that important information.

The training of each team included the methods for requesting an artillery fire mission, requesting air support, and for requesting emergency medical evacuations. Again, every team member knew what was required and the learning of the reports was mandatory.

The older Marine noncommissioned officers in 3d Force shared their combat experiences whenever possible, and those lessons learned from their days of combat in Korea and their stories of earlier tours of duty in Vietnam were always considered an important part of our training. All of our instructors said that they owed their success and their current existence to the high quality of training they had always received.

By the end of seven days of intensive training, our teamwork had improved significantly. We had demonstrated that we had learned our lesson in the fundamentals of patrolling, but classroom instruction was only a small part of the process. The real proof would be in applying what we had learned around the company area to life in the bush. Each additional phase of our training program had to be successfully demonstrated by each team member before we would advance to new subjects.

The proper handling of ropes, the correct tying of knots, and the knowledge of when a particular type of knot was called for became second nature to every man. There was great emphasis placed on reviewing the basics of map reading, the use of the lensatic compass, and plotting exact locations. This skill was also demonstrated several times per day by each team member to the satisfaction of the platoon sergeant and platoon commander.

On the evening of our final day of training, Staff Sergeant Williams and Corporal Bishop were told to report immediately to the operations hootch. The rest of the team waited for their return by the large green conex box that we called the club. Our company strength was so small that we did not have the luxury of an enlisted club, a staff NCO club, nor an officer's club. Our club was a large metal box designed for shipping military cargo. It was the size of a small tool shed, and its contents were protected by piles of sandbags. The stacked cases of Carling Black Label and Falstaff beer that were kept in our club were not refrigerated, making the coolness of evening the best time to enjoy sharing a warm beer. The company policy on alcohol consumption was "two beers per man, per day," and warm beer to a Recon Marine was always better than no beer at all.

When Staff Sergeant Williams and Corporal Bishop returned to the club, our guess as to why they had been called over to the S-3 hootch was quickly confirmed—we would leave the following afternoon for another mission across the DMZ.

Corporal Bishop was assigned as our new team leader. He had been an assistant team leader in the first platoon before the company reorganization, and this new mission was his first opportunity to demonstrate his skills as a team leader, under the silent but constant supervision of Staff Sergeant Williams. This nine-day mission on the DMZ would be similar to our last patrol. We were going to look for another 300-millimeter enemy rocket-launching site, believed to be located south of the Ben Hai River.

Kegler was our team pointman; Corporal Bishop walked second, and carried his own PRC-77 radio. Staff Sergeant Williams would observe the team from his number three position. I walked at position number four, Silva was a rifleman at position five, and Keaveney was our M-79 blooperman at position six. The number seven position was taken by Corporal Jenovich, the assistant team leader and secondary radio operator. Last, but not least, was Private First Class James Furhman, tail-end charlie. Our official team name was "Snakey One Three" (first team, third platoon), but our radio call sign was simply Snakey. We would share each other's company every hour of every day for the next seven months.

Our rough ride to Con Thien was without incident. We arrived at the Army camp late in the afternoon. We staged our gear and

Staff Sergeant Williams, Bishop, and Jenovich went down into the comm bunker to get the latest extended weather information and to make sure that there had been no change to the long list of different radio freqs and call signs for our artillery and air support.

When the team leaders came back to our staging area, Bishop called for a team meeting to pass the word. "This mission will not be a cakewalk across the DMZ. The guys in the comm bunker say that there is a tropical storm headed this way, and it could be here within forty-eight hours. If it gets any bigger it will become a typhoon, and we'll be out in the middle of it. We'll leave here at first light. Get some sleep."

The nine-square-kilometer area of the DMZ that was our recon zone was west of Con Thien, and our direction of march did not include passage through the minefield that bordered the northern edge of the camp. By noontime of our first day, we had moved about three kilometers west of Con Thien. Bishop had radioed in our location, and following his report, he received word that the tropical storm was on a steady course that would have it come ashore within twenty-four hours. It had been upgraded to a typhoon. Our orders were to continue the mission so we moved northward all afternoon without any sightings.

By late in the afternoon, a rapid change in the weather began. The blue sky was quickly overcome by the formation of steel gray clouds, and the change in humidity caused giant thunderheads to appear in the east along the coast. By the time we had moved into our first harbor site, we knew that the heavy rain was but a few minutes away. We set up our claymore defense.

One of the problems with the PSIDs was that their sensitivity caused them to transmit each time there was a great clap of thunder, whenever raindrops landed on the seismic spindle, or whenever artillery shells landed nearby. To the person assigned to radio watch, the beeping sound of the PSID was always assumed to be caused by approaching enemy soldiers first, and artillery fire or acts of nature came second. It was more than confusing to try and tell the difference between the two possible sources, particularly at night and compounded by the noise of a thunderstorm.

By midnight the temperature had dropped from the humid nineties to a very cold sixty-five degrees, made worse by an increasing wind. It was impossible for any of us to sleep. By first light the wind had become a constant forty-knot gale, and the people in the rear said that the strength of the typhoon was to intensify by late afternoon. They also said that we were to continue the mission and "be in your reconnaissance zone no later than 1600." As the heavy rain continued to fall, our primary concern was to quickly find an area of shelter and not be caught on the low ground.

By 1700 we were in our second harbor site and surrounded by the thick stalks of bamboo. The height and density of the bamboo helped to break the force of the wind, but the noise of the swaying and rubbing stalks masked all other sounds. Our position made the best of a bad situation. Even with PSIDs and claymore mines in place, our ability to rely on them was greatly reduced and put us at great risk.

At 2330 I was due to take my turn on security watch. I awoke to the shaking of my shoulder by Keaveney, and he didn't have to whisper for fear of his voice being heard. He said that the radio-relay people had passed new information to him that indicated the typhoon was due to come ashore within two to three hours. The force of the wind was expected to be in excess of 120 miles per hour. We were to consider taking every precaution possible to protect ourselves. This advice came from people who were dry, warm, and safe, thirty feet underground. We both laughed like hell when he had finished reading those words from the pale yellow pages of his dripping little message book.

As I sat in the dark with my back against my rucksack listening into the radio handset, I tried to visualize the experience of a hurricane named Carol, the one that caused tremendous damage to the New England states in 1956. I witnessed great oak trees, pines, and beech trees that were ripped up by their roots and thrown around like so much kindling. As kids, we thought that it was a great event. No school was scheduled for the day before the storm hit, and we were able to go outside and play as the eye of the great hurricane passed by. It took days for my father to repair and restore power to our small village. Scores of people were hurt, and the cost of the damage was in millions of dollars. That had been more than a dozen years ago.

The idea of being out on fairly open ground as the typhoon came ashore and passed over us took on a new dimension—concern. The wind and rain increased to such a degree that by midnight we had each taken out our Swiss seats and tied the twelve-foot lengths of nylon line around our waists, looping them through the larger stalks of bamboo.

How the seven Marines around me could sleep while the velocity of the storm increased to a great and roaring howl with the rain beating down so hard was difficult for me to imagine. There had been no training for such an event. Now we were tied to bamboo and hoping not to be blown away by the wind. I thought that perhaps my teammates weren't really asleep. Perhaps they were all lying there like me, shivering, soaked, and silent, but still awake and wondering to themselves, just like me, why in the world were we really out in the middle of a typhoon.

As our turns on security watch rotated, the black of the night slowly turned into the dark gray of a morning storm. The message traffic that was passed from our operations people during the night had said that we were to stay in our harbor site until the storm had passed.

The wind died down with the first light of morning, but the driving sheets of rain continued, relentless. Covering ourselves with our ponchos had been a futile attempt at staying dry. The skin on our hands was wrinkled and white from the constant immersion in water. We were given the signal to eat, and in an attempt to get warm began making coffee.

The making of good C-ration coffee in the field is an art form. Each man has his own style, one that he has perfected over many mornings in the bush, where a cup of good-tasting coffee is considered the mark of an experienced man. There are rules: the coffee cannot be made to taste like instant coffee; it cannot be served lukewarm; it must not be too sweet, or taste bitter; it is not made black. Good-tasting C-rat coffee is a coveted prize. It is sometimes shared, but only a short taste was ever offered—to show those of lesser culinary experience what good-tasting coffee is all about. The coffee-making ritual begins.

A coffee cup begins its life as a small, green can of apple sauce, pitted apricots, or fruit cocktail. Once the selected can is removed from the rucksack, its lid is punctured with a John Wayne can opener that hangs from the dog-tag chain. The dog tags are always taped together, silenced. The lid of the can is opened three-quarters of the way around, then pried up and backward, and the edges are then pinched together, forming a convenient metal handle. The original contents of the can are immediately eaten with a white plastic spoon that is always kept in the left breast pocket of the utilities. The empty can is not cleaned out with water—that would be a waste of precious water—and the residue of the heavy sugar syrup will sweeten the taste of the coffee.

There were two methods for heating water in the bush. Using a heat tablet is one method; the second, and more preferred method, is begun by lighting a match and igniting a small teaspoon-size piece of white C-4 plastic explosive. It burns white-hot, taking less time than the blue heat tab to boil the water. One brown packet of instant coffee is laid aside. One or two sugar packets are also set aside, depending on the maker's taste. Powdered-cream-substitute packets are used in the same manner. Once the water is brought to a boil, the instant coffee is slowly stirred in, followed by the addition of the cream substitute and sugar, in that order.

The hot coffee can is raised slowly to the lips; the can is held by the metal lid handle with only the thumb and index finger. The first sips of the hot coffee go always to the maker. The taste is his mark. If it passes his quality test, then and only then is it shared. As the can cools, it is cradled in both hands for warmth.

As a departing gift, Hospital Corpsman First Class Solis had presented me with a cardboard box that contained twenty-four one-ounce bottles of brandy. These bottles were marked "medicinal purpose only." It was decided that if ever there was a time to use brandy, this morning was the time. So for those members of the team who wanted to add some extra kick to their coffee, a one-ounce bottle of brandy was ceremoniously poured into each green coffee can or canteen cup that was offered up.

As the ritual of the making of morning coffee ended, Bishop gave orders that we were to check and clean our weapons. The constant downpour of water did them little good, but they would be totally useless if they were not lubricated and protected against rust. So that, too, was a daily ritual in the bush.

Corporal Bishop had been given the word for us to continue moving toward the northwest, and our slow rate of travel over wet and muddy ground put us into our recon zone by late in the afternoon of our third day. We had seen no movement, encountered no trails, and we had found no fresh tracks. The rain continued to pour down, and the low ground had absorbed all of the water that it could possibly handle. By late in the afternoon, and with no relief from the rain, Kegler began his search for our harbor site area. The area that we had moved to gave us protection from the wind but not from the rain.

It was a miserable time. Everything that we carried in our packs was wet. Though we had wrapped our extra clothes in plastic and tucked things deep into the recesses of our rucksacks, all our extra uniforms, sleeping shirts, and socks were thoroughly soaked. By the time we had put out our standard PSIDs and claymore defense, it was dark. Our last verbal radio transmission pinpointed our location, and we settled in for another night of waiting out the constant downpour.

We continued to operate within our nine-click area for the next five days. The rain would subside to a drizzle from time to time, but it never stopped. As we moved throughout our zone, we could only imagine what the storm damage would be like when we returned to Quang Tri. But for the present time, our attention was focused on what was happening to us there on the DMZ and in trying to locate the enemy rocket site.

On our eighth day into the mission, we moved down from an area of high ground toward a bombed-out area that appeared to have once been a very small village. The area was dotted with huge bomb craters filled with water. As we left the protection of cover from the dense vegetation, we moved through these instant swimming pools that had been made so many months ago. One by one, on signal from the man in front, we would slip down into the water-filled craters and cross through them. We tried to maintain our balance as we moved forward, but the weight of our gear caused us each to sink chest-deep into the water. When the tail-end charlie emerged from the last crater, Bishop called for a rest. Our movement through the cratered area had made no immediate difference in our comfort. We had been wet for eight days; what was a chest-deep wade through a bomb crater to us?

During the rest, Staff Sergeant Williams motioned to Kegler to lean his head forward. Kegler bowed toward Williams, and as he did this, the staff sergeant pulled a large green leech from the side of Kegler's neck. It was at least four inches long. The look of surprise on Kegler's face was mirrored on our own as the big leech turned over and over in the palm of Staff Sergeant William's hand. It hadn't been on Kegler's body long enough to attach itself to his neck; its searching movement had caught William's eye and immediate attention.

As Staff Sergeant Williams studied the leech, he drawled, "That one I could see. Y'all better check each other out and see who has acquired any new friends." It was another lesson learned and passed on. He said that the large green water leeches lived in the water of the bomb craters and whatever passed through the craters would become a host to the fast-swimming leeches. Welcome to the DMZ.

The morning of our ninth day brought only more rain. We had finished patrolling the entire recon zone, and we were now located at our last rallying site before beginning our return trek to the southeast.

The last position that we occupied before our departure home was called third base. It was a good boost to our morale to be at third base. It meant only one more night on the DMZ and only one day's walk back to Con Thien. We would get mail; we would get

Team Snakey: Corporal Ted Bishop, "Doc" Norton, Donnell Kegler, and
Paul Keaveney.

Team Snakey's death card
used to mark dead NVA in the
A Shau Valley.

A Marine on rappel during training (note lack of helmet and gear).

A Marine rappelling during a mission, with helmet and gear.

Results of a B-120 rocket attack on 3d Force Recon Company Area, Quang Tri, September 1969. Fourteen Marines were wounded.

From left to right: Colonel James, Captain Norman Hisler, Major Alex Lee, and First Lieutenant C. C. Coffman.

"Doc" Norton, Phu Bai, 1969.

3d Force Recon's parachute loft, October 1969.

Soviet 12.7mm antiaircraft gun captured in A Shau Valley in 1969.

Bamboo irrigation system used by the NVA.

Left to right: Lance Corporal Rowley, Corporal Premmel, and Corporal Moss. In background are team members preparing for a mission.

Lance Corporal Paul Keaveney, September 1969.

Lance Corporal Sexton before a patrol.

Sexton's K-bar knife and day and night flare, damaged by AK-47 round.

Zulu relay shot down on Hill 883, December 1969.

clean, dry, and drunk. For the first time in nine days of constant rain, the hint of a smile would appear from time to time, to form across the bearded faces of each one of us. We began our slow walk to Con Thien.

When we were two clicks away from the perimeter of the base, Bishop radioed our position to the relay-site comm moles and told them to pass the word that we would be entering friendly lines at noon. He wanted to make absolutely sure that our movement beyond the wire would not be mistaken for that of an approaching NVA patrol. Our signal at the wire would be a white flare fired by Keaveney from his M-79.

When we passed the last strands of tanglefoot wire, we were finished. It was the end of a long and uneventful mission. Our backs were bent from the weight of our packs. Our boots were heavy, caked with the thick, red mud of Con Thien. We were exhausted. Miraculously, our six-by truck had made it from Quang Tri to Con Thien, and we moved like a band of old men toward the back of the truck. It took two men to throw each man's pack into the bed. We sat in reflective silence all the way back to the company area, inwardly pleased that we had survived the typhoon and had been able to continue the mission. The discovery of the elusive rocket site would have to wait for another time.

Not all of our missions would include finding the enemy. Many of our sister teams experienced the same long and difficult missions during the typhoon and during the subsequent monsoon season. The enemy seemed to have disappeared. He went underground. He moved only short distances and primarily at night. We would change our tactics to find him.

By the end of the second mission, I felt that I had been fully accepted by the members of my recon team. I was physically fit, I tried to pay close attention to everything that was happening in the bush, and still remember why I was there.

My being a Navy corpsman was *never* viewed by any Marine in the company as a handicap to their success in the field. My team members knew that I was capable of doing everything that they could do, and they took pride in teaching me all that they knew about patrolling. We were brothers, and there was absolutely no doubt in my mind that any one of them would protect me with his life as they knew that I would do the same for any one of them.

—— TEAM MEMBERS ——

DURING THE MONTH OF SEPTEMBER 1969, THE SOUTH Vietnamese province of Quang Tri received more rain than had previously been recorded in any thirty-day period in Vietnam. The constant rains of the monsoon season caused the roads to be totally impassable to all but the heavy tracked vehicles; even the tanks and tank retrievers were unable to negotiate the deep red mud. Visibility was reduced to feet, rather than miles, and that made use of helicopters for team insertions impossible. The weather may have temporarily slowed our ability to patrol, but it did not stop us from training. Training was a continuous event in 3d Force Recon.

We knew that as soon as the rains lifted and the skies cleared, our team would be fragged for a mission. We had spent the past wet and dreary weeks in preparation for our next assignment, and during that time, we had gotten to know one another on a very personal level.

It was not at all unusual for us to share with one another the contents of our mail from family and friends. We always shared the care packages that we each had received from home. Even though cookies, brownies, and other homemade treats arrived stale, flattened, or totally unrecognizable, it was the daily sharing of those personal gifts that helped to strengthen the bonds between team members. Each man in our team was special.

Corporal Ted Bishop came from the small town of Lufkin, Texas. He was always happy and said that he found his happiness in reading and studying the Bible. His position as our team leader gave him a high status within our platoon, and he never abused his authority. He was personally interested in each one of us, and his interest was genuine. He was a reader, and in the spare time that was ever made available to a team leader, he could be found reading. He was also a poet. He shared his poems with us and took great pride in his written work. Bishop was also an athlete, having played various sports in high school. We were pleased that he was our team leader, and he represented us well, being even tempered and meticulous in his attention to detail.

Lance Corporal Paul Keaveney was nicknamed the Ol' Man because he was the oldest lance corporal in our platoon. According to his teammates he was, at twenty-seven years old, the oldest lance corporal in the entire United States Marine Corps. Born in Massachusetts, he claimed Florida as home. His parents owned a paint company in New Smyrna Beach, where they also raised champion American quarter horses as a hobby.

For an older guy who obviously came from a wealthy family, his personality seemed to fit perfectly into the chemistry of our team. He was married, had no children, and spent his off-duty time sketching short-timer's calendars for Marines in the platoon. Keaveney had told us that he planned to become an artist. He had graduated from college with a degree in fine arts and had wanted to broaden his horizons by becoming a combat artist. Somewhere along the line he had crossed paths with a Marine Corps recruiter who had told him that the possibility of becoming a combat artist existed in the Corps. Keaveney was trusting enough to believe him, and by the time that he arrived in Vietnam, he still believed that there was such a requirement for artists. The staff sergeant at the division order-writing desk in Da Nang added fuel to his fire by telling Keaveney that if he truly wanted to see and draw any combat up front and close he should volunteer for duty with a force recon company. He did.

Staff Sergeant Danny Williams came from the back woods of Ohio. By the time he was twenty-two years old, he had completed his first tour in Vietnam with the grunts (1965–66), and his experience with an infantry "letter" company had been extensive. He was a skilled woodsman. He knew the history of the development of small arms better than anyone in our platoon, and his ability to teach the intricacies of combat patrolling and the proper use of supporting arms lent to his credibility. His word was law. There was no reason for any of us to go to outside the platoon with a problem; Staff Sergeant Williams was the problem solver of the third platoon.

James Furhman came from York, Pennsylvania. He was married, and he shared with us the fact that his wife was due to have their first baby sometime close to Christmas. Furhman was an outstanding athlete, having played varsity baseball and football in high school. He was a rifleman and was as dependable as any man in our team. He had a great sense of humor and was generous.

Lance Corporal Silva was a Mexican-American who came from Flint, Michigan. He was a real loner, soft-spoken and quiet. He said that he had been a member of an outlaw motorcycle gang before joining the Marine Corps. He carried an ice pick on his harness.

Corporal Jenovich, our assistant team leader, called Philadelphia, Pennsylvania, home. When Corporal Jenovich joined our platoon and team, he was getting short. He had spent most of his tour as an assistant team leader in the first platoon, completing at least twenty reconnaissance missions. He was street smart and worked well with Corporal Bishop in running our team. He took his work seriously, particularly in teaching us the finer points of map reading.

These individuals represented a cross section of the youth of America in 1969. Some came from wealth, some were poor, some well educated, and some were street smart. Each one of them was determined, dedicated to the team, and proud. Individually they would appear to the casual observer to be "average kids." But as members of a well-trained Force Reconnaissance team, they were collectively smart, aware, and capable of independent action and great destruction. Each one was individually secure, dependable, and a thinker. Collectively, we had learned to draw on our individual strengths, and now we worked best as a well-trained team.

The extended period that we spent confined to the company area due to the heavy rains of the monsoon season was viewed as valuable team-training time. Our skill in immediate-action drills improved. We constantly practiced how to break through different types of ambushes and probes. None of the time spent training was ever considered wasted time or redundant. We knew from past experience that response time was the key to staying alive.

Staff Sergeant Williams had designed his continuous training with one goal—that the team could continue to operate no matter who was in charge. He said that his personal experiences in combat had taught him that Marines would not always rally around the senior man in a combat situation gone bad. He said that they would gravitate toward the person who they believed would have the best chance to keep them alive, regardless of his age or his rank.

Experience, knowledge, and demonstrated skill were the tools of his success, and he wanted to be sure that each one of the members of his platoon was more than capable of keeping himself and all others alive, too.

Staff Sergeant Williams encouraged free thinking. He believed that every idea was worth pursuing if it could contribute to the team's ability to stay covered, concealed, and undetected.

Each day after classroom and practical training ended, Staff Sergeant Williams called the platoon together for a meeting. His approach to these gatherings was based on his philosophy of good training. We were told to break out our notebooks.

"None of us are gonna be here forever. I want you to remember that as we are taught how to do new and better things, we must remember *how* we were taught so that we can pass it on to those that don't know. Each member of the team should consider himself to be a teacher. If I get killed or wounded, I want Sergeant Garcia to be able to step in where I fell. I want you assistant team leaders to be prepared to be team leaders. I want all of this good patrolling information written down in your little green notebooks so that if some son of a bitch steals your notebook, he will learn something when he reads it. We all seem to be physically able to hump in the bush all day long. But the physical part only gets you there. It is the mental part that lets you do the real reconnaissance work. You guys know that I ain't been to no college like Bishop, and I can't draw no pictures like the Ol' Man, but I have been able to remember enough stuff from what I was taught in the grunts to keep my ass in one piece once the shit hits the fan. I want all you Marines, and the doc, to know what I know. We'll stand a better chance at staying alive if we think first, and act on it second."

Staff Sergeant Williams had Bishop lay his M-16 rifle down on a foot locker that was covered with a green bath towel. Bishop had found a roll of green duct tape, and he had used strips of the tape to cover the black plastic stock and forestock of his rifle. With the aid of a surgical scalpel, he had cut away leaf-shaped areas of the green tape, producing a beautifully camouflaged pattern on his rifle.

"This here is a good example of free thinking. It is simple, it is effective, it gives us an advantage, and we have enough green tape to camouflage every weapon in the platoon. If you'll pass Bishop's rifle around, you'll see some improvements that have been made to it. There is a strip of white tape applied to the front sight post. The tape will help you get a faster sight picture in reduced light. There are three sections of cleaning rod taped to the right side of the forestock. The reason that there are *three* sections is to give you the right length of cleaning rod to extract a jammed cartridge casing. There is nothing more useless in combat than a jammed weapon. Please notice, too, that there is no sling on this rifle. Slings and sling swivels make noise. Tape the sling swivels down against the stock, and there will be no more noise. Good job, Corporal Bishop.''

Sometime during Williams's assessment speech on Bishop's rifle, First Lieutenant Coffman had quietly walked into the hootch. Normally the platoon sergeant would have called the Marines in the hootch to stand at attention, but Coffman had waved a signal to Staff Sergeant Williams not to do this, and to continue on with his class.

First Lieutenant Coffman's interest in our team training was not a passing curiosity. As the company's operation and training officer, his personal concern for what we were learning was demonstrated daily.

Lieutenant Coffman was considered a living legend in the world of Marine reconnaissance operations. He had trained in areas of Indochina, had been involved with the design and testing of military parachutes and scuba equipment, and he had written military training manuals on small-unit patrolling. Having risen in rank from private to gunnery sergeant, he had then received a battlefield commission to the rank of first lieutenant. His nickname was Bucky, but he was also known as Igor. He was on his third tour of duty in Vietnam. He had been awarded the Navy Cross by President Johnson during his last tour in Vietnam, and it was casually mentioned from time to time that he had also been the recipient of two Silver Stars and three Bronze Stars, and had been awarded the Purple Heart seven times.

"I want to talk to you briefly about patrolling. During the last couple of weeks we haven't been able to get away from the company area because of the rains. The roads have been useless and our birds don't fly when they can't see. So, when we are in the rear, we train. The training that you have been going through has been well-planned, and I have seen a lot of hard work being done by each one of our teams. Before any of you mount out for our next mission, I wanted to take this opportunity to address each of the teams and give you my thoughts on the art of patrolling.

"Combat patrolling and reconnaissance patrolling are built of the same design. We sometimes use exotic methods of insertion and extraction to get us into and out of our areas, but the principles of what we do once we get there are still the same.

"We may think that a grunt platoon makes too much noise. They give themselves away. We use stealth and concealment to hide ourselves because six men cannot afford to be seen. In fact, if we get ourselves involved in a firefight, nine out of ten times it is because we have done something stupid.

"Our job here is not to get involved in running gunfights with the NVA or Vietcong. That's what the grunts get paid for. They run combat patrols. We are supposed to find gooks, follow gooks, report on what they are doing, and then kill them scientifically. That is why you have spent so much time in learning how to communicate, breaking contact, and in practicing your immediate-action drills. That is why you have been constantly practicing calls for artillery fire, and learning how to use close air support. Our teams are designed to be small to give us the advantage in hiding, but what we lack in formal fighting size, we make up for by using our heads.

"In the days to come I will be teaching some new classes that I know will help you. These will be tactics learned from the Gurkhas. I have watched them train and have been with them in the bush. They are the finest jungle fighters in the world. I think that we can take a page or two from their book and make it work well for us. These classes will be fun; look forward to them. I can promise you that they will prove to be valuable, and may save your lives. The S-2 reported to the company commander, just a little while ago, that it looks like there may be a good break in the monsoon rains. It may be clear enough to fly by tomorrow. If that happens, then Snaky will be our first team out of here. Corporal Bishop, come with me."

When Bishop returned from his initial briefing with Lieutenant Coffman, he called for a team meeting. We were fragged to recon an area around the Hai Van Pass, north of Da Nang and south of Phu Bai. He also said that the word around the CP was that the entire company was leaving Quang Tri, and moving to the airstrip at Phu Bai, forty miles to our south. We began to get our gear ready for a mission.

——— PHU BAI ———

IN SEPTEMBER OF 1969, THE 3D MARINE DIVISION BEgan to "stand down" and prepared to sail for the island of Okinawa. The 1st Brigade of the 5th U.S. Mechanized Division remained in Quang Tri Province along with half of the ARVN (Army Republic Vietnam) division to guard the DMZ and the Laotian border approaches into I Corps.

This was the second increment of the U.S. troop withdrawal from Vietnam and it was announced on September 16, 1969. Of a total of 45,000 Americans to be redeployed by mid-December, 18,483 were Marines, which was the majority of the 3d Marine Division in I Corps. Additionally, a proportional share of Marine aviation assets and service units would leave Vietnam, too. Headquarters, 3d Marine Division, and the 4th Marines were sent to Okinawa. For the 40 months of combat in Vietnam the 3d Marine Division claimed 28,216 enemy killed, 499 prisoners taken, and 9,626 weapons captured.

Third Force Reconnaissance Company "belonged" to the III MAF (Marine Amphibious Force), commanded by Lieutenant General Herman B. Nickerson, and General Nickerson had operational control over both the 1st and the 3d Marine Divisions operating in I Corps. Subordinate to the III MAF commanding general was Major General Ormond R. Simpson, commanding general of the 1st Marine Division, and the commanding general of the 3d Marine Division, Major General William K. Jones.

As our teams from 3d Force Reconnaissance Company were the "eyes and ears" for Lieutenant General Nickerson, the two division commanding generals relied upon the Marines of the 1st and 3d Reconnaissance Battalions, respectively, to conduct ground reconnaissance and observation in support of their divisions. (This simple explanation of "who worked for whom" is essential in understanding the role of 3d Force Reconnaissance Company as opposed to the role of the reconnaissance battalions of the two divisions.)

In October of 1969, 3d Force Reconnaissance moved forty miles south of Quang Tri to occupy a company area adjacent to the airstrip located at Phu Bai. The responsibility for patrolling the DMZ had been handed over to the 5th Mechanized Division of the U.S. Army, and our small company of 120 Marines and five corpsmen had new patrol areas that were of significant interest to General Nickerson. These areas included the Hai Van Pass, located south of Phu Bai and north of the city of Da Nang, and the A Shau Valley, located forty miles west of Hue and immediately adjacent to the Laotian border.

Our company compound at Phu Bai was a much-welcomed improvement over the small green plywood hootches that we had called home in Quang Tri. This new company compound was comprised of six two-story wooden barracks called Butler buildings that had once been occupied by members of the Marine air wing. The company had also laid claim to several small supply warehouses, a new sick-bay hootch, and a parachute loft and scuba-equipment locker.

Our company sick bay was located directly across from the flight line of the Phu Bai airstrip. The only facility that we lacked was a mess hall, and that problem was easily overcome by our sharing of the existing mess hall belonging to the air wing personnel who had remained at Phu Bai. There was rumored to be an enlisted club close by, but permission for any of us to use the club had not been given pending final word from Major Lee, our company commander.

The company's relocation plan had allowed only one week to dismantle everything that we had owned in Quang Tri, convoy personnel and all equipment south, and reorganize and reassemble ourselves at Phu Bai. Fortunately, the weather had cooperated with the plan. The lack of heavy rains made the difficult move that much easier.

The logistics section of the company had sent an advance party to Phu Bai while most of us had remained in Quang Tri, dismantling. This plan had paid off by enabling us to arrive in the new compound ready to move in.

Third Force Recon was not considered to be fully operational until our arrival at Phu Bai, but once we had entered the company compound, Major Lee expected the teams to be ready to go to the bush, and orders for several recon missions came to the company the day that our platoon rode into the new company compound.

Staff Sergeant Williams had now been placed in command of our platoon. First Lieutenant Hensley had received orders sending him back to the States, and a new platoon leader was due to report in and take his place, but until that happened Staff Sergeant Williams was in charge.

He called for Corporal Bishop and gave him the word to immediately report to the company operations hootch for a premission briefing.

When Corporal Bishop returned to our barracks from the S-3 (operations) shop he called for a team meeting and passed the word to prepare for a mission scheduled to leave the following morning. He said that he had been told that our relocation to Phu Bai had been carefully designed to allow us the opportunity and advantage to use available helicopters and OV-10 Bronco observation planes to study possible reconnaissance areas from the air before the actual team was scheduled for insertion. From then on, we would be inserted and extracted by helicopter, and not have to take long and surreptitious walks into our recon zones as we had done on the DMZ.

The new policy was designed to give each recon team leader enough flight time to personally view the proposed recon area's terrain, note and plot the location of any usable helicopter landing zones (HLZs), check for the location of possible trails, and locate water.

The theory was that the North Vietnamese soldiers who were operating in the south had become so accustomed to the presence of U.S. aircraft overhead that they would not fire skyward and draw unwanted attention to their staging areas. If that held true, then our premission flights would not be shot at, and our intention of putting reconnaissance teams into a suspected enemy area within the next day or two would not be compromised.

Just before noontime the team escorted Corporal Bishop and Staff Sergeant Williams to the flight line. They wore their 782 gear and carried maps in their trouser pockets. Each boarded an Army Huey helicopter that was prepared to take them on their area overflight. We gave them thumbs-up and then walked back across the street to prepare ourselves for the first company formation of 3d Force Recon at Phu Bai. Williams and Bishop were scheduled to return by 1500.

The command "Fall in and cover down" was given, and the four platoons of 3d Force stood at the position of attention. The company first sergeant had taken his position in front of the company.

First Sergeant Lonnie Henderson, USMC, was an imposing figure. Standing six feet eight inches tall, he had been in the Marine Corps forever and had never been known to smile. The only physical change to his face that even approached something resembling a smile was when the first sergeant filled his lower lip with an oversized pinch of Skoal. He had a well-known reputation within the company for being knowledgeable and for being fair in his dealings with us. He considered all of the Marines in the company to be "his Marines," and he knew by name each and every Marine and corpsman who stood before him at this company formation.

"Stand at ease. I have some words to pass along to all of you, and I want to make sure that every man in this company gets the word. First off, the members of the advance party that were sent down here about two weeks ago have worked their asses off in trying to get our company area squared away before the rest of us arrived here. The old residents left it looking like hell. It is our home now, and we will make it better than we found it. You will not fuck this area up. Staff Sergeant Tate and his people from the S-4 shop deserve our thanks for the job that they did so that we wouldn't have to do anything more than throw our packs on a rack and get back to work. We appreciate their efforts. Second, we are new to this area, and people don't know us or know what we do. Keep it that way. We gather information; we don't spread it. There are a bunch of slimy fuckin' hippie wing-wipers living across from our mess hall. Keep away from them. They are a mob of unprofessional, undisciplined, lazy shitheads and are known to use dope. If I even *see* any one of you Marines within ten feet of one of those long-haired Army assholes, I'll put my size fourteen boot so far up your ass that you'll taste boot leather for a week. Do I make my simple feelings clear? We are here to work hard, and when time permits, we will play hard. This company is a tight unit, and we are professionals. I know that you will not let me down. Our company commander has approved the use of the enlisted club for the grades of sergeant and below. They serve only sodas, beer, and wine. The club shows a movie each night at 1700. It is free. If you are not on security watch, or on the reactionary force roster, you may go to the club. One last thing, company PT will go at 1500 today. Company, ATTENTION, dismissed."

When we left the formation, we walked back to the barracks to get our gear packed and ready for the next day's mission. Staff Sergeant Williams had already picked up ammunition bandoleers and C rations before he and Bishop had left and had dropped them off inside the barracks.

We began to choose the type of food we would carry for what we had been told was a four-day mission. The amount of food taken was always dependent on the length of the mission. Any mission that was scheduled to last for more than six days allowed each man to receive one case of C rations, twelve individual meals. One case of twelve dehydrated meals, called "long rats," was divided between two men. Normally, the canned fruit (apple sauce, apricots, peaches, pears, or fruit cocktail) from the C rations were the first items to go into a rucksack. Coffee, powdered cocoa, and candy were next. The larger cans of meat and potatoes, chicken, or spaghetti, called "heavies," were less desirable because of their weight. The packaged long rats weighed next to nothing and replaced heavies whenever they were available.

Our routine for preparation was always the same. Food, new ammunition, extra clothing, special equipment, batteries, and notebooks were packed and made ready. The assistant patrol leader would read from a team checklist, and each special piece of gear was produced and checked for proper operation. The last pieces of equipment to be gathered were items like the claymore mines, PSIDs, starlight scopes, plastic explosives, and grenades. Fresh water, because of the desire for its taste and a dislike of its weight, would be the last item on each man's list.

By 1600, Staff Sergeant Williams and Corporal Bishop had returned safely from their flight. We had spent the afternoon packing the last of our gear, and finished off our checklist by test-firing our weapons. Corporal Bishop held an inspection and passed his final instructions to the team.

"Our team is scheduled to leave Phu Bai tomorrow morning at 0700. We will be inserted by helo into an area north of the Hai Van Pass. There have been reports of gooks using a trail system that leads up and over the pass toward the city of Da Nang. We'll be put in on the low ground, check out a nine-click grid area, and we'll be back here four days from tomorrow."

The honor of being the first team from 3d Force to be operational from Phu Bai went to Team Snakey. We would not have artillery in general support of our mission, but the proximity of the airstrips at Phu Bai and Da Nang meant that we could have protection from above within ten minutes. We had looked over the maps of the area where we were to operate, and the dark color of the contour lines meant that we would have to move through some extremely difficult and mountainous terrain.

By 2000 our preparations for the mission were completed, and for the first time in what had been a very busy day for all of us, Corporal Bishop, Lance Corporal Keaveney, and I asked Staff Sergeant Williams for permission to leave the area and to take a look at our new club. Of course Staff Sergeant Williams knew that this would be our last night in the rear, and he also knew that he needn't caution us about overindulging in beer. Off we went.

The Marine enlisted club at Phu Bai was probably no different from any other Marine enlisted service club that was located in a combat zone. Dimly lit, always crowded, smoke-filled, and smelling like a combination of stale popcorn and urine, it served its purpose—a cheap, loud, and obnoxious place for Marines to go and have a couple of beers with their friends.

The presence of an enlisted club was a great boost to the morale of the men in the company. No one in 3d Force had ever complained about the old conex box club at Quang Tri because that was all we had. It was so poor an example of an enlisted club that it appealed to the image of any Force Recon Marine. Nothing, short of not having a club, could have been worse, and that was exactly why it was so highly regarded. The Quang Tri club had been legend.

As the three of us sat at one of the many tables, we talked quietly about our next day's mission. We were really pleased with the prospect of finally putting together all of our continuous training into reality so soon after arriving at Phu Bai. We would get to operate as the team that we had become, and we felt confident in our abilities to do a good job of it.

After we finished the second round of beers, Corporal Bishop decided not to push a good thing too far, and he suggested that we walk back to the company area to be in the barracks by 2100. Without any argument from us, we started to walk out of the club.

"Hey, are you guys from that Marine Recon company that pulled in here today?" The staff sergeant who was assigned as the club manager waved us over toward the bar and pointed to a Marine who sat alone at a table in the corner. "That Marine has been in here since we opened at 1630. He's so shit-faced that he can't walk. I shut him off from the bar more than an hour ago, but all he wants to do is sleep. Whenever I try to wake him, he stands straight up and yells, 'Force Recon, oooh rah' at the top of his lungs and then falls back into his chair in a stupor. How about waltzing your buddy back home and put his butt in the rack? I sure don't want any trouble in here tonight."

The Marine who had let it be known throughout the club that he was from 3d Force Recon Company was a PFC in the second platoon. He was something of an established character within the ranks of 3d Force Recon. He had a good reputation in the bush and was an accomplished tracker. Using his field skills, he had obviously discovered the pleasures of the club as soon as he heard that it was located nearby.

We walked softly over to the PFC's beer-can-covered table, and we took a hard look at him before deciding on whether or not to wake him. Corporal Bishop shook his shoulder. The Pfc. started to rise up from his chair, but before he could yell "Recon," Corporal Bishop slapped a hand over his mouth and told him to open his eyes. The PFC recognized Corporal Bishop after a few moments of corrective blinking. Staring back at Bishop, he slurred, "Hey, Corporal Bishop, let's go back to the barracks." So without any further incident developing, the four of us began our quarter-mile walk toward the company compound.

The Army engineers had been stationed at Phu Bai long before the arrival of 3d Force Recon Company. As part of their field sanitation program, and in their attempt to shield the people of South Vietnam from the sight of soldiers urinating in public, they had built devices known simply as pissers all over the area. A pisser was a fifty-five-gallon fuel barrel that was buried into the ground to within a few inches of the rim. The top of the barrel was covered with a single layer of window screen that kept cigarette butts, rodents, and dirt from falling into the barrel. A drainage system was hidden in the bottom of the barrel. Usually, the location of a pisser was marked by two large pieces of painted plywood that would shield the user from public view.

As the four of us walked back toward the 3d Force Company area, the Pfc. was positioned and supported between Keaveney and me. He was trying very hard to walk forward, but too many beers had clouded his brain, and his efforts were marginal at best. It was not an easy task to take the PFC's arms over our shoulders and guide him back toward the company, but we were making good progress only because we were sober. Besides, he was one of us, and he would have returned the favor.

After walking the PFC several hundred yards in the direction of the company, we stopped for a rest. The private was getting better at locomotion, but it was still apparent that he would need our help to make it all the way back.

As we began our second effort walking arm in arm, the great PFC suddenly disappeared. The momentum of our stride had taken Keaveney and me forward several steps before we realized that our drunken buddy was gone. In the light that only a half-moon can provide, we watched in utter amazement as a human head slowly rose from the ground. The watery cry of "Heeeelp meeeee" came from the center of the moonlit face, and we realized what had happened.

By a stroke of luck, Keaveney and I had passed to the sides of an abandoned pisser, but not the PFC. His short, alcohol-induced steps had carried him into and under the contents of a large drum of old urine.

The shock of what had happened could not have been any greater than the hilarity of seeing our buddy treading water, or more accurately, urine, below the surface of the ground. His cries for help fell on deaf ears as he struggled to get a grip on the rim of the hidden barrel. The PFC was much more awake now than when he had started his journey home, but the smell of him was overpowering. He felt for the rim of the barrel and slowly lifted himself out of the pisser, then pushed himself out of the barrel. He was on his hands and knees when he reached out for us. It was like a scene from a horror movie, and all we could do was laugh and think that "there, but for the grace of God, go I."

With only several hundred feet to go before entering the company area, Bishop, Keaveney, and I shouted words of encouragement and direction to the semiblinded, stinking, and staggering PFC. As he came nearer to us, our pace quickened until we got to the steps of our barracks. Once inside and safe we bolted the door shut and waited for the sound of the PFC to pass by as he moved toward his platoon's barracks. He must have heard the sounds of our laughter as he went off into the night.

KEAVENEY'S BEAR
———— STORY ————

AT 0600 WE LEFT THE MESS HALL AND WALKED BACK to the building that had become the operations and training center for 3d Force Recon. All of our gear had been staged in front of the building. It was only a matter of putting it on and going through our last-minute equipment check before Corporal Bishop passed the word for Team Snakey to move out toward the flight line and to the waiting helicopters.

Before our move to Phu Bai, we had been training with elements of the 101st Airborne Division, and particularly with the helicopter pilots and crews of the 2d Squadron, 17th Air Cavalry. This Army helicopter unit was located northwest of Phu Bai at Camp Eagle, and used the small but fast Huey helicopter. The pilots were Army warrant officers, and virtually every pilot in their organization was no older than any of us. They were great guys to fly with, and their courage and reputation were well known. They considered our mission to be their mission, and their presence added to our morale, for anyone who was injured or wounded knew that a helicopter emergency evacuation would be less than fifteen minutes away.

Our experiences with the Marine Corps' CH-46 helicopters had not always been good. The CH-46 was designed as a medium-lift aircraft, and its size required a large area from which to take off and land. We had learned that large, slow-flying things tend to draw lots of fire from the enemy, and being inside a large, slow-moving target was not viewed by most of us as the happy event of the day.

Our team's mission was scheduled to begin with a liftoff from the Phu Bai airstrip at 0800, fly south toward Da Nang, and then be inserted into our zone, north of the Hai Van Pass.

Just as it had been in Quang Tri, those team members of our

platoon and the people from within the company who were not going on missions still came to the flight line to wish us all luck and a safe return. The helicopter pilot, copilot, and the two door gunners were already strapped inside, and, with the rotors of their bird turning, they were only waiting for us to climb aboard before we lifted off.

The door gunners had M-60 machine guns positioned on each side of the helicopter; the outer sliding doors had been removed for ease of getting into or out of the bird quickly. Both guns were fed from full cans of belted ammunition. One other Huey was scheduled to fly with us as an escort, and we welcomed the presence of the additional gunship and its firepower.

Our helicopter picked up and hovered only a foot or two above the metal runway matting before it began to move slowly forward. The pilot was skillful in his maneuvering of the bird between the large steel revetments that protected the other helicopters that were parked by the flight line. With three of us seated along each side door of the Huey, our weight seemed to balance out, and we began to move down the long axis of the runway. The second bird traced our progress.

Corporal Bishop had flown with this same helicopter crew during his premission flight, and he had been recognized by them as one of our recon team leaders and was quickly given a communications helmet to wear so that he could talk with the pilot and copilot as we flew along.

The rest of us sat in silence studying the ground below. We were not strapped into the Huey in any way, and the sudden shifting of our positions during any quick banking turn would have meant our instantly falling out of the helicopter from an altitude of four or five thousand feet. A secure hand hold was our only assurance of remaining inside and seated as we gained altitude. We flew wearing all of our gear because we had been trained to exit the helicopter just as it touched down. Sometimes we were not even given that luxury of a true landing.

The flight toward our recon area lasted less than half an hour. We could see that clouds were beginning to move in from the ocean, and by late in the morning, we would be operating under heavy cloud cover. It seemed that there would never be any relief from the daily rains of the monsoon season.

The signal to get ready was given by Corporal Bishop once he and the pilot had agreed on the primary HLZ. We dropped down and made two false inserts. One Huey would dip down well below treetop level, and as the first bird raised up above the trees, the second bird would drop low, appearing to take the first Huey's place. The maneuver was designed to confuse the watchful little eyes of the North Vietnamese because it was their standard policy to send out a patrol and to check out every sighting of a helicopter landing within their area of operations. The false insert was designed to make their searching an impossible task.

As our Huey dropped for the third time, we knew that we were going in for our insertion. The door gunners prepared their weapons, and as the two machine-gun bolts slammed into their firing positions, the gunners assumed a new posture with their fingers on the triggers and their eyeballs roving the HLZ for the hint of any "unnatural" movement. We tried to listen for enemy rifle fire.

As soon as the landing skids were about six feet above the ground, we jumped out. The force of the rotors had pushed the elephant grass downward and revealed a hard, level surface. Within seconds the Huey went from hovering overhead to a nose-down, tail-up bird, moving rapidly forward out of our area.

We knelt in our HLZ long enough for the Huey to move away, and then Kegler started to move out toward a saddle of two great hills to our west. Our plan was to move away from the HLZ as quickly as possible and to get ourselves to elevated terrain that would give us a better view of the area.

We were already at a disadvantage by being surrounded by the mountains that made up the Hai Van Pass area. The low ground was not the best place to be, and Corporal Bishop was in no mood to keep the team still. We moved three or four hundred yards away from the HLZ, then we waited.

The wait served two important purposes. When we flew we did not wear hearing protection, and the whine of the helicopter's jet engines and the staccato sound of the blades desensitized our hearing. Once we had been inserted, it usually took ten minutes before our hearing returned to normal.

The second reason for waiting was to observe the HLZ for the likelihood of a searching enemy patrol. The helicopter pilots who brought us into the landing zone were still circling in the area, and they would remember their reference points to the HLZ. If the North Vietnamese did have a unit patrolling close to our insertion point and we could immediately detect and report its position and approach, the NVA would be a much easier target for the gunships to pick up on because of the pilot's familiarity with the landing zone.

As soon as Corporal Bishop had established communications with the radio-relay site, he signaled Kegler to move out toward the distant saddle. By noontime we had reached the area that Bishop thought would provide us with both the elevation and view needed to observe a trail that had been plotted during the premission flight. The cloud cover had continued to roll into the area, but our visibility had only been reduced to less than a mile.

As we set up to monitor the trail, we staged our rucksacks near the base of a tree and took out several pairs of 7×50 binoculars. With three team members watching both ends of the trail and the surrounding area, we felt confident that our position would allow us the luxury of staying hidden for several hours.

Keaveney's hand went up and signaled "freeze," and the other two pairs of binoculars turned in the direction of his. Two North Vietnamese soldiers had come into view and had continued to move along the trail that ran below our position and across our forward view. The first soldier wore a tan short-sleeved shirt, dark green trousers, and had black rubber sandals on his feet. He had a small rucksack on his back and carried an SKS rifle at the ready position. He wore nothing on his head.

The second North Vietnamese soldier was larger than his comrade. He was dressed in the same color uniform, wore a helmet, and carried a new AK-47 rifle in his left hand. He continued to motion to the first soldier to continue to move forward along the trail.

Our view of the trail enabled us to observe an unobstructed section of it that was at least a hundred yards long. The beginning of the trail came from the edge of a streambed and moved around the side of a hill that was about three hundred yards to our front. Kegler had put us in the best spot possible for observing anyone's approach. We had the safety of the hill behind us, and two claymore mines were set on both sides of our position. All that was required was to observe this trail, count North Vietnamese soldiers as they moved from north to south, and immediately report the sightings back to the radio-relay site.

By 1630 we had counted twelve North Vietnamese soldiers, most carrying weapons, who had used the trail and were headed south. The very first individual whom we had seen, and later dubbed Tonto, was observed three more times, guiding North Vietnamese soldiers along that section of the trail. We assumed that the North Vietnamese had a staging area fairly close by because the turn-around time for Tonto was less than one hour between sightings. We were told to remain at our position and to continue to monitor the traffic. At 1800 Corporal Bishop passed the word to move into our harbor site.

Kegler had looked for a place that would satisfy our needs, and we moved to an area that was closer to the trail. Bishop had called in our location, and he had plotted the location of the streambed and the area where the trail disappeared around the side of a hill. If our position was discovered by the North Vietnamese, air support would know where we were in relation to those two physical locations.

The rains started to pour down on us just after we had moved into the harbor site. Radio communications with the radio-relay team remained good. Losing comm would mean having to move in the darkness until we found an area that was good for our personal security and good for radio reception.

By midnight the rumble of thunder and the flicker of lightning announced the passing of another cold front. I had been on radio watch since 2300. Our previous observation position had not required any of us to move, we weren't tired, and the usual half-hour radio watch had been extended to a full hour. I woke up Corporal Bishop and handed him the radio handset. A military watch was strapped to the handset, and the small, luminous face and hands now indicated midnight. I pulled my "bush cover" over my face to keep out the rain and tried to cover up under my poncho liner. I was less than two feet away from Corporal Bishop who sat upright against his radio and pack, listening to the sounds of the night.

Keaveney began to move on the other side of Bishop, and I could hear his voice as he whispered to Bishop, "Bishop, tell Norton to get back into the harbor site." Bishop didn't move, but waited a few seconds before answering. Again, Keaveney whispered, "Bishop, did you hear me?"

Corporal Bishop said, "What makes you think he's outside the harbor site?"

Keaveney said, "I thought I saw him walking around out there."

Bishop's arm moved away from his side and he put his hand on my head, confirming his thoughts. "Norton's right here."

Keaveney whispered, "Well, if he's right there, then who the hell is that?"

I had moved my bush cover from my face and tried to rise slowly to see just what Keaveney was staring at. At the same time, I moved slowly to unsnap the leather strap that held my .45 Colt in its shoulder holster. Peering over Bishop's shoulder, I strained to look through the rain-covered lenses of my glasses and waited for the next flash of lightning to illuminate the spot where Keaveney believed he had seen something move.

Within seconds the sky lit up and showed the silhouette of someone moving away from us, not more than twenty yards to Keaveney's right. Another flash of lightning and the figure had moved, but he appeared to be heading away into the heavy rain.

Bishop did not wake the rest of the sleeping team. There was no reason to start moving men around in total darkness or to risk panic. Three of us were awake and alert, and we remained that way for at least an hour.

Whoever or whatever had been moving past us in the night was gone. When the first light of day came through the thick jungle canopy, Keaveney and Bishop crept over to examine the area for tracks, but the continuous rain had washed away any real sign of our visitor, and the wind had covered any other signs of disturbance. When they returned, Bishop asked if anyone had moved outside of the harbor site during the night to answer nature's call. No one had.

We knew that the North Vietnamese moved constantly at night. We rarely did since the areas that we operated in did not ''belong'' to us, and it was wiser to remain hidden at night than to move around in unfamiliar territory.

Perhaps he was just a lost gook. Perhaps he had been the last man in the column of a patrol. He had wandered into and out of our lives like a ghost, but there was no doubt in Bishop's, Keaveney's, or my mind that what we had seen was a real human figure moving in the night's rain.

In the morning the radio-relay site passed the word to Corporal Bishop that we were to move parallel to the trail and follow its course for another click, hoping to discover whether or not it did lead toward the location of an enemy base camp.

Bishop knew that we would have to climb up and over a huge hill in order to put us into a new observation position, and he gave the signal to saddle up. By late in the afternoon, we had moved only nine hundred yards forward but six hundred yards vertically. The steep slope of the hill made our movement slow and tiring, and the night's rain added to our difficulty. Four steps forward meant sliding three steps backward, and our route had kept us from being able to watch the trail that we wanted to observe. We stopped as we crested the hill and were finally rewarded with a better view of the trail than we had believed possible. Visibility was good, and the trail was now several hundred yards below us.

There were no signs of any heavily used trails nearby, and the steep slope that we had just climbed would not be a likely avenue of approach by enemy patrols. Kegler and Bishop had already begun to observe both ends of the trail, and with Silva and Furhman acting as our security team, Keaveney and I were signaled to hurry up and eat. Within fifteen minutes we all had rotated in turn, from observing, eating, and being on security watch. We had seen no new enemy movement along the trail.

Kegler and Furhman were sent out to locate a harbor site, and they returned quickly with news of discovering a fresh trail not more than two hundred yards from where we sat. The position we had was defendable, although it didn't offer us the protection and concealment found in a good harbor site. Bishop decided not to move nearer the hilltop so late into the day in search of a better place to hide and to sleep.

Kegler and Furhman left our position again, this time with the PSIDs and claymore mines, and returned to our harbor site as the last of the evening light faded into darkness. We knew the features of the ground around us, and we had studied where every tree and bush were located. We did not want to mistake the shape of a tree for that of an enemy soldier, open fire, and give away our location. The thought of last night's mystery visitor was in every man's mind. We could still observe the direction of the trail, and if the North Vietnamese began to move with the assistance of night lights, they would be easy for us to detect.

The night passed slowly with our assignment to radio watch, again lasting one hour. Sometime during the middle of the night, a slow drizzle began and continued until first light. Bishop contacted the radio-relay site at dawn, and new information was passed. He took out his notebook and copied down grid-square coordinates. That meant that we were to move again. We had covered half of the area of our original recon zone, but the desire for new information concerning who was using that trail required us to relocate.

Corporal Bishop said that we were moving to a hill approximately two kilometers away, where there had once been a U.S. Army defensive position. We were told to move to the old position, determine if the North Vietnamese that we had seen the day before were using or improving it, and then remain in the vicinity for our helicopter extract, now scheduled for late in the afternoon.

The news of an extract, a day earlier than originally scheduled, was a welcome piece of information, but the idea of moving through an old defensive position meant moving across open terrain, and that was not news well-received. We moved downhill, and Kegler gave the hand signal to freeze. He had come upon a section of the same trail that he and Furhman had discovered the evening before, and now we went to work.

The first priority of our team was to secure each end of the trail to permit two team members time to take a series of photographs, recover some soil samples, and record signs of recent use. Corporal Bishop would decide whether to set up for another period of observation or to rig up booby traps for those who walked that trail.

Since we already knew that the area was used by a number of North Vietnamese soldiers, our ability to observe and report on their activities remained good. There was certainly enough cover and concealment provided by the heavy vegetation, but that worked both ways—if we could hide, so could they. Our choices of observation sites were also good because of the many areas of elevation throughout the Hai Van Pass area. The only serious drawback to our remaining close to the trail was that the constant rainfall reduced the availability of dependable aircraft support. "They don't fly when they can't see" was the standard line used to describe air support.

There was just enough time left to set up one good booby trap on the trail, then to move out of the area toward our new objective, the old defensive position. Bishop pointed to Kegler and then to me. We knew what he wanted us to do.

Our method for emplacing booby traps had been rehearsed many times under the guidance of Staff Sergeant Williams. He had said that "only terrain would dictate what we could or could not do," and this flat stretch of the narrow trail, with thick growth on each side, made our plan possible.

Kegler produced a large, lime green white-phosphorous grenade and one M-67 fragmentation grenade. They would serve as our greeting to the next unsuspecting travelers on the trail. We cut four strong sections of bamboo for stakes that were not more than six inches long. The first two pieces of cut bamboo were sunk into the ground on opposite sides of the trail, less than a foot from trail's edge. The second two pieces of bamboo were also hidden opposite each other, and were implanted about twelve feet from the first set of stakes. The white-phosphorous grenade was secured to one stake, and the frag grenade was wired to the opposing stake. White dental floss was run across a green camouflage paint stick, making the floss appear to look like a typical section of green and white jungle vine. The dental floss was then run from the frag grenade up the trail and around the stake that was on the same side of the trail, across the trail, around the second stake, and back to the white-phosphorous grenade. Once the grenades were wired to the stakes and the dental floss length was cut, the floss was secured to the cotter pins on each of the grenades. The success of our booby trap was left up to the North Vietnamese.

The design of this particular booby trap would allow for an unsuspecting group of North Vietnamese to walk into the kill zone and continue to move past the fragmentation and white-phosphorous grenades. Their point man would then trip the dental floss "vine" that was strung at ankle height, and with any luck, the pins would be pulled out of the two grenades just as the second or third man in the column was opposite the grenade stakes.

If the enemy approached from the opposite direction, the blast of the two grenades would still have the desired effect, though our setup was primarily intended for movement north to south.

Setting up the booby trap took less than five minutes from the time the stakes were cut until the trail was swept clean with a handful of ferns to hide evidence of our work. The location of the booby trap was plotted less than one kilometer from the defensive position we had been instructed to locate and observe.

By 1400 we had moved to an observation point several hundred yards above the old defensive position. It was the size of a football field. The edge of the position dropped steeply for several hundred yards and was heavily overgrown with shrubs and small trees. The outlines of old fighting holes could still be seen along the crest of the northernmost hill. Barbwire covered with vines was still strung around the perimeter of the position. There was no evidence of recent use, but only close inspection of the site would confirm our observations.

Bishop had contacted the radio-relay team again and had passed the word about the location of our booby trap. During the same transmission we learned that a Marine Corps "weather bird" was scheduled to pick us up at 1630 in the afternoon. We would be able to observe the old position for a short while longer and then plan our approach and inspection prior to the Huey coming in for our extraction.

The defensive position was at least six months old, and the jungle was quickly reclaiming what had once belonged to it. The fighting holes were full of stagnant water, and the steel engineer stakes that held up the barbwire were rusted and falling down. The open ground showed no sign of recent traffic, and our inspection of the site was radioed back to the rear.

Corporal Bishop had Kegler lead us away from the open area, and we positioned ourselves under several small trees on the far right side of the crest of the hill. Our secondary radio was turned to the incoming helicopter's frequency, and we waited to hear from the approaching pilot as the time drew nearer for our extraction.

"Team Snakey, this is Snow Bird two seven. Over." Bishop took the handset and confirmed our position with the yet unseen Huey. The pilot wanted us to mark our position with a yellow smoke grenade so that he could confirm our location as he made his first pass over the landing zone. His request for a position mark branded him as a rookie and placed us in a very bad situation.

Once we popped a yellow smoke grenade, our position would not only be known to the "green pilot" but to the rest of the residents of the Hai Van Pass. We would become an immediate target for any gook mortar team within range.

"Snow Bird two seven, this is Snakey Actual. Over."

"Go ahead, Snakey."

"A yellow smoke is a no-good at this time. We have confirmed recent enemy sightings in this area and don't want to invite trouble. Over."

"Understand, Snakey, what do you want?"

"Snow Bird two seven, when I have a visual of you, I'll give you a clock position of our pos when you make your east to west pass. Over."

We could see the Huey before we heard him. The wind was blowing toward the east, and the sound of his rotos could not be heard until he was right on top of us. "Mark, Mark, Mark, Snow Bird two seven. We are at your eight o'clock, and holding a position at the east side of the large open area that you just passed over. Over."

"Understand your location, Snakey. I'll make one more pass before I come in on a final approach. Over."

The Huey circled around the hill and came in fairly low. We could see the pilot's head move as he studied the ground below. He didn't like what he saw.

"Snakey, Snakey, this is Snow Bird two seven. I see only one spot that will take this bird, but it looks like there is a tree stump too close to the center of the landing zone. What is that thing?"

The pilot was right, there was a large old tree stump that stuck up about four feet from the center of his landing zone. It was not the only place where he could land, but it was the one that he wanted, and we were at his mercy.

"Snow Bird two seven, this is Snakey. Over."

"Go ahead, Snakey."

"Snow Bird, why don't you take off for about ten mikes, and we'll blow the stump out of the zone. We'll give you a time hack, and you watch the landing zone. When the stump blows, you can come in right behind it. Over."

"Understand, Snakey, we'll leave for ten minutes. You clear the stump from the zone, and then we'll come in. Over."

One of the items that each member of our recon team carried inside of his rucksack was C-4, white plastic explosive, more powerful than TNT. A little C-4 went a long way. It could be molded like dough, it could be burned without the danger of explosion, it was waterproof, and it took an electrical blasting cap to set it off. We used C-4 to heat our water, and it was sometimes used in the construction of booby traps, or to blow up trees, enemy bridges, or bunkers.

We pooled together about five pounds of C-4 from all of our packs. Kegler and Keaveney took the C-4, some blasting caps, and fuse and headed out to the stump to rig up the explosive charge.

A one-pound block of C-4 would probably have been sufficient to destroy the stump, but the weather was turning to rain again, and we did not want to spend the night near the old defensive position if we didn't have to. Our ticket home was now one explosion and less than eight minutes away.

Kegler and Keaveney had rigged up a weatherproof fuse lighter to a very long section of blasting fuse and had stuffed the entire arrangement into a hole at the base of the tree stump. They moved back to our position and waited for the explosion.

For whatever reason the pilot couldn't wait until the C-4 went off. We had no reason to contact him until after the stump blew, and we assumed that he would approach our position once we had given him the all clear, but he was impatient for something to happen.

Bishop pointed to the approaching Huey. "What the hell is he doing?" The helicopter continued to move closer to us and was now inbound toward the landing zone. "Doesn't he know the C-4 charge hasn't blown yet?"

The whole area shook as the C-4 blew the stump skyward. The placement of the charge underneath the stump had not caused it to blow into a thousand pieces; instead it went straight up like a great ugly wooden missile, right at the approaching Huey.

The reaction of the pilot was instantaneous, and he pulled the Huey into a sharp roll away from the flying stump. It had already passed by him as the helicopter pulled away. "What the hell are you bastards doing? I waited out for ten minutes, and now you guys tried to blow us out of the sky. You can find a new way to get back to Phu Bai. Tell your people in the rear what happened. Enjoy the rain. Over and out.''

The weather-bird pilot headed home with no obvious appreciation for us or the spot that we were now in. Anyone within five miles of our position would have heard the sound of that C-4 explosion, and they could rightfully assume that someone on the ground had caused it. Single explosions do not usually originate from the sky.

Corporal Bishop contacted the radio-relay site and explained in detail what had happened. We were told to find a harbor site and wait for the word on a new extraction time, dependent now on the availability of aircraft and, as always, on the weather.

We moved away from the old defensive position and set up on the opposite side of the landing zone. If we had been seen, our last position would be vacant, and we would at least have an open area on our right side to use as an escape route away from the landing zone. Our new position was right on the edge of a very steep slope, and the angle would make any approach toward us impractical at best. We had set out PSIDs and claymore mines and waited for nightfall.

The muffled sound of the exploding grenades and the faint orange-white flash of light in the distance meant that our booby trap had finally worked as planned. The North Vietnamese were on the move, and probably headed in our direction to investigate the source of the great explosion. We went to a 100-percent alert. No small-arms fire was heard, and there was no sound of Chicom grenades exploding near the location of the booby trap. We could have caught six of the North Vietnamese in our trap or perhaps only one. We would never know for certain what had caused the booby trap to detonate, but someone or something had tripped the vine and had been caught unaware as shrapnel and burning white phosphorous showered an area around the narrow trail. We sat in complete silence.

Furhman was the first one to hear the noise. He said that it sounded like a can being dropped onto a rock. We were all awake and ready for the possibility of an enemy probe. Half an hour had passed since the sound of the booby-trap explosion, and we continued to sit motionless, listening for the approach of the North Vietnamese.

This time the sound was clear, and it sounded like metal banging against metal. The noise repeated itself several times in rapid succession, and there was no doubt that someone was approaching our harbor site, climbing up from below. The occupants of the old defensive site must have thrown their trash into one area, and whoever was climbing the steep hillside had now blundered into the trash pile.

The clouds had begun to break apart when we moved into our harbor site, and the light of a half-moon gave us a limited visibility of one hundred yards. Kegler and Furhman were studying the area where the noise had originated with their 7×50 binoculars. "I see movement down below," whispered Furhman, and Kegler nodded in agreement. "It looks like one gook still headed up this way." The sounds of the cans being scattered around grew louder, and now there came a new sound. The moan of someone in pain.

Corporal Bishop whispered, "Maybe one of the gooks who got caught in our booby trap is headed this way. When he hits that strand of barbwire, I'll throw out this willy-pete (white-phosphorous) grenade, and I want Keaveney to hit 'em with the first shot from the blooper." Keaveney positioned himself next to Bishop, and the rest of us remained ready to fire downward over the crest of the rim as soon as the white-phosphorous grenade illuminated the area around the trash dump.

The crouching form of the lone soldier was outlined against the wire when Bishop threw the heavy grenade out of the harbor site. The weight of the grenade and the angle of the slope caused it to continue to roll downhill, and it detonated behind its intended target. When the phosphorous cloud spread out and away from the point of detonation, the area lit up to reveal a large black bear standing erect and headed in a growling panic straight for Keaveney.

The unmistakable sound of the blooper was cut short by the impact of a 40-millimeter, high-explosive round hitting the bear square in the chest. The body of the bear was thrown backward and it rolled down the slope and into the brush.

"Holy shit, did you see that?" Keaveney had quickly reloaded his M-79, but the rest of us peered over the edge of the rim in disbelief.

The sound of the wounded bear thrashing around below could still be heard as Keaveney spoke. "I never knew they even had bears in Vietnam! That bear must have been living off the garbage that was thrown over the side. I'll be goddamned. Wait till the guys in the platoon hear about this."

Kegler looked over at Keaveney and spoke. "Ya know, Keaveney, for an ol' man who has humped that blooper for the past six months and not fired a single round, I wouldn't be so damn fast to tell anyone that the first and only thing I've shot was a gook bear.''

There were no more sounds to be heard from below our hasty position. Corporal Bishop decided that it would not be wise to move again during the night, so we spent the entire time awake and alert for any sounds of movement.

Our communications with the relay site had remained constant, and Bishop received another radio transmission before first light saying that the morning weather bird would be available and in-bound for our extraction at 0600. The word was also passed during the early-morning transmission that a more experienced helicopter pilot would be assigned to take us home from the Hai Van Pass. The pilot from the day before had been grounded.

– NOVEMBER TRAINING –

BY THE FIRST OF NOVEMBER 1969, 3D FORCE RECON
Company had been given new and greater areas of operational
interest in which to operate, still within the great boundaries of I
Corps. These new areas of operation ranged from the Hai Van
Pass, located north of Da Nang, to the provinces of Quang Nam
and Da Krong, the A Shau Valley, and to our old stomping
grounds, the demilitarized zone.

The great variation in the physical topography and elevation of
these new areas, slated as our reconnaissance zones, ranged from
the sea-level plains along the coast, west, to the mountainous
areas of the Laotian border. Because of the great variation in the
terrain and given the distance from Phu Bai to the new areas, all
of our recon team insertions and extractions were to be conducted
exclusively by helicopters flown by the 2/17th Air Cav.

We had always walked out onto the DMZ during our patrols
from the U.S. Army base at Con Thien. Recon team insertion onto
the demilitarized zone by helicopter was considered impractical
because the flat terrain of the DMZ would make the insertion
obvious and immediately compromise it.

Major Lee, Captain Hisler, and First Lieutenant Coffman had
carefully studied our new areas of responsibility, and they planned
a detailed company training schedule that was designed to meet
the demanding challenges and requirements of this new, but yet-
unseen territory. The emphasis on our new training would consist
of rappelling techniques, the use of close air support, and ad-
vanced patrolling classes. Our training began immediately with
First Lieutenant Coffman setting the stage with a detailed history
of the A Shau Valley.

The A Shau Valley was located about thirty miles southwest of
the imperial city of Hue. The floor of the valley ranged in eleva-

tion from 1800 to 2000 feet, with the highest mountaintops in the valley exceeding 7000 feet above sea level. The angle of slope of these mountains was usually between forty to sixty degrees, and some slopes were viewed as absolutely vertical. The A Shau Valley was over forty kilometers long.

Two old, abandoned airstrips, built long ago by the French, were located on the floor of the A Shau Valley. Ta Bat airstrip was in the northwestern portion of the valley, and A Shau airstrip was fourteen kilometers southwest of Ta Bat. The narrow Rao Lao River ran the length of the valley, and as it passed by the abandoned airstrip site at A Shau, it disappeared underground less than two kilometers away into neighboring Laos. Highway 548, which began in Laos as Route 923, ran up the entire length of the valley and paralleled the Rao Lao River, never less than one hundred yards away.

The A Shau Valley had not been subjected to the chemical defoliant known to us as Agent Orange, so the entire area was lush, green, and covered by a thick evergreen forest of great trees often reaching eighty feet. The forest and jungle now hid enemy bunker complexes, supply dumps, staging areas, hospitals, and numerous antiaircraft positions.

First Lieutenant Coffman detailed the physical appearance of the area with a terrain model. He explained that the A Shau Valley had been used during the French Colonial days of the late nineteenth century as one of the principal capturing and hunting areas in Vietnam for the Bengal tiger, wild boar, and various types of ape.

Since the beginning of the war in Vietnam, the valley had been the primary infiltration and supply route for the North Vietnamese Army, but no recent intelligence on enemy activity had been obtained from anyone on the floor of the A Shau Valley for nearly one year.

The mission given to 3d Force Recon was to patrol this enemy-controlled area and report our findings to the III MAF and U.S. Army's XXIV Corps headquarters as soon as possible. But, prior to the first planned insertion of a team, we would undergo additional training and prepare for the missions that lay ahead. We began our new training with rappelling classes.

Rappelling is a mountaineering technique that enables a climber to descend rapidly over the face of cliffs and vertical walls. Wearing a specially designed web harness, the climber is attached by a steel snap link to a secured or anchored line. The climber is taught how to control his rate of fall by braking his descent at different intervals until he safely reaches level ground.

Rappelling was being taught to all the team members of 3d Force Recon because of the difficult terrain within our new area of operation. It was also planned for us to conduct rappelling operations from both the Army Huey and Marine CH-46 helicopters because our teams would be inserted and extracted from locations where the helicopters could not safely land.

First Lieutenant Coffman and his training NCOs from the S-3 shop had located an unused observation tower that was within walking distance of the company compound. The tower was forty-five feet high and was easily transformed into our new company rappelling tower. A thick steel bar was bolted above the floor of the observation platform, and two rappelling lines were secured to it. With one-half-inch sheets of plywood nailed between the supporting legs of the tower, the telephone pole–size legs had become a wall.

The majority of the team members in 3d Force had received instruction in rappelling either before reporting for duty in Vietnam, or during the Force Recon Indoctrination Program (RIP School) that had been conducted in Quang Tri during the early summer. Nevertheless, every team member in the company received rappelling instruction.

First Lieutenant Coffman was positioned on the rappelling tower when we arrived to begin our training, and his instructors were standing in front of the tower. Every man had brought his Swiss seat rope along, and classes began immediately with a review of the proper manner in which to transform the coiled section of nylon line into a Swiss seat harness. Once this instructional class was finished, we lined up in front of the observation tower's ladder to begin our individual rappels.

First Lieutenant Coffman ensured that each man had come to the top of the rappelling tower with his Swiss seat tied properly and had correctly inserted his steel snap link to the Swiss seat. Once the lieutenant's physical inspection of the nylon lines and snap links had been completed, he told each man to look directly at him as he spoke.

"This Swiss seat harness is designed to support your weight comfortably. The two nylon lines that you will descend on will not break, and the snap link will not open up if you have put it on correctly. You must have total confidence in your equipment and your instructors. Remember, if you take care of your gear, it will always take care of you."

A rappelling demonstration was performed by the training NCOs for the benefit of those Marines who had never before rappelled. At the bottom of the tower stood the "belay man" whose job was to watch the student rappeller. In the case of an emergency, the belay man knew how to separate the rappelling lines, safely braking anyone's fall.

After each man had climbed the ladder to the top of the tower, he was told to stand on the rappelling platform, facing the instructors with his back toward the ground and with his boot heels hanging over the edge of the platform. Each man was given the go-ahead command and then lowered himself to a position perpendicular to the face of the rappelling tower wall. Each man would sound off, yelling his name, followed by the words "on rappel," and then descend in a series of two or three bounds to the ground below. From the safety of ground level, it looked like a piece of cake, but from the unnatural position of one standing backward and at the edge of the high tower, it was not so easy. For the first timers it was quite an experience. I climbed the tower and met face-to-face with First Lieutenant Coffman.

"Good morning, Doc. How are ya? Just pay attention to me, do exactly what I say, and you won't have any troubles with this. Okay? Place the rope in the open gate of your snap link like you were shown in class. Walk over here to the edge of the platform and turn around, facing me. Now with your line in your right hand, put your hand into the small of your back and slowly lean out over the edge. Do not look down."

I did as the lieutenant told me to do and quickly found myself horizontal to the ground forty-five feet below. I didn't like it.

"Now, look at me and listen. Flex your knees and give yourself some slack in the line at the same time. Now practice bouncing out from the edge of the platform once or twice and then you're on your own. Don't forget to sound off or you'll be doing push-ups all morning long."

Watching him and listening to what he was telling me to do, I didn't have time to think about being scared. It worked like a charm. First Lieutenant Coffman had easily made a difficult experience into a good time. Many of us had no appreciation for heights, but his personal approach to our individual problems—and his reassurance for our safety—had put each one of us at ease.

By the end of the first training day, we had progressed from simple rappels while wearing only our utility uniforms to fast rappelling, wearing all of our equipment and weapons. The feeling of accomplishment was contagious and lasting.

The second day of training was more involved than the first. We learned how to rappel down the front of the rappelling tower wall, face first. This was called the Australian Rappel Method and, by descending face first, enabled the climber to use his weapon during the descent. The use of weapons was demonstrated, using blank ammunition.

The last portion of our rappel training was learning the technique of lowering injured or unconscious individuals down the rappelling line. The method was first demonstrated for us and then tried by every team member. No one was injured and everyone enjoyed learning what was the most difficult and potentially dangerous part of the class.

Major Lee stood before the company formation at the end of the second day of our training and announced that we would begin rappelling from helicopters, starting the next morning. He had met with the pilots from a Marine CH-46 squadron at Da Nang and with the Army pilots from the 17th Air Cav squadron to brief them on our training requirements. With the pilots and helicopter crews closely involved in our training, there would be less reason for error when the need for rappelling was required during missions.

First Sergeant Henderson and Gunnery Sergeant Hamilton had years of experience as teachers of mountaineering and rappelling techniques for the Marine Corps, so they were given the responsibility of coordinating our training with the Marine and Army helicopter teams. There was no difference in equipment or principle used for rappelling down the face of a cliff or from the back of a helicopter.

When the Marine CH-46 landed near our company compound, we were given detailed instructions on how the rappelling bar would be rigged to the inside of the helicopter, what size and length lines were to be used to rappel with, and exactly how the lines were to be secured to the rappelling bar. All that remained was for the recon teams to suit up, get into the helicopters, and begin rappelling from a height of about fifty feet.

Doc Montgomery was a hospital corpsman second class who had been with the company for several months when the new training began. He had not been assigned to any one particular team, and his normal duties centered around maintaining the company sick bay. It was, however, company policy that all corpsmen would actively participate in all the training, and on our first day of helicopter rappelling he stood with the rest of us, waiting to be taken up inside of the CH-46.

First Lieutenant Coffman had conducted his short refresher class on the ground prior to the first liftoff, and he had covered all aspects of what would be required of us to get through the helicopter rappelling. Montgomery, unfortunately, had not paid attention to what was said. When the first load of Marines took off, Montgomery was tapped as being the first one to rappel from the tailgate of the hovering CH-46.

First Lieutenant Coffman and First Sergeant Henderson had positioned themselves in the rear of the CH-46. Doc Montgomery was told to move to the rear of the helicopter and lock himself into the rappelling lines. Once he had done that, he was told to lean backward, get some slack in his line, and kick off from the tailgate, rappelling the fifty feet down to the ground.

He panicked.

He had not taken out enough slack in the rappelling line to allow himself to get away from the helicopter, and when he leaned out over the edge of the tailgate he fell backward and immediately found himself upside down and underneath the green bird, much to the amusement of those of us observing his predicament from ground level. His feet were firmly planted on the underside of the helicopter, his head pointed straight down toward the ground, and he still held the rappelling line in his hands.

First Sergeant Henderson moved to the lip of the tailgate and yelled down to Montgomery to loosen his grip on the rappelling lines. Montgomery wore a pair of thick leather gloves for protection from rope burn, but he ignored the advice of the first sergeant and continued to hang upside down. His refusal to let go and to trust his fall to the belay man on the ground did not sit well with the first sergeant, nor with First Lieutenant Coffman. When the lieutenant took the place of the first sergeant, his advice was also ignored by the frozen Montgomery, who finally solved his own problem by slowly releasing his death grip on the rappelling lines, then creeping down the lines to the safety of mother earth. He had violated all the principles of rappelling safety we had just learned, and that was unforgivable.

The CH-46 continued to hover until the rest of the recon Marines rappelled, without any problems, to the ground, and then the CH-46 landed less than a hundred yards from the training site. The first Marine to emerge from the bird was First Lieutenant Coffman, and he was hot.

"Where's that goddamned idiot squid Montgomery?" We knew what was about to happen and we catcalled and cheered as Doc Montgomery presented himself to First Lieutenant Coffman. "Turn around and bend over, Doc." When Montgomery had assumed the proper position he was unceremoniously booted square in the ass, and he landed hard on the ground with the lieutenant standing over him. "If we had been inserting you into a red-hot LZ and you pulled that kind of shit, I would have shot you dead. You're lucky this is only a training lesson. Now get your dented ass back inside of that helicopter and get ready to rappel out of it like you were taught." No other incidents interrupted training during the rest of the day. The situation created by Doc Montgomery was noticed, was addressed, and was corrected. That was the way that things were done in 3d Force.

First Lieutenant Coffman had scheduled a series of patrolling classes for the teams following our four days of rappelling instruction. He began his class with a detailed history lesson, the first time that the history of the people of Southeast Asia was addressed to any of us as a prelude to patrolling techniques.

"The Gurkhas of Nepal are considered to be the finest infantrymen in the world. During the next few days I want to teach you as much as I possibly can about the tiny hillmen of India, and you will learn what makes them so dangerous. The reason that we will become more than familiar with the Gurkhas is that the missions that we will be involved with are very similar to the operations that the British conducted when they led the Gurkhas against the Japanese Army in Burma during World War II."

That entire day First Lieutenant Coffman detailed the history of the Gurkhas, describing their customs, character, history, and unique fighting and patrolling skills. Every Marine listened intently as new and more interesting material was presented. The Gurkha mercenaries were described as honest, hard, incorruptible, and skilled in the art of jungle warfare. We learned that they were recruited from their mountain homes at the age of seventeen, but most had begun their preparation for life in the military when they were seven years old, and by the time the average recruit presented himself for recruitment, he had ten years of preparation time behind him.

The Gurkhas, we were told, do not lie. Their word was their bond, and that one great characteristic made them invaluable to the British. What they reported as having been observed on their patrols was the absolute truth. If they saw ten Japanese soldiers, they reported ten. If they saw no one, they reported seeing no one. The point was easily made: we were expected to do the same thing.

First Lieutenant Coffman brought his kukri to the next day's class. He explained the history and design of the famous Gurkha fighting knife, and he began to describe the tactics that he had learned from the Gurkha patrols in Malaya. His knowledge came from his experiences with them. "The Gurkhas have perfected several types of ambush that I want you to practice. They are simple but effective. The first one that we will study is the prisoner snatch. . . ."

When his description was completed, each team organized itself accordingly, and we were taught the technique for the surprise taking of a prisoner. The prisoner snatch was very simple in design, and it appeared to be easy to execute. In practice, the actual execution of such a tactic would not be so easy.

First Lieutenant Coffman explained the technique. "Terrain will dictate whether or not you'll be able to pull off a prisoner snatch. The first key to success is to find and observe a trail that is used frequently and to locate a section of that trail where it turns sharply to the left or to the right. The setup would be the same as for a hasty ambush. Four men will position themselves next to the trail where the vegetation offers them the best concealment. The fifth man will position himself, hidden, at the bend in the trail, and able to fire on full automatic down the long axis of the trail into the kill zone. The sixth man will be positioned on the opposite side of the trail, unarmed, and directly across from his four teammates. When the right size group of gooks is sighted approaching, the team will move into position. Knowing that the point man is never the leader of the group, we assume that the number two or three man in the group is in charge. He's the one we're after. Let's say that it's number three. Once he gets across from our hidden-and-unarmed man on the opposite side of the trail, our man dives across the trail taking out their number three man. Our man at the bend in the trail fires his weapon low and straight down the long axis of the trail. The other four men take out the rest of the gooks, and the team moves out of the ambush site with the prisoner. Any questions?"

There were plenty of questions concerning the likelihood of our employing such a tactic, but the lieutenant took each of our questions and answered the concerns that we each expressed. We had learned a new tactic, but whether or not we would put it to use remained a big question in all of our minds.

We learned new tactics that ranged from how to position ourselves for better defense while inside our harbor sites, to better methods of hasty ambush. The new training was designed to give us the advantage over a numerically superior enemy. The Gurkhas had fought against thousands of Japanese in the jungles of Burma with only the smallest-sized units, and they had been successful.

They accomplished their missions by using their heads, practicing stealth, and by using their knowledge of the enemy.

We were preparing ourselves for recon missions against the North Vietnamese Army in the A Shau Valley, and like the Japanese soldiers of Burma, the North Vietnamese had been secure in their territory for a long time.

On the morning of November 6, Corporal Bishop was told by Staff Sergeant Williams to report to the S-3 shop for a premission flight brief; we had again been fragged for a patrol, and while Bishop was gone, we prepared ourselves for a four-day mission.

THE BOMB DAMAGE
- ASSESSMENT MISSION -

THE MORNING SUN WAS BURNING OFF THE GROUND fog, and as we flew above the jungle, the dark shadow of our helicopter was cast onto the trees flashing below. Our destination was, again, the Hai Van Pass, and our mission was to locate the base camp of the North Vietnamese soldiers who we had observed moving along their trail several weeks earlier.

The November weather was changing, and the brief period of unusually sunny days we had just enjoyed was soon to become days of heavy rains. The opportunity to get several recon teams inserted into the Hai Van Pass area depended on the window of good flying weather for our helicopters. Major Lee accompanied one team in the lead CH-46 and First Lieutenant Coffman was with us in our own "frog." He was engrossed in a thick paperback.

According to rumor, there had been a series of high-level meetings to decide who would fly our insertions and extractions, the Marines or the Army. This helicopter insertion was considered to be something of a test case that would help to resolve the issue, and that was one reason that our company commander and our operations officer would be present on the insertions and extractions.

The sound of the CH-46 rotors changed as the pilot slowed the airspeed of his bird. That was always the first clue that we were close to our insertion point. We each took up a firing position beside an open window and watched as the two escort Cobra gunships made fast, low passes over the intended LZ. There were no white muzzle flashes of ground fire, and there was no sign of any movement in or near the landing zone as our pilot flipped the switch that lowered the tailgate ramp into its landing position.

Before the ramp was fully down, we were out of the back of the helicopter and pushing our way through the tall elephant grass. Kegler had seen the best possible position for us to move toward just before we landed, and the patch of tall elephant grass gave way to a small open area that we quickly passed through. We looked back to see that our CH-46 was still in the landing zone. Bishop's concern was not centered so much on the helicopter, but on our being able to get away from the LZ as quickly as possible. Within four or five minutes we had moved several hundred yards away from the noise of the helicopter, but it still sat, blades spinning, in the LZ. That was not a good sign.

Corporal Bishop contacted the pilot and asked him what the trouble was. The immediate radio reply was that a hydraulic line had ruptured and it was being repaired by the crew chief. The pilot added that he didn't like sitting on the ground any more than we liked seeing him there. The longer he sat with his rotors spinning, the greater his chances were of becoming a target, not to mention his compromising our insertion.

The change in engine sound caused by the increase in rotor RPMs indicated the fast lifting of our frog out of the landing zone. He had been on the ground for almost ten minutes. The question in our minds was whether our insert position had been compromised.

We moved again and headed toward a series of small rolling foothills that were less than three kilometers from the trail we had observed several weeks earlier. It would take us most of the afternoon to get into an elevated position good enough to allow us to observe the trail.

As we moved slowly through the brush, the wind picked up and rain clouds moved in over us. By late afternoon Bishop had brought us into a place that overlooked a streambed, and through our binoculars we could make out the definition outline of a trail that ran beside the stream. Bishop and Keaveney watched the trail, Silva and I were on security watch, and Kegler and Furhman took advantage of the observation time to eat before we would move to the night's harbor site.

The rain that had started earlier as a slow drizzle had become a steady, heavy downpour. As the temperature decreased, a wet, thick fog moved in and covered the area, stopping our observations. Radio communication was excellent, and we had no trouble in letting the people in the rear know exactly where we were located and what we had been observing. We left our observation point and moved a short distance away to the harbor site. Immediately after arriving at the site, Keaveney and I were told to go out and place the four sensors and claymore mines in the standard defensive pattern. When we returned to the team's location, Bishop passed around a slip of notebook paper that listed our names and the times that we were assigned to radio watch during the night. The first night was uneventful, except for the heavy rainfall which made our four PSIDs register continuously.

At first light I woke up and reached for my glasses, which I had folded and placed inside of my bush cover. I pulled a small piece of green colored face cloth from my right breast pocket which I used to clean my lenses. For some reason I couldn't see clearly from my right eye. When I finally sat up straight and tried to put on my glasses, Keaveney stared at me, and reaching toward my face, he said one word, "leeches." The ground was crawling with them.

I took the small signal mirror from my breast pocket and looked into it. It reflected the picture of two grape-size black leeches that had attached themselves to my right eyelid during the night. They were fat with my blood, and their bites had caused my eyelid to swell half shut.

There were several bush techniques that I had become used to in dealing with the uninvited little carnivores. Applied directly to the leech's body, a lit cigarette immediately caused it to release its grip and drop off. The same satisfactory results were achieved with a good squirt of insect repellent applied to the leech, and, from time to time, my surgical tweezers were used to remove the leeches from the arms, necks, and heads of team members. With my fingertips, I removed the two swollen leeches from my eyelid and placed them on the ground.

Silva was watching me, and he studied the two squirming leeches on the ground. Without a word he threw his ice pick straight into the first leech, retrieved his pick and hit his second target on the first try. Smiling, he held up his pick for all of us to admire, the leeches now looking like two black olives on a bloody red swizzle stick.

The leeches that we had encountered on past missions traveled on the floor of the jungle in a constant search for blood from any host. They moved with a deliberate, caterpillarlike motion. Once they had firmly attached themselves to their host, they filled themselves with the blood of their host until they were full to the point of bursting, when they would release their bite, fall to the ground, and begin to digest the blood, then repeat the process as often as was necessary. An anticoagulant made their bite mark bleed for several hours after they had fallen away. We had been told that leeches could transmit a serious disease known as leech-bite fever.

The constant presence of leeches affected each of the team members differently. Some viewed the leeches nonchalantly, as nothing more than an ugly pest. Others cringed at the sight of them and moved themselves and their gear out of the leeches' path.

For the first time in four months, Lance Corporal Silva sounded philosophical when he spoke. "One good leech reminds me of a six-man recon team. He moves slowly, deliberately, and with one purpose. He finds his victim, which is always bigger than himself. He attacks it in his own way, drains it a little, hurts it a little, and slips away, unnoticed, ready to do it all over again. If that ain't recon, then that ain't shit!" He was right.

After finishing our daily routine of cleaning weapons, replacing radio batteries, repacking gear, eating, and recovering the PSIDs and claymore mines, we moved from the harbor site toward a new observation position, still overlooking the trail beside the streambed.

At 0900 Bishop spotted the first traveler, a young kid clad in black pajamas. He was moving very slowly along the edge of the streambed, and he kept turning around. He appeared to be looking back for someone, still unseen, and asking for direction.

Now because of the amount of time our CH-46 helicopter had spent repairing itself on the ground during our insertion, we assumed that the North Vietnamese knew, or at least suspected, that we were in their area. This trail walker confirmed our suspicions.

We had been told that the NVA had a reputation for treating the local Vietcong badly, and if the opportunity to use a young VC kid presented itself, they would always use a dummy to walk as a point man on their trails. They would watch him, checking for the possibility of an enemy ambush or booby traps, and follow only after being assured that the trail was safe. We believed that this VC kid was their unarmed bait.

We were hidden less than two hundred yards above the trail, and our concealed position was very good, giving us a direct and unobstructed view of at least forty feet of the trail. Numerous boulders broke the steady rush of the stream as it ran southward. The stream did not appear to be more than ten feet wide or four feet deep, but the sound of the rushing water was a concern. The noise masked any sound that we might make around our observation position, but it also served to hide the sound of anyone approaching. Bishop had seen the VC on the trail before he had heard him, and this added to his concern.

As the lone VC began to climb up a small rise on the trail, a voice called out, halting him. We watched as two uniformed NVA soldiers moved up to join the young VC. The first soldier was wearing the typical NVA uniform—a dark green shirt, tan trousers, sandals, a light pack, pith helmet—and he carried an SKS rifle. The second NVA was dressed the same as the first one, but he wore no pack at all, and on his right hip was a black holster, which identified him as either a senior noncommissioned officer or, more likely, as an infantry officer.

The three men talked for several minutes, and once their conversation ended, the young VC started to move ahead of the two NVA soldiers who remained standing by the edge of the trail. We watched them until they disappeared from our view, and Bishop immediately radioed back the news of this important sighting. The mood of the team had changed dramatically.

The three enemy soldiers had passed within easy killing distance of our OP, but our mission was to observe and to report on the enemy, not to engage them in a firefight. The question of whether or not we would see any NVA had been answered. What remained to be learned was who they were, where they were going, and how many more enemy soldiers were using that one trail.

We continued to watch the section of the trail for more than an hour where the lone VC had first emerged, but there were no other sightings. Bishop motioned to all of us to gather around near his pack, leaving Kegler to watch the trail. "Watching those three gooks pass by made me think about Lieutenant Coffman's prisoner-snatch technique. If we could find a section of this trail that had a right-angle turn and good cover on both sides, then we might be able to pull it off."

Bishop left with Kegler, and while the rest of us remained at the OP site watching the trail and acting as security, the two of them went out in search of a place that would offer us the chance at grabbing an NVA prisoner. Within half an hour they had returned to our OP, and Bishop started to draw his plan out on the ground. We drew close to listen to him.

"If we plan this right, I'm sure it'll work. We found a place about four hundred yards from here where the trail goes uphill, and there's one good section with a lot of thick cover where we can stay hidden to within four or five feet of the trail's edge. From this new location, we can see back down the hill to where that first VC appeared this morning. We'll try to get set in place for the ambush this afternoon. By the looks of those dark clouds coming in, it will soon be raining hard, which means that any gooks who are headed this way will be walking with their heads down. Having to walk uphill, if they're wearing a heavy pack, will be double insurance that they'll move with their eyes looking down on the ground.

"Kegler will be at the bend in the trail, here. You four will set in here, with a space between Keaveney and Doc. I'll be on the opposite side of the trail and take out the one gook. The signal to fire will come when Kegler opens up on full automatic. Once I grab that gook and cross over to our side, Kegler will be able to see me and so will the rest of you. His firing straight down the trail and your cross firing will ensure that we can blow away the rest of the group. We'll stage our packs here. Doc, once I grab their man and cross over to our side of the trail, I want you to stuff and tape that gook's mouth shut and then tape his hands behind his back.

"We need to consider two other things: first, we have to have good visual signaling ability with each other; and second, if anything should go wrong and we need to call it off, the signal to stop will be our freeze signal. Now, take five minutes, think about everything that can go wrong with this plan, and we'll talk about 'em, one at a time.''

There were no objections to Bishop's plan, provided all the conditions were met. Bishop had good reason to feel confident: the terrain was in our favor, the bad weather was on our side, we had practiced the technique at Phu Bai numerous times, and we had the nerve to do it. We moved out. Within half an hour we arrived at the place that Bishop had selected.

We took only our weapons, our web belts, and our harnesses. Our packs were stacked and hidden about thirty yards behind us, and we were able to watch the trail from both directions once we had crawled into our positions.

I could see Keaveney to my left, and Silva was to my right. Kegler could see Silva at the bend in the trail. Furhman was turned to the right side of Keaveney, and sat with his binoculars watching the spot from where the first VC had appeared earlier in the morning. Keaveney and I could see Bishop on the opposite side of the trail. We sat in the rain and waited.

I had placed my M-16 beside me and had removed the .45 Colt automatic from my shoulder holster, holding it cocked and in my right hand. I sat upright, watching Bishop watch me. I had taken one small battle dressing and one roll of tape from my medical bag and placed them on the ground next to me. If Bishop did manage to grab one NVA soldier, I was ready for him.

We had sat in place for nearly half an hour, when Furhman

touched Keaveney and signaled "freeze." He studied the area with his binoculars for several more seconds before slowly raising his right hand. His fingers unwound from his unclenched fist; one, two, three, then four fingers showed. His signing that four enemy soldiers were approaching was passed to Bishop, then to Silva, and down to Kegler, whose position protected our left side in the ambush.

Four NVA soldiers had emerged from the jungle and were moving slowly up the trail toward us, four hundred yards away. Each of us watched one another, waiting for more signals to come from Furhman, which would help to tell us what gook was to be the best target of Bishop's attack.

Furhman continued to view their progress. His next signal would be a distance estimation so that we could prepare ourselves for the ambush. His hand moved again, but this time it was a repeat of the first signal, "freeze," followed by a flash of three fingers. Three more NVA had suddenly appeared on the trail behind the first four. That signal was passed on to Bishop, Silva, and Kegler, sending a rush of adrenaline through all of us. Seven NVA soldiers meant that no attempt would be made at grabbing one of the passing men.

Bishop signaled "move back slowly," then rose and crossed the trail to the safety of our side. We began to move back and away from the ambush site, trying to put distance and vegetation between us and the edge of the trail. Furhman could still see the first four NVA and signaled to us that we had less than two minutes before they would pass through our killing zone. Any more movement from any one of us might be heard by the approaching soldiers, and with so little time for planning, we remained frozen in our new positions less than ten feet from the trail.

Furhman had remained in his concealed position until the first four NVA disappeared from his view, moving into a small dip on the trail. He chose that moment to move back toward us and then crept up next to Bishop. "I counted twenty-three NVA headed toward us. Let's hope that none of them decides to take a head call off of the trail, or we're in some damn serious trouble."

We were at the mercy of fate. By pulling back just a few feet from the edge of the trail, what we had gained in better conceal-ment we had lost in the ability to observe. By then no one had a clear view of the trail except Kegler, and we hoped that none of the NVA had any view of us. All we could do was sit motion-less in the rain and wait for the approaching column to pass by. There is no way to describe the feelings of complete alertness, fear, apprehension, and excitement that ran through us. We could not move; we could not talk; we could not motion or even whisper to the man beside us. To do so would invite immediate reaction from the NVA. Our fear was not only in being discovered but for each other.

I believe that such feelings are instinctive. They begin the first time we play the game of hide-and-seek. The excitement builds as we stay hidden, waiting for that one moment of possible discovery when the seeker passes by. We pray to be invisible. It was like that alongside the trail, but the stakes were higher. This was no school-yard game; this was the ultimate game: life or death. Even though we had trained for the possibility, we had never been so close to the enemy before.

Their singsong voices could be heard before we began to hear the muffled sound of their boots on the muddy trail. They shouted back and forth to one another in short, clipped phrases as they passed by, unaware that we sat not more than ten feet away. My pulse was racing and I prayed that the sound of my heart pounding through my chest would not be heard by any of the NVA walking on that trail. I knew that Bishop and Keaveney could hear the pounding; it must have been that loud.

As long as their voices could be heard, as the blurred green forms continued to pass by, we were safe. But what were we to do if they suddenly stopped? What if one of them had seen us? Would he turn and fire at us, or would he shout and alert the column to throw grenades at us? The sound of those North Vietnamese infantrymen moving along the narrow trail in the rain continued for what seemed like hours, and still no one in the team moved.

There is a rhythm to the sound of men moving along in a column. If they are uniformed and carrying the same type of equipment, then the same noises are repeated over and over as each man passes by. It was that rhythm that we each listened to, hoping that it would not stop abruptly.

When the only sound to be heard was the patter of raindrops, Bishop slowly raised his head and looked to his left and to his right. It had taken ten minutes for the column of NVA soldiers to pass. He motioned to Furhman to move back and look down the trail for stragglers while the rest of us began to creep back to our packs and the secondary radio.

It took another five minutes before Kegler crept over to join us in our little staging area. He whispered to Bishop that he had counted sixty-two North Vietnamese soldiers as they had passed by him! He said that most of them carried rifles, some carried sacks of rice, and six men had carried RPG-7 grenade launchers on their shoulders. He had been less than six feet from the edge of the trail.

We moved away from the trail as quietly and as quickly as possible. The rain continued to fall, and it helped to mask our noise, but Bishop knew better than to go back the way we had come. The greater problem was not so much in knowing what direction the NVA trail took, but more importantly, we did not know where the long column of NVA soldiers had gone. It could have stopped and rested only a hundred yards away.

Bishop had staged his radio pack with the rest of our gear when he had decided to be the one to grab the passing enemy soldier. We had not been in communication with our radio-relay site since staging our packs, and the people in the rear needed to know what we had just seen, and we needed to know what they wanted us to do about it.

As we started moving away from our staging area one of the men turned and spoke to the team leader. "Bishop, I don't want you to get too mad or nothin' at the way I smell, but I pissed my pants when all of them gooks walked by me." No one laughed. As Bishop adjusted his pack, he said, "I'd rather have you here alive with me, reeking of piss, than to be up in heaven, listening to you tell me about it." We moved out to find our harbor site and radioed back the events of our last half hour.

By the time we had found a good harbor site, it was dark. Bishop changed radio batteries and contacted the relay site, filing a lengthy SALUTE report and requesting air support for the next morning. Within an hour the rain had stopped, and warm winds swept into the Hai Van Pass. It was safe enough for us to take turns eating a cold evening meal.

When Bishop had talked with the people in the rear, they had told him to sit tight, plot the course of the trail, wait for morning, and then see if we could locate the staging area that the North Vietnamese were using as their base camp. We did not attempt to put out our PSIDs or four claymore mines for fear of making too much noise, but Bishop did double the number of men on radio watch, believing that two pairs of ears were better than one.

I was wakened by Kegler, who was on radio watch with Bishop. My watch showed 0400, and as I sat up, Kegler asked me again if I was awake. When I answered, "yes," he told me to take a few deep breaths, smell the air, and then tell him what I smelled. The strong smell of boiled cabbage was in the air. Kegler had told Bishop that he had smelled the cabbage, but Bishop wanted another opinion, and for whatever reason, I was the one chosen.

Bishop told Kegler and me to wake up Keaveney, Silva, and Furhman. If we could smell the cooking fires of the NVA, they couldn't be too far away from our harbor site, and they must have sent some of their people out to gather wood for their fires.

Once all of the team was awake, Bishop contacted the radio-relay site and reported the new situation. We knew that plans were being made by Major Lee and Lieutenant Coffman to get our air support ready for use once we had located the NVA base camp. The smell of boiling cabbage was a good indication that our job of finding the NVA was going to be made much easier than we had expected.

No one wanted to try to locate the NVA by paralleling their trail; there were too many of them and not enough of us, and we had been taught never to walk their trails. Our plan for the morning had been to locate their encampment by patrolling, if it was within our reconnaissance area, then call in air support to bomb the North Vietnamese and their base camp into oblivion.

Bishop received a radio transmission with instructions to locate the suspected cooking fires and report our location and observations of the area as we patrolled. By 0600, the morning light began to brighten. We had eaten, checked and cleaned our weapons, and repacked our gear, ready to move out. When Bishop had finished his detailed map study, he gave Kegler the new compass heading.

Bishop knew that our direction of travel would now take us up to the top of another hill, and according to our maps, we would be able to look down into a large but narrow draw that appeared the most likely and closest place that would be used as an enemy base camp area. The wind that carried the smell of cabbage was coming from that draw, over the hill, and down to our harbor site, so Bishop's reason for moving in that direction made sense to us.

By 0730 Kegler had threaded his way across the face of the hill, and we found ourselves on a ridge line looking down into the deep draw. Several thin columns of white smoke rose from the edges of the long draw, so we set up to observe the area, this time putting out claymore mines and PSIDs to help our hasty defensive plan. The draw was several hundred yards long, and the steep angle of the two opposing hills that made up the draw protected it well from aerial observation. It was the genius of the North Vietnamese to choose draws and valleys as their staging areas. The camps were next to impossible to hit with long-range artillery fire: because of the high trajectory of our shells, artillery could not hit between hills. The only way to engage them was to kill them scientifically, with the use of Marine close air support.

Our training at Phu Bai included planning for close air support, and as we watched the draw for additional signs of enemy activity, Bishop was busy with his map and compass, writing down coordinates and the best approach for air support, enabling the aircraft to find the draw in poor weather and then drop their ordnance between the hills and down the long axis of the protected draw.

A short while later we had been told that four Marine A-6 Intruders and one OV-10 Bronco observation plane would be on station to support our request for a close air attack on the enemy base camp. The attack aircraft would be over us within twenty minutes.

The key word in the phrase "close air support" is *close*, and that is because of the close proximity of the friendly forces on the ground in relation to the enemy target. The draw from where the smoke was rising was less than three hundred yards below the hilltop that hid us. That was close enough for us to observe the North Vietnamese encampment and still be able to adjust the bombing missions of the four A-6s with the help of the OV-10.

The Marine's A-6 Intruder was an all-weather attack aircraft capable of carrying thousands of pounds of bombs, rockets, and missiles, delivering all of them with great accuracy onto any selected target in all types of weather, night or day.

The OV-10 Bronco was a Marine twin-engine, two-seat aircraft that was equipped with radio gear that let the pilot and the aerial observer stay in communication with both the attacking aircraft and with us on the ground. The OV-10 would assist the fast-moving A-6s to adjust their bombing strikes after the initial target run.

Six limitations had to be considered in making use of close air support: the radius of action, a consideration based on fuel and ordnance load; the pilot's time on station, how long the A-6s were able to stay above us; radio communications (not a problem, we could talk with our relay site and the OV-10 pilot); identification of the target; description of the target, grid maps, geographical reference points, and good descriptive communications; and weather. The last consideration was the most important element. Weather was the greatest limitation simply because if you can't see the target, you can't hit it.

The news that A-6s were the support aircraft was significant because of their all-weather capability. If the pilot and aerial observer in the OV-10 knew their job, then the A-6s would be more than able to drop forty thousand pounds of Mark 81 or Mark 82 bombs straight down the draw, even if the target was masked in rain and fog.

"Team Snakey, Team Snakey, this is Lunch Meat four zero. Over." The OV-10 was "up" on our radio freq, and the pilot wanted to know as much about the suspected base camp area as we could tell him. All of the pilots had been briefed on our patrol reports during the night. What they needed to know was whether or not there were any antiaircraft gun positions there, too. Bishop gave the OV-10 pilot as much information as was requested. We had not yet seen the OV-10, nor had we heard the sound of his twin engines as he flew closer to our hilltop. What he wanted to do was to gain some altitude and then glide by the area to orient the aerial observer to our position and to the exact location of the base camp. We were instructed to give the pilot a clock reference of our location after he made his first pass over us.

We were surrounded by tall trees that made it difficult to watch for the approach of the Bronco, but Bishop's description of the target and his skill at reporting our exact grid location gave the pilot several reference points to plot and helped in guiding him over the target.

The A-6 Intruders were standing by not more than twenty miles away. Their presence would only be made known to the North Vietnamese as they pulled out of their bomb run over the draw.

The OV-10 made two low-level passes over the area, and our exact position was marked and noted by his aerial observer. All that remained for the OV-10 to do was to fire several white-phosphorous rockets into the draw so the fast A-6s would have a mark on the ground to aim at when they sent their ordnance tumbling into the enemy camp. Our job would be to observe the bombing, send necessary adjustments up to the OV-10, plot the location of antiaircraft fire, and watch for secondary explosions. The OV-10 pilot radioed Bishop that he was making his first run at the target and that he would fire two willy-pete (white phosphorous) rockets on his pass. The air attack began.

The first flight of two A-6s was called in from its holding pattern and immediately picked up on the splash of white smoke and orange fire spreading out from the center of the draw. The aerial observer in the OV-10 radioed that the two attack aircraft were "coming in wings level and cleared hot," meaning that our small patch of earth was about to start shaking.

The first load of bombs landed right in the middle of the protected area where the pillars of smoke had risen earlier in the morning. The earth below us erupted, as great chunks of dirt and trees and brush blew away from the center of the bursting bombs. The ground beneath us shook, and we tried to find cover.

Several automatic weapons chattered skyward, but there was no sound of machine-gun fire. On the second pass the effects were the same, although the bombs had hit farther up the draw than the first strike. The muffled sounds of secondary explosions were heard after the second pass, assuring us that our call for fixed-wing had been good.

The pilot of the OV-10 radioed to Bishop that enemy soldiers were running for the safety of the adjacent hillside after the first air strike. The second run at the target had enveloped the area at the base of our hill. The OV-10 observer radioed that the last two A-6s were headed in to drop ordnance on the burning and smoking area that had once been the NVA base camp. In all, four passes were made into the draw.

Our secondary radio was linked to the radio-relay site, and Keaveney had kept them informed of what was happening while it was happening. As the OV-1O remained over the area, the Marine A-6s headed back toward their base at Da Nang, radioing that they had been "happy to be of service" in answering our request for help.

There was no way to know what had actually happened inside the enemy base camp. We had no clear view of the area from where we stood, other than to have seen the smoke of the fires, and having known that we smelled the aroma of cooking food. The fleeing enemy soldiers and the sound of secondary explosions added to the probability that we had hit a base camp, but it would take a visual inspection of the draw to satisfy the people in the rear.

Within several minutes the radio call came in to Corporal Bishop that we were now tasked to conduct a bomb damage assessment (BDA), and that meant taking a walk through the draw that had just been heavily bombed. The idea did not sit well, considering that after we had stuck one hell of a big stick into a hornet's nest, they wanted us to count dead hornets. Of course, we knew it would happen. Our mission was to collect information, and since we had asked for a heavy hand in dealing with the enemy base camp, we were expected to report on the results first hand.

Bishop passed the word that we would wait for several hours before making our move down from the safety of the hill and into the draw. Our hilltop was defendable, and the wait would allow us time to plan our route and to observe the area, hoping to see any movement from below and still be able to recall the air support if necessary.

By 1100 we had seen no signs of movement. The area continued to smoke, and several small fires burned along the far hillside, but there was no sign of enemy soldiers moving below or headed toward us. Bishop had radioed back his reports of the bombing to the rear, and told them his plans for conducting the BDA. They understood his reason for not caring to rush into the bombed-out area until things had cooled down considerably.

Kegler led the way down from our hilltop toward the far side of the draw, and the area that we moved through was covered by double canopy, two levels of trees. The double canopy enabled us to stay well hidden as we dropped down below the two hundred meter level of the hill. When we took our first break, we began to study the results of the bomb damage, still several hundred yards away. Within seconds of focusing his binoculars on the damaged area, Kegler's hand signaled "freeze," and we got down and assumed a ready-to-fire position.

Kegler was watching two NVA soldiers who sat upright against the trunk of a large tree. They were uniformed, but they wore no helmets. Their weapons could not be seen, and they didn't appear to be wounded. There were no bandages on them, and there was no obvious evidence of injury. We studied them for more than fifteen minutes. No one approached them, they did not speak to one another, and this led us to believe that they were dead.

The two NVA soldiers were about two hundred yards from where we sat, and Bishop handed me his binoculars and told me to watch them to see if I could tell whether or not they were breathing. It didn't appear so, and closer examination with a spotting scope revealed the stain of blood coming from each one of the soldiers' ears and running down their necks. We held our position for another half hour, reporting this information back to the radio-relay team, then we were told to move.

Bishop's plan was to skirt the edges of the draw, and that would allow us the opportunity to view the two NVA soldiers and observe the damage from opposite sides of the area. The move took three hours of skillful maneuvering on the part of Kegler to get us to the other side of the draw. Once in our new position, we set up to observe what remained of the enemy base camp.

We could see several bamboo hootches that remained standing, having once been lashed together with wire and vines. Several ruined NVA packs had been abandoned and left out in the open, and several sacks of rice had been ripped apart by the flying shrapnel, but still there were no signs of life. We moved in closer to the edge of the draw.

If anyone had survived the bombing attack, they had not remained in the draw. We found several pools of blood, and we saw what appeared to be pieces of bodies, but the damage done to the area was complete. We assumed that the two dead NVA soldiers who were left behind had died of concussion. We believed that they had been underground somewhere during the attack and their bodies had been left behind.

As the late afternoon sun began to cast long shadows across the bombed-out draw, we moved up to higher ground and awaited word on the time of our scheduled helicopter extraction. Kegler had found a suitable harbor site for our night's sleep, and as always, we went through the ritual of setting up our defense, putting out our PSIDs and claymores, keeping two men on radio and security watch throughout the night.

At first morning light of our fourth day in the bush, the radio-relay team contacted Bishop and informed him that we were scheduled for extraction by CH-46 at 1000 hours. The grid coordinates of the pickup point were plotted, and we moved from our harbor site to a position nearly two kilometers away from where we had spent the night.

On time, the first of two Marine CH-46 helicopters came into view, and Lieutenant Coffman's voice came over the radio, letting Bishop know that he was aboard. Our extract from the Hai Van Pass area was completed without any untoward incidents, and we landed at Phu Bai just before noon on the tenth of November. As we walked down the ramp of the CH-46, we saw Major Lee walking with another team from the back of the second CH-46. We were met by the company first sergeant; company gunnery sergeant; our platoon sergeant, Staff Sergeant Williams, and the rest of the men in the company. They had waited for the return of the two reconnaissance teams before beginning to celebrate the Marine Corps' 194th birthday with steaks, shrimp, and cold beer.

The final patrol report that was filed on the BDA did not indicate that we had killed sixty-two North Vietnamese soldiers. We knew that number had passed by us on the trail, and we knew that a base camp had been destroyed, with secondary explosions occurring as a result of the bombing. But like the Gurkhas of Nepal who Lieutenant Coffman held in such reverence, we reported only what we had seen and knew to be true.

· THE RIFLE INSPECTION ·

THIRD FORCE RECONNAISSANCE COMPANY SAW SOME new personnel during November 1969. Our platoon leader, First Lieutenant Hensley, had departed Vietnam for the States and was replaced by an infantry officer, First Lieutenant William Singleton. Staff Sergeant Williams remained our platoon sergeant, and Sergeant Garcia became our platoon guide.

A First Lieutenant Robinson went to work for First Lieutenant Coffman in the company's S-3 shop, as did another new man named First Lieutenant Black. These officers would have no direct impact on us until later. But training between missions was continuous under the guidance of Major Lee, Captain Hisler, and Lieutenant Coffman, and they included the new officers in that training.

The use of the rappelling tower was now a standard event, and as information became available concerning our new areas of operation, the training placed greater emphasis on rappelling and the techniques required to haul equipment vertically. Gunnery Sergeants Hamilton, Collins, and Bilodeau had extensive infantry and reconnaissance backgrounds. Their ability and enthusiasm in teaching classes to team members always made for interesting times whenever the three of them got together.

One morning First Lieutenant Coffman had scheduled a class at the rappelling tower to teach vertical haulage. As part of the instruction, he and his training NCOs had set up a slide-for-life line that would allow a Marine to hook himself to it with several snap links and quickly descend to the ground in what can best be described as a controlled crash.

From the starting point, high up on the platform of the tower, to the end of the slide-for-life was no greater than 120 feet, but with the starting height at least forty feet above the ground, the downward speed was considerable. The speed of the individual descending the line was controlled only by using his boots for brakes.

Lieutenant Coffman was on top of the platform, making the final adjustments to the slide-for-life line, when our platoon arrived for training. Our team was told to climb to the top of the tower to receive instructions before descending the slide. First Lieutenant Singleton had climbed to the top of the platform prior to our arrival and was observing the new training as part of his education with the company S-3 (operations) shop. We had seen him walking around the company area but none of us had yet spoken to him.

With the lines secured and final instructions completed, Lieutenant Coffman began to tie himself into the slide to demonstrate how it was done and to reaffirm his statement that he would not have any of us do something that he would not do himself. At that point Lieutenant Singleton spoke with Coffman and told him that if he was being considered a candidate as platoon leader, then here was an opportunity to show "his men" that he would lead the way.

Lieutenant Coffman was not convinced of Singleton's ability to properly demonstrate the slide-for-life without having practiced the technique before, but Singleton insisted, and Lieutenant Coffman gave him the benefit of the doubt. We looked at one another in silent amusement wondering what kind of individual would insist on trying an untested system in the hopes of looking good in front of his platoon. We found out.

Lieutenant Coffman began to explain the best way to travel down the slide-for-life and the techniques for braking but he was cut short by the anxious lieutenant's words. "I seen this done before, and there's nothing to it. Just give me some room to get a good start, and my demonstration will be just as valuable as yours." Without any more conversation between them, the new lieutenant hooked himself onto the slide with his steel snap link and then took a running leap from the platform.

The line was tied off well, and it supported his weight perfectly, but the angle of descent made him pick up forward speed as soon as he left the tower. By the time he neared the ground, he was moving fast. The anchor point for the slide-for-life line was a telephone pole, and there was a large knot tied in the line several yards ahead of the pole. Lieutenant Singleton had not first brought his boots up and onto the line as we had been instructed to do, and when his feet slammed into the ground, his left ankle twisted around into the opposite direction of travel.

The pain of his sprained ankle almost caused him to pass out; it would have been better for him if he had. The Marines on the ground unhooked him from the slide-for-life, and Lieutenant Coffman, using the slide as he had instructed us, was at the injured lieutenant's side in seconds. "Doc, get down here with your Unit-1, and get this peckerhead over to sick bay."

The ride down was not a problem, and as soon as I was next to Lieutenant Singleton, the training officer had the rest of our team join him on the ground beside the injured officer.

"Here is another perfect example of someone who does not pay attention. I told you men how to use your boots to slow your descent along the line. Now you can see what happens when you do not listen. I want you to take a look at the lieutenant's ankle and remember just what a good sprain looks like. If this happens to any one of you while you're on a mission it will decrease your security by fifty percent. It will take two people to carry one injured man, and that only means big trouble. When Lieutenant Singleton came out here this morning, I'm sure that he didn't realize what a valuable training aid he would become. We should thank him for his assistance."

With those words, the platoon members cheered and applauded as Lieutenant Singleton was led toward a jeep that would eventually take him to the Army's 85th Evacuation Hospital, located on the opposite side of the airstrip at Phu Bai. His ankle was in a cast for four weeks, but he remained with 3d Force Recon, working on the company's training schedule within the S-3 shop.

Team training at Phu Bai continued at a fast pace, centered on the preparation for a mission inside of the A Shau Valley, and our close association with the soldiers and pilots of the 2/17th Air Cav continued to grow. We practiced rappelling techniques until it became routine for us to exit a hovering helicopter from a line, sixty feet in the air.

Every team member became familiar with the use of the special equipment used to extract an injured man from the jungle. The jungle penetrator was such a device. The penetrator was shaped like a tear drop, which allowed it to pass through the trees, and it consisted of three steel blades suspended from a cable that was attached to a winch located on the outside of the helicopter. Once the penetrator was lowered to the injured man, the blades were unfolded, and they became a seat for the injured man to sit on while he was hoisted back into the hovering helicopter. The trick in using the jungle penetrator was in making sure that the seat hit the ground before anyone touched it. The static electricity from the helicopter came straight down the cable, and anyone foolish enough to grab the swinging but ungrounded penetrator would quickly find himself flattened by the electric shock that was generated from above.

The longer that we remained in our company area, the more we were expected to participate in the mundane, garrison-type duties. These included standing guard duty, being available for morning and afternoon platoon training, and running morning and afternoon physical fitness training. One morning, during the last week of November, Staff Sergeant Williams returned from a meeting that was held by the commanding officer. When he entered the squad bay, he told us to assemble outside.

"I have some word to pass, and I want you to hear it from me, first hand. As of today, Lieutenant Singleton has been assigned as our platoon leader. I know that we have not had a platoon commander here for a long time, but the company commander wants to put these newly joined lieutenants to work. I'll still be the platoon sergeant, and Sergeant Garcia will be our platoon guide. You all know how I expect our chain of command to work. I can also tell you that First Lieutenant Singleton has an outstanding record coming from the grunts and that he has seen his share of combat, up front and close. He will be here at 1300 today to hold a rifle inspection."

This news of a rifle inspection caused a great many odd looks to occur on the faces of the men in the platoon. We had never had a formal rifle inspection during the past five months. Sergeant Chapman, Corporal Swederski, or Corporal Bishop had always been the ones who were responsible for ensuring that our weapons were cleaned to their satisfaction. We prided ourselves on keeping our weapons immaculate and operational. Staff Sergeant Williams could walk through our squad bay at any time and know that if he picked up a rifle or a pistol, it was clean and ready for use.

Our training for the morning was to conduct a series of immediate-action drills in and around the company area. The drills would last until 1100, and then we were to break for noon chow. The rifle inspection scheduled had thrown a monkey wrench into our plans by requiring us to spend additional time cleaning our weapons in order to meet the new lieutenant's requirements.

The cleaning of weapons, as it was performed in garrison, was quite different from the way it was conducted in the field. The field cleanings were fast and expedient, as opposed to the many hours that were taken to clean rifles and pistols after returning from a mission.

Lance Corporal Keaveney carried an M-79 grenade launcher as his T/O (table of organization) weapon. There was no place for such a weapon at a rifle inspection, and Staff Sergeant Williams told Keaveney that on this occasion he would be required to fall out with his M-16. Keaveney kept his issue M-16 in a footlocker underneath his rack and after rediscovering it among his extra 782 gear, he saw that it was red with rust and had become filthy since being placed in his footlocker some weeks before.

When Keaveney learned that the M-16 was the only weapon to be inspected by our new lieutenant, he made a beeline for the shower, taking along his M-16. We had found no harm in taking our M-16s into the shower when we returned from missions, and using the hot, soapy water, we frequently began rifle cleaning with a good scrubbing while we washed. The smaller parts of the rifle's firing mechanism were brought along, disassembled, and kept covered with WD-40 or some other cleaning solvent in an unused ammunition can.

After taking more time than usual to shower, Keaveney scrambled to get back to the squad bay, got dressed in the proper utility uniform, and then began to fine-tune his weapon for the inspection. At 1250 Staff Sergeant Williams called on us to fall in for rifle inspection. Keaveney was late, and was the last to fall in, ready for our platoon sergeant to present the platoon for the first time to the new platoon commander.

We had fallen in by teams, and as Lt. William Singleton limped into view, still wearing his cast from the slide-for-life accident, Staff Sergeant Williams called the platoon to attention. The lieutenant instructed Staff Sergeant Williams to precede him through the inspection and to have Sergeant Garcia take the appropriate notes, recording any discrepancies found during the inspection.

The lieutenant began his detailed rifle inspection with Corporal Bishop. He noted, out loud, that "your cover is dirty, your glasses still carry traces of green cammie paint, your utilities have several holes that need patching, and your boots are not spit-shined."

While the lieutenant was inspecting Corporal Bishop's rifle he asked him several questions on general military subjects, testing Bishop's knowledge and noting his ability to answer questions under pressure. Our team leader answered the lieutenant's questions quickly and correctly. Once finished with Bishop's rifle, the lieutenant spoke to Staff Sergeant Williams saying that the condition and cleanliness of the weapon was "noteworthy."

The lieutenant executed a right face, took one pace forward, halted, executed a left face, and stood directly in front of me. My T/O weapon was the .45 Colt automatic, and fortunately for me, Staff Sergeant Williams had spent some time in preparing me for "inspection arms" with the pistol. The precise movements are, of course, different than those done with a service rifle and it must have taken the lieutenant by surprise as I went through the motions of pulling back the slide and inspecting the chamber of the pistol before presenting the weapon to him for his detailed inspection. I had practiced to the satisfaction of the platoon sergeant.

The lieutenant turned his head in the direction of Sergeant Garcia, who was doing his job as the platoon guide by keeping a list of the noted discrepancies.

"Dirty cover, missing buttons on his utility blouse, unshined brass, and the heels of his boots need to be replaced. His pistol is immaculate."

The lieutenant's critical comments regarding the condition of our uniforms were loud enough to be heard by every Marine in the formation. It was apparent that he was some sort of a perfectionist and while our collective appearance was disappointing to him, he was pleased with the attention that we had given to our weapons.

"Doc, how much time did you spend on cleaning this pistol?"

"I guess it was about half an hour, sir."

"How much time did you spend on getting your uniform ready?"

"I didn't spend very much time on my uniform, sir."

"Why is that?"

"I think that having a clean pistol or clean rifle is more important than having my boots spit-shined or all of my buttons sewn on my pockets, sir."

"You do, huh?"

"Yes sir, I do."

"Well maybe you'd care to enlighten me as to why you think that way."

"Well, sir, I think that you would rather know that we can strip down a rifle or a pistol and keep it clean and operating than to waste time spit-shining boots that will be dirty in ten minutes or sewing on buttons that I don't need."

"What do you mean, you don't need?"

"Sir, those buttons didn't fall off, I took them off because they get in the way when I need to get into that pocket in a hurry."

My answer seemed to satisfy his curiosity and he did not proceed any further with his line of questioning. He just glared at me before turning to his right to position himself in front of Lance Corporal Keaveney.

Once the lieutenant had centered himself on Keaveney, he waited impatiently for him to go through the maneuvers of inspection arms and to present himself and his weapon ready for inspection. He snatched the M-16 from Keaveney's hands and began to comment loudly on what he was finding wrong with the rifle. "Dirty butt plate, dirty rear sight, dirty magazine wall, dirty front sight, dirty flash suppressor." Then he looked down the barrel of the rifle and squinted, saying, "Dirty barrel, too."

The last part of Keaveney's weapon that Lieutenant Singleton wanted to examine was the chamber. Evidently he had seen something in or near the chamber that raised his curiosity, and this caused him to stick the little finger of his right hand up and into the tight chamber, twisting his finger around in the process. He removed his little finger from the chamber and brought it up close to his nose, studying the foreign matter that was wrapped around his finger like a ball of steel wool.

"What the hell is this?" His question was asked of no one in particular, but Staff Sergeant Williams and Sergeant Garcia leaned closer to see what he was talking about.

"Keaveney, do you know what this is?"

"No sir, I don't."

His face getting very red with anger and his voice rising in utter disbelief, the lieutenant held up his shaking finger and yelled, "What the hell is that?"

I looked at the lieutenant's finger and said, "It looks like pubic hair to me, sir."

He looked ill. "Pubic hair? Pubic hair? Yeeccch, take back this goddamned rifle, Lance Corporal Keaveney!" When Keaveney took the rifle from Lieutenant Singleton's hands, the entire platoon began to laugh. There was no stopping it. Sergeant Garcia began to snicker, Staff Sergeant Williams's jaws were noticeably tight. He was trying desperately to keep his composure, but it was no good. The spell of rigid formality had been broken by the discovery of pubic hair inside of Keaveney's rifle.

Our new lieutenant walked away from his first formation, still trying to flick hair from the little finger of his right hand. He was disgusted, mortified with what he had found inside of Keaveney's M-16, and professionally embarrassed at his loss of bearing. To make matters worse, he didn't walk away, he limped away, and that made the event even more hilarious.

Staff Sergeant Williams glared at us all, and he tried hard not to find the humor in the disaster of the rifle inspection, but he couldn't do it. He dismissed his platoon and followed after the lieutenant, hoping to convince his new boss that this was an isolated incident. We waited for an explanation.

Keaveney had left his rifle in the long metal sink that was commonly used in our head. He had placed his rifle over the one large drain hole and as the water drained out all of the refuse in the sink passed through the magazine and chamber of Keaveney's M-16. He had come to the platoon formation, never having looked inside the chamber of his rifle until the lieutenant had reached for it.

Our new platoon leader never conducted a formal rifle inspection again. Unknown to us, this event marked the last time that we would stand together as a platoon. It was also one of the last times that we would share a humorous situation together. The eight reconnaissance teams of 3d Force Recon Company were committed to patrol inside of the A Shau Valley several days later.

A SHAU VALLEY (THE ——— BEGINNING) ———

IN DECEMBER 1969, 3D FORCE RECONNAISSANCE COMpany was under the operational control of Lt. Gen. Herman Nickerson, Jr., commanding general, III Marine Amphibious Force, Fleet Marine Force, whose headquarters was located in Da Nang. General Nickerson needed to know exactly what North Vietnamese units were operating inside the A Shau Valley and what were their routes of entrance and egress.

The celebration of the lunar new year, the Tet holiday, would occur on the last day of January, and General Nickerson did not want to be surprised by a communist attack on the American Forces in I Corps, as had happened in the famous "Tet Offensive" the year before.

The warrant officer pilots of 2/17th Air Cav had become regular visitors to our company operations room during November, and they had been tasked to plan for and provide us with the helicopter support required for our team insertions and extractions within the A Shau Valley, scheduled for the two months prior to Tet.

The A Shau Valley was located well outside the limits of any friendly supporting artillery fan, and that meant that our team's request for friendly fire support could be answered only by close air support. The distance and hilly terrain between the A Shau Valley and Phu Bai also meant that all of our team's radio communications would be dependent upon one radio-relay site that would have to be established and defended inside the valley.

As dawn broke on the thirteenth of December, 1969, three flights of Marine F-4B Phantoms were called upon to blow the top off of Hill 883, located on the eastern side of the A Shau Valley, halfway between the old French airfields of Ta Bat and A Shau. This coordinated plan also called for a formation of escorted Army Hueys to land three teams from 3d Force on top of Hill 883. Once the hilltop was secured the Marines would build and defend a 292 radio communications site, known as Zulu Relay, enabling three of our operational teams to be inserted into the valley. Their patrol information would be received on Hill 883 and then relayed back to Phu Bai.

The first day of the new operation got off to a very bad start. The Marine close air support came in on time, the bombs hit the sides and top of Hill 883 as planned, but that first attack did not neutralize the entrenched antiaircraft guns of the waiting North Vietnamese Army.

As the first Huey began its final approach onto Hill 883, two camouflaged Soviet 12.7-millimeter antiaircraft guns opened up from an adjacent undamaged hillside less than five hundred meters away. The lead Huey took four 12.7 rounds through the Plexiglas cockpit, blowing the head of the pilot into the rear of his own Huey. That bird, crowded with its pilot, copilot, two Army door gunners, and one six-man recon team, pitched wildly as the co-pilot tried in vain to wrestle the controls from the dead pilot's hands. The Huey crashed on its side in the landing zone and immediately began to burn.

The second Army Huey, trailing behind the lead bird, came under immediate fire from the same gun emplacements, and it, too, crashed and burned just behind the wreckage of the lead bird. One Army light observation helicopter (LOH, pronounced "loach") that came in close to the crash site was hit broadside by an enemy RPG-7 rocket, and it exploded in midair like a well-hit skeet target, instantly killing the two Army warrant officer pilots inside.

Within seconds, six Marines were injured and three of the Army's Air Cav personnel were dead. The Marines who survived the destruction of the first two helicopters managed to salvage the 292 communications equipment from the two burning Hueys. As the emergency radio call went out for additional close air support, the Marines on Hill 883 dug in and began to construct the radio transmission site, set up their defense while waiting for dust-off helicopters to arrive and evacuate the injured and the dead.

Team Snakey was inserted in the northeastern part of the A Shau Valley at approximately 0700 that same morning. We had witnessed the bombing attack on Hill 883 and the subsequent downing of the three Army helicopters while we sat in our Huey and orbited an area near our insertion point. We were to observe the floor of the A Shau Valley and immediately report all sightings of enemy activity to the radio-relay site on Hill 883. We were scheduled to be out in the bush for five days.

Kegler, Bishop, Keaveney, Silva, Furhman, and I had been on the ground for no more than ten minutes when we heard the first rifle shot fired from a hilltop several hundred yards away. We had been inserted into a small open area at the base of a long finger that rose gradually from the valley's floor to an elevation cresting more than two thousand feet above us. We had assumed that it would take us all day to complete the climb to the top of the hill to set up our observation position, but the sound of the single rifle shot quickly changed our plans.

We had no way of knowing who had fired the shot, exactly where it had originated, or why the shot had been fired. There was no impact near us and no additional firing. There was no reason for us to return fire. Our questions came automatically. Have we been seen by an enemy unit? Was the single shot a signal to another unit, or was it the shot from a nervous and undisciplined young NVA soldier hidden in an ambush site? Do we continue to move, or do we remain hidden and temporarily safe?

Bishop kept us in position for another half hour, waiting. We heard no other sounds, and we saw no movement, but as we resumed our long climb up the finger, we could only hope that we were not walking into a well-planned ambush.

The brush that we had moved through at our insertion point had now given way to an open forested area that required us to increase the distance between one another as we moved. It was difficult to communicate between one another across such large intervals because our signals and gestures were hard to give, receive, and be clearly understood. The poor alternative, our team's traveling closer together, invited the prospect of us all being killed in one well-executed enemy ambush.

By noontime we had moved to a new position better than halfway up the finger, and our stopping place allowed us to look back down onto the floor of the valley. It was a beautiful place. The mountaintops were shrouded in thin white clouds but the sun continued to shine through, revealing the great lush green valley. We could see several long waterfalls as they cascaded through the rocky saddles of the mountain range on the opposite side of the valley. That was Laos.

It was perfectly quiet with the exception of the calling of an occasional black crow or some other forest birds, and that was a good sign.

For a long time we studied the new area, plotting reference points such as uniquely configured hilltops, visible roads, the waterfalls, and several large green open areas that appeared to be cultivated fields. That long valley in South Vietnam was one of the most beautiful and peaceful places any of us had ever seen. The A Shau Valley could easily pass for the Garden of Eden.

By late in the afternoon we had positioned ourselves on a rocky ledge just below the crest of the mountaintop. The ledge offered an unobstructed view of the valley floor, and as the evening clouds began to drop down around our mountaintop, we watched in amazement as points of light began to appear in isolated areas around the broad expanse of the valley. The lights were stationary, unlike those of any moving vehicle headlights, but for us to see so many of them in an area that was owned and operated by the North Vietnamese Army was grounds for significant concern.

We had been able to maintain good radio contact with the relay site from the time of our helicopter insertion, and despite the situation that existed on top of Hill 883, the communicators were always up on their radios. Our report of observing those lights in the valley was immediately passed back to Phu Bai, and our transmissions were soon answered by requests for the plotting of all of the light positions and the grid coordinates of all visible trails and roads.

Bishop wanted to be able to observe and report on the visible trails and roads during the night. We had brought along two Starlight scopes for just this purpose. The Starlight scope could be fastened to the receiver of the M-16 rifle or held in the hand. The scope was a four-power device that functioned as an electronic image intensifier. A very good eight-degree field of view was found in the most limited lighting. Through the eyepiece of the Starlight scope, we could watch the lights in the valley below and report on which ones went out and which remained on or moved. It took little time for us to realize that we were surrounded by the lights. As the evening fog closed in around us, we began to hear something new, the sound of distant hammering.

Our recon team's radio frequencies were known to our sister teams, and it was possible for us to listen to the conversations that took place between other teams and the relay site. This was one way that we kept ourselves informed to what was happening in the rear and with our sister teams without jamming up the limited radio frequencies.

Our radio report of what sounded like hammering generated a great deal of interest from the people in the rear. The radio operators at the relay site on Hill 883 had reported earlier that they were preparing their defensive positions, but they also expressed concern at the possibility of being a target for an enemy mortar and ground attack. The presence of Marines on top of Hill 883 had been made known to all of the inhabitants of the A Shau Valley earlier in the day, and as the afternoon light turned to evening shadows, the team observation reports of lights and the sound of hammering gave the Marines at the relay site good reasons to be concerned for their own safety. We could hide, they could not.

Our team reconnaissance zone was nearly five miles north of Hill 883, and while we had a good line-of-sight communication link to the relay site, we could offer them no real assistance if they did become the target of an infantry probe. We moved into our harbor site and waited out the night.

The second day began with Bishop receiving a message that instructed us to remain close to our position. The other two reconnaissance teams had also reported seeing lights during the night, and we were told to observe the various roads and trails for possible use by the North Vietnamese during the day. As we sat in our OP, we began to hear the sound of single shots of rifle fire coming from different locations along the valley floor. We could only assume that the rifle shots were some kind of all-clear signal used by NVA moving along hidden trails. By late in the afternoon of the second day, we had reported at least a dozen signal shots having been fired.

The evening of the second day brought rain, and our ability to report on the lights in the valley diminished with the decreasing visibility.

A radio message from the relay site during the early morning of our third day required us to move over the crest of the mountain and begin reconnaissance of a small valley. The night's rain had been constant and that made our progress very slow due to the slippery condition of the ground.

Kegler had started to follow a natural turn in the terrain, and as Bishop walked at a distance behind him, he signaled back to me to freeze. I relayed the freeze signal back to Keaveney and waited for Bishop's next move. He moved forward to the spot where Kegler was last seen and then he disappeared. I waited for several minutes before moving up to where Bishop had once stood. The ground revealed his tracks moving forward, but I could see neither Bishop nor Kegler ahead of me. I signaled back to Keaveney that I was moving forward to find them and for him to come forward to my position.

I began to move around a large outcropping of vine-covered rock with my rucksack pressed tight against the rock wall. The ground was covered with a soft but thick fernlike vegetation, but it continued to support my weight as I moved slowly forward. Suddenly, the vegetation parted beneath my feet, and I fell straight down twenty feet to the ground below. Beside me lay Kegler and Bishop, both suffering from having had the wind knocked out of them but otherwise unhurt. My fall had been exactly the same as Kegler's and Bishop's. With any luck, Keaveney would soon be joining the three of us.

Kegler and Bishop had immediately come over to help me get on my feet, and they checked to see if I had been injured in the fast fall. I hadn't, but I knew that Keaveney, Furhman, and Silva still remained above us, and they were about to repeat the same fall. The distance between us had kept each man from hearing the fall of the man he had followed. The situation was turning out to be far more humorous than dangerous.

It would be only minutes before Keaveney's curiosity would take over, and he would move forward to find out what had happened to me. Bishop looked at his watch and signaled "one minute" to Kegler and me, trying to predict the time of the sudden arrival of our M-79 from twenty feet above, and it happened just that way.

The advantage of being on the soft ground below gave us the opportunity to watch the heavy mat of vegetation above us as it suddenly gave way to the weight of a man carrying a sixty-pound pack. When Keaveney reached the point of no resistance, he, too, came crashing down, landing in a heap at our feet. Two minutes later Furhman arrived in the same manner.

We could not help but laugh. With our hands placed over our mouths to keep from being heard, we stood with tears in our eyes, laughing at the helplessness of the one man left to fall down and join us.

Silva had been given one of the Starlight scopes to carry in his pack but instead of putting the scope inside of his rucksack he had positioned the heavy scope across the top of the pack. Now the five of us stood by, unable to warn Silva as to what was about to happen.

Silva weighed about 140 pounds, less than anyone else in the team. This slight advantage in less body weight allowed for him to cross over the area where the four of us had fallen through, but, nonetheless, the ground gave way to Silva, too.

The difference in Silva's fall was that as he fell forward the heavy weight of his pack and upper body caused him to fall head first. His left foot wedged itself in the crotch of a small tree, eight feet above the ground. This sudden stop temporarily broke his fall, but it also caused the Starlight scope to hit Silva in the back of the head, knocking him out cold. He hung upside down and unconscious in the small tree.

Hands held tightly over our mouths did no good at stopping our laughter. It was hilarious. We had patrolled together for months without making any unnecessary sounds. We had prided ourselves at keeping quiet, but this time it did no good. We let it all out.

When we managed to free Silva from the tree, we were relieved to find that nothing more than his pride had been damaged, along with his gaining an egg-size lump on the back of his head. He had come to while hanging upside down.

Our noise had not lasted even as long as it takes to relate the incident, but we were concerned that our laughter had been heard, so we stayed where we had landed for several more minutes before continuing down the steep side of the mountain.

By early afternoon of the third day, Kegler had brought us to an opening that widened into an old burnt-out area. The outline of a single trail was easily seen as it entered the open area from the valley floor. We radioed our new position to the relay site and set in to observe the trail. By late that afternoon, we had seen nothing except one small herd of bush pigs rooting around the base of the trees at the edge of the forest opening. We moved away from our OP to a harbor site several hundred yards off.

The evening of the third day brought more heavy rain into the A Shau Valley, and our radio-relay site prepared us for the possibility of being extended for another day because of predicted bad weather.

The fourth day of observing the trail below us proved uneventful, but the operations people back at Phu Bai wanted us to remain in our OP to monitor it. We moved to a fourth harbor site. (We never used the same site twice.) The heavy rains continued to restrict our observations.

Our new harbor site offered the team a better shelter than our previous positions had because it had a small rock ledge which provided us with some overhead cover from the rain. It could accommodate only three men, but it was a welcome relief from the constant downpour, and we used the spot to cook and eat one hot meal during the day.

After two days of observing the trail with no sightings, we were told to continue to the outer limits of our reconnaissance zone. After studying the map, Bishop chose what looked like an easy route that would take us an additional two clicks from our current position. We repacked our equipment and began to move out on the morning of our sixth day in the bush. We had seen no signs of the NVA, we had heard no rifle shots fired, and there was no sound of hammering.

By late in the afternoon of the sixth day, we had arrived at the outer edge of our recon zone and were able to look down at the floor of the A Shau Valley and onto one of the green cultivated fields that we had seen through our binoculars and reported the first day.

They were, in fact, cultivated and were obviously being maintained by someone to grow a variety of vegetables. Weeds that once competed with the vegetables were dead and brown where they had been pulled from the ground and thrown off to the side of the garden. A bamboo irrigation system was visible, running from the edge of the jungle straight into the cultivated field. This Oriental watering system relied on a gravity flow originating in the high ground. Thick bamboo tubes carried mountain water. They were suspended by cut stalks of bamboo formed into large Xs, placed along the slopes at short intervals and ending at the edge of the cultivated fields. We radioed back the grid location and a description of the field and moved in close enough to photograph the unique discovery, hoping that our helicopter extraction would allow for the timely development of our camera film.

Bishop was told to set up another OP, and we began our sixth day by monitoring the cultivated fields from a distance of several hundred yards. By late in the afternoon we had seen no one, but we did report the several rifle shots that we had heard during the day. As we moved back toward higher ground and the safety of a new harbor site, heavy rains closed in around the A Shau Valley.

We received an extended weather forecast from the Marines at Zulu Relay during the night, and because the weather was not expected to change for at least twenty-four hours, our extraction was postponed for another day. Although this news was not what any of us had wanted to hear, there was nothing that could be done about it. Our ability to observe the cultivated fields or any area of greater distance was made impossible by the heavy rain, so all that remained for us to do was to sit and wait for a break in the weather.

Noon of the seventh day brought no relief from the rain. It was miserable, not only for us but for the other teams as well—sitting in the rain, unable to speak, and having only to wait for the weather to clear, giving our helicopters the opportunity to retrieve us.

Bored with the prospect of having to remain in place for hours, Bishop passed the word to Zulu Relay that we were going to check out the origin of the bamboo watering system. The bamboo supports ran back into an area that was within our reconnaissance zone. With any luck, we might find out more about who was using and guarding this irrigation system.

Kegler was given a new compass heading to follow, and as we moved away from the cultivated fields, we began a long, slow climb toward the eastern rim of the A Shau. We passed through an area thick with wait-a-minute vines, and they were appropriately named. These green and yellow jungle plants had small black hooks that protruded all along the edges of the vine. The hooks were strong enough to rip through our heavy web gear, so our light utilities stood no chance of survival. To fight against the vines was a losing battle, and by the time we had passed through them, we had each suffered enough rips and tears in our clothing to realize that our uniforms would be useless after our return to the company area.

It was our standard practice to walk slowly for several hundred yards and then to stop, look, and listen. The brief halts gave us the opportunity to rest, and more important, to study the areas that we were passing through. It was usually during those stops that we could observe the important details of the area that would have simply been overlooked while we were on the move.

Bishop and Furhman had been scanning the area ahead with their 7×50 binoculars, and they noticed what appeared to be two huts built up off of the ground in trees, like two well-made tree houses. Bishop quickly reported the information to the radio-relay site and informed them that we would remain at our new position to see whether or not the huts were being used.

By late in the afternoon, we had seen no one approaching or leaving the area around the huts. In the pages of his notebook, Keaveney drew several sketches of the two structures. Bishop decided to take a chance and move the team closer so that he and Kegler could see what was inside.

We moved slowly past the opening in the trees that had revealed them and once we were in a position to cover Bishop and Kegler from anyone approaching from the back side of the jungle, they moved to a spot beneath the two trees that held the huts off the ground.

The ground at the base of the trees had been marked with small boot marks, but the rain had washed most of them away, making it impossible to tell exactly how fresh the tracks might be. Inside the first hut, Bishop found a small iron pot, two used oil lamps, and some old cooking utensils. He put the iron pot into his pack as a souvenir.

There were no other signs of recent use, no discarded papers, equipment, or ammunition. The second hut was outfitted like the first one except for several new conical hats made of palm leaves that had been left on the floor of the hut. One well-used oil lamp was hung on the wall.

We reasoned that the place was probably used as a rest area by the NVA or possibly by the unseen men who tended the cultivated fields, but no more than that was revealed by our inspection.

We left as quietly as we had come, and as we moved away from the small clearing, we found a place where sections of bamboo had been freshly cut, stacked, and covered with palm leaves.

Perhaps these small items were part of the answer to the questions of the hammering sounds and the many lights that we had heard and seen several days before. The bamboo irrigation system would certainly require maintenance to replace the old and broken sections of the bamboo watering tubes, and the old oil lamps were obviously the source of some of the lights that were observed within the valley. Here, at least, was what appeared to be good physical proof of recent activity within the area.

By nightfall Kegler had guided us into another harbor site, and Bishop radioed back our situation report to Zulu Relay. As he was finishing his radio transmission, he was informed that a break in the rain was due to occur during the night. The people in the rear wanted to know if we would be in a position and ready for an extraction scheduled for 0600. The recommended grid coordinates for the point of extraction were less than five hundred meters from our position.

The news of our possible extraction was very welcome. More than seven days' patrolling a twelve-click reconnaissance zone in constant rain had begun to take its toll on the physical condition of the team members. Our feet were the biggest problem because we had always taped our utility trousers into our boots to keep the leeches and night-crawling insects from getting on our legs. Wearing two pairs of green socks served to cushion our feet, but once they became wet, the socks acted like wet sponges and caused a condition commonly known as immersion foot. The only relief from that condition was to thoroughly dry our feet and apply foot powder to the affected areas. That was impossible to do in the bush, and we would have to wait until we all returned to Phu Bai before we could treat the problem.

At approximately 0600 on the morning of 20 December 1969, the voice of the pilot of a single Army Huey, referred to as the weather bird, came up on our radio frequency.

"Team Snakey, Team Snakey, this is weather bird Mike two seven. Come in. Over." And with those few words, we knew that our extraction from the A Shau Valley was assured. We returned to our airstrip at Phu Bai before 0800, anxious to get to our team debriefing and to find our Christmas meal.

We were greeted at our debriefing session by Major Lee, Captain Hisler, and Lieutenant Coffman, and as we all stood to leave the room following our debrief, Major Lee said, "You will be taking two additional Marines with you on your next mission—Lieutenant Singleton and a Vietnamese-language interpreter. You'll leave in the morning on the day after Christmas."

—— CONTACT! ——

OUR TEAM HAD PLANNED TO ATTEND THE CHRISTMAS
Eve service in the small air wing chapel, followed by a long-
awaited trip over to the enlisted club to watch a movie, but our
team leader had just returned from a new mission briefing session
and he wanted to pass along some early word before we scattered
ourselves around the company compound. As we sat and waited
for Corporal Bishop to return to the platoon's squad bay, two
Marines entered our living area and walked down to join us. First
Lieutenant Singleton had brought a lance corporal with him to sit
in on Corporal Bishop's team meeting.

The lance corporal looked scared.

It was unusual for anyone considered an outsider to be present
when we discussed our plans for a mission. Staff Sergeant
Williams was always welcome to sit in with us at the team meetings because he had run the bush with us and with two other teams
within the company. The same acknowledgment of respect was
given by each team to Major Lee, Captain Hisler, and Lieutenant
Coffman, but this visit was something new. As the two of them
pulled up chairs and took out their green notebooks, Bishop
walked into the squad bay.

"The reason that I called for this team meeting, is to go over
our team rules before we go to the bush with two new people.
Eight men on any reconnaissance patrol creates a number of problems that don't exist with a six-man team, so if you will please
bear with me for a few minutes, sir, I'll tell you how we operate,
in front of all of my team's members so there will be no questions
once we get on the ground.

"I am the team leader and what I say in the bush goes, regardless of who is senior in rank. Lance Corporal Keaveney is our
assistant team leader, and he will be the one who will tell you when

you can eat, when you can shit, when you can sleep, and when you will be on a radio watch. The doc, here, is the 'medical actual' in this team, and what he says goes in all matters relating to first aid and to the medical condition of any team member. Kegler is my point man, and he leads the direction of the team according to my compass heading and his own good common sense. We have been together every day, as a team, for four months, and we don't want the simple mistake of a new member to get us into any trouble, let alone cost us our lives. Tomorrow morning we will fall out with all of our gear for my initial equipment check and to go over the specifics of our mission. Be here at 0730 with all of your gear on and do not be late.''

Following that statement Bishop introduced the other members of the team to the lieutenant and to the lance corporal. Bishop then told Furhman that he would be responsible for looking after the lance corporal's welfare. When he finished passing the word, he stood up and walked out of the squad bay, the rest of us following in trace. We walked over to the company's sick-bay hootch and once inside, knowing that neither the lieutenant nor the lance corporal had followed, Keaveney began to talk.

"Bishop, I can't believe that little speech you made back in the squad bay. What's gotten into you, anyway?"

"First Lieutenant Coffman took me aside after his team meeting in the S-3 shop and told me to get their attention. Singleton came to us from the grunts, but he has no real reconnaissance experience, and the lance corporal was sent to us from the intelligence section because he went to a Vietnamese language school. He's supposed to have the equivalent of a tenth-grade Vietnamese reading and writing level, but he has never even been in the field for one single day. Do you feel real comfortable in the A Shau Valley looking after these two?"

Bishop's point was immediately understood. We had taken ourselves for granted, knowing that after so many months together, we could depend upon one another. It was not easy for us to assume the responsibility for one new man and give to him the trust and confidence that we automatically gave to one another. Now, we were supposed to accept the two new men and get them ready for the bush within two days.

There was nothing that we could do to change the situation. The lieutenant had been given the okay by our company commander to join the patrol, and Bishop had voiced no objection. The lance corporal might prove useful if we ever got close enough to listen in on a conversation between North Vietnamese soldiers, but we seriously doubted the likelihood of that ever happening. We discussed the changes that would be necessary, and finally, accepting the situation, we left the sick-bay hootch and walked down to the chapel. We now had more reason to pray for divine guidance than we had before.

The Christmas Eve service was attended by virtually every team member in the company. To observe the men on a daily basis, it would appear that none of them would own up to being overly religious, but that was not true. Each of us usually sought his God in his particular way, and at a particular time, but the mutual uplift from that particular service strengthened each team member and, consequently, each team.

When the Christmas Eve service ended, we walked, as a team, from the chapel to the enlisted club, where we had planned to watch the movie *Grand Prix*. The small club was a gathering place for all off-duty Marines, and Christmas Eve made the intended celebration that much more of a special occasion. Beers, as usual, cost twenty-five cents, the popcorn was free, and the movie was to be the great drawing attraction for the holiday.

As the lights inside of the club were turned down, the projectionist turned on the film before a packed house. The movie had only played for two minutes when the screen suddenly went blank. This immediately caused loud catcalls and the shouting of long epithets aimed at the sexual preference of the projectionist's mother. It was apparent that the piousness of those of us attending the Christmas Eve service had been lost somewhere between the chapel and the enlisted men's club.

When the lights were turned back on, the projectionist, some poor Marine lance corporal, announced in an amazed voice, "There's no film!" Someone had spliced the lead of *Grand Prix* onto a canister of blank film, which had been traded for the last movie that was shown in our club. Fearing for his life, the lance corporal announced that he did have one additional, but untitled, movie that he could show in place of *Grand Prix*. The news only settled the crowd temporarily, but within a few minutes the lights were dimmed once again, and the title *Kiss the Other Sheik* appeared on the wall.

The movie was a grade-B film about an English-speaking Arabian sheik who purchased blond, blue-eyed American women to fill the ranks of his harem. The incredible stupidity of the movie's plot was surpassed only by the terrible acting. It was not the best film to show to more than fifty Marines from 3d Force Reconnaissance Company who were angry over being screwed out of the better movie and loaded on cheap beer.

From out of nowhere, a K-bar fighting knife was thrown across the crowded room, embedding itself in the wall used as the screen for the movie. With the knife now superimposed into the face of the leading man, the lights went on in the club, and the movie projector was mysteriously kicked over on its side. The club manager tried to restore order, but his shouting fell on deaf ears. Then the manager announced that he was closing down the club. Full and half-full beer cans were thrown at the screen, and a mass exodus began, Marines tipping over the tables as they emptied the club. Shouts of "kill the manager" and "burn down the club" were echoed outside as we walked dejectedly back to the platoon squad bay.

The evening proved not to be a total loss because, during our absence, Staff Sergeant Williams had received the incoming mail for the platoon. There, lying on the racks throughout the squad bay, were care packages and mail from home. Soon, tins of smoked baby clams, Kool-Aid, home-baked cookies, rum-soaked fruit cakes, and other goodies, all packed in stale popcorn, were laid out to be shared. There was more than enough food to satisfy the hunger of everyone in the platoon. We celebrated Christmas Eve, 1969, in style and together, because we were all the family that we had.

Christmas morning was not much different from any other morning within the company area. When we returned from breakfast at the mess hall, we began to organize ourselves for Bishop's equipment inspection. Furhman had done a credible job in taking the lance corporal linguist under his wing and in preparing him for the mission into the A Shau Valley, but we were all surprised to learn that he would not be present for the inspection.

We learned from Furhman that when the linguist had returned to the company area from the mess hall, he had been volunteered to attend the Bob Hope USO show at Camp Eagle. The company gunny needed bodies to fill the unscheduled quota for the show, and as the linguist passed by the formation of Marines going to the Army's camp, he was ordered aboard the truck. Our equipment inspection went off on time despite his absence. Bishop knew that Furhman had not been present to intercede on the lance corporal's behalf, and we would have to wait for his return from the USO show before the detailed equipment inspection could be completed.

At 1700 the lance corporal and a half dozen other lucky Marines returned to the company area from the USO show. We had spent the afternoon writing letters home and making final preparations for the bush. Furhman immediately collared the linguist and spent the remainder of the evening teaching him the finer points of packing gear, followed by a short lecture on never again failing to keep his team leader informed of his whereabouts.

Bishop had scheduled the final team briefing for 2000 and began the meeting with a description of the new area that we would patrol and what we could expect to find during the next six days in the A Shau Valley. Our liftoff time was set for 0700, which meant early chow, final inspection, and the test-firing of our weapons before moving over to the airstrip and the waiting Hueys.

Three recon teams were scheduled to be inserted that morning and, for once, the weather looked good. We had become accustomed to patrolling in the heavy rains that South Vietnam was subjected to, and our ability to patrol and observe was always diminished by the bad weather. To see a morning begin with clear skies and sunshine was an unusually good sign.

Our eight-man reconnaissance team, fully loaded for an extended period in the bush, took up more than the usual amount of floor space in the Air Cav Huey. We could not split the team into two groups, so the pilot elected to drop one door gunner to give us the space needed. In addition to the three teams headed into the A Shau Valley, several Hueys carried a resupply of food, water, mail, and additional ordnance for the Marines sitting on top of the Zulu Relay site. As usual, Major Lee and First Lieutenant Coffman were aboard a command and control Huey to observe the insertion of the teams, the extraction of teams in the field, and to make aerial reconnaissance flights over other parts of the A Shau Valley.

The nine-kilometer grid that made up our reconnaissance zone included our insertion point onto an elevated plateau area less than four hundred meters east of the Laotian border, west of the abandoned A Shau airstrip known on our maps as Thuong Luong. Our mission was to monitor a trail network that was suspected as being one of the better infiltration routes of the North Vietnamese soldiers moving from the safety of Laos into South Vietnam.

As we flew out of Phu Bai and headed northwest, we were met by two Marine Cobra gunships assigned as our escorts. The Cobras were always a welcome sight and their arsenal of Zuni rockets, 40-millimeter grenades and 7.62 miniguns made them more than capable of suppressing any enemy ground fire that might be in or near our landing zone. We entered the southern mouth of the A Shau and were greeted with a bank of fog that covered the eastern side of the valley. The fog would mask our arrival, and with any luck, our insertion would hardly be noticed as we spiraled downward and onto the green plateau. We made one false insert, dropping down and through a narrow draw half a mile from our intended landing zone. The pilot banked the helicopter over toward the southwest edge of the A Shau and put us down onto a small grassy hilltop, six hundred meters above the valley floor. We got a thumbs-up from the pilot and door gunner and were off and moving into the jungle as he flew to rejoin the other Hueys.

Our first rest stop was several hundred yards south of the insertion point, and having climbed up and over the nine-hundred-meter mark on the map, we paused to look and listen while regaining energy lost to the climb. Communication with Zulu Relay was good, and as Bishop spoke, giving them our location, they mentioned that they were receiving their resupply by the Army Hueys.

According to our maps, an old trail ran beside a stream as it passed through a very narrow draw approximately four hundred meters below our position. Bishop wanted us to set in and observe the trail and the stream, hoping to observe frequent North Vietnamese travelers and radio back their movement to Zulu Relay. We moved downhill toward the stream and began to hear the sound of rushing water. As we approached the stream, we could see that the old trail marked on our maps was still there on the far side of the water.

The only way to know if the trail was being used at all was to physically inspect it. That meant that two of us would have to move to the right and left limits of the trail and set in as security while two other Marines moved forward to inspect the trail. The remaining members of the team would stay put and be ready to react if anyone appeared at either end of the trail. Bishop signaled to Silva to take the right end of the trail, Kegler took the left end, and Bishop and I went forward to take a look.

The evidence of frequent and heavy usage was obvious. Boot prints were clearly visible as were the tire-track marks of the famous Ho Chi Minh sandals commonly worn by North Vietnamese soldiers. Two thin sets of bicycle tracks had hardened in the mud on the edge of the trail. We bagged several soil samples, noted the number of different-size tracks and their patterns, and returned to where the rest of the team lay waiting. After plotting the exact location of the trail, Bishop contacted the radio-relay site and reported our new position. We spent the remainder of the afternoon observing the trail, but no one walked past us. Our first day ended with a spectacular view of the sun setting over the mountains that marked the Laotian border.

By twilight we had moved to our harbor site, and Bishop told Silva and Kegler to take the linguist along with them to teach him how our PSIDs and claymore mines were positioned and hidden. When they returned to the harbor site, the assignment list for the night's radio watch was passed around. The lance corporal would be following me from 0100 to 0200.

Just before midnight, Kegler woke me and gave me a few minutes to clear the cobwebs from my brain before handing me the radio handset and the PSID receiver. Kegler told me that only one message had been received during the night from the Zulu relay site. They reported seeing lights on the valley floor. A steady rain had begun to fall, and as usual, our PSIDs were registering as the heavier raindrops landed on the sensitive equipment.

My turn on radio watch went by slowly and was compounded by the difficulties of having to sit motionless, watching and listening for the possible approach of a North Vietnamese Army patrol, and by not being able to see clearly through rain-covered glasses, having to constantly wipe them clear.

The harbor site did not offer the usual concealment of the thick and protective vegetation that we normally sought, because the growth at higher elevations consisted mostly of scrub brush and tall trees. Each time that we moved into our harbor site, we tried to allow ourselves enough daylight to be able to study the immediate area. Each team member knew exactly where the rest of the team was sleeping. The location of trees, stumps, bushes, and, most importantly, the makeup of the terrain were noted by each member of the team because what appeared as a tree or a stump during the fading hour of twilight could easily look like a man, or several men, in the imagination of whoever was on radio watch during the night.

The lance corporal was due to follow me on radio watch. The procedures that we routinely used on radio watch had been explained to him several times before we left Phu Bai. But this would be his first time on watch. When 0100 finally arrived I woke him up, and once I was sure that he was awake and alert, I handed him the radio handset, the PSID receiver, and the two claymore mine hell boxes. I told him that I would be sleeping next to him but if he had any questions or thought that he heard anything out of the ordinary to wake me.

The lance corporal tapped me on the shoulder. When I sat up, he whispered that all four of the PSIDs were registering movement. I told him that the rain was making them go off and not to worry about it. I laid back down, and not two minutes had passed before he tapped me again. "Doc, I think I hear something." I sat up and listened to the night sounds, but could hear only the soft hiss of the radio handset and the constant falling of rain. "What do you hear?"

He whispered that he thought he had heard a chopping sound coming from the rise above us. I listened for a while longer but could hear no such sound. I told him that if he heard the noise again, to wake me. Several minutes passed, and again, I felt the familiar tap on my shoulder. He whispered, "Doc, the PSIDs have stopped going off, but it's still raining. How come?" I explained that it was not unusual for that to happen when it rained. I told him that sometimes the sensor spindles didn't get hit by the rain, and they would stop registering. This explanation seemed to satisfy him, but not more than a minute later he tapped me and said that he thought he had heard the chopping sound again. My patience was being tested, and I cut him short. "I'm wide awake and not more than two feet away from you. I do not hear any goddamned chopping noises. If you're sure that you hear something, then I'll wake up Bishop and we'll check it out. Did you hear something or not?"

"Well maybe I imagined it, but I thought I heard something."

Bishop sat up. "What's going on?" I explained to Bishop. Then Keaveney sat up and wanted to know what was happening. Bishop explained it all to him. The four of us sat listening for ten minutes but could hear nothing other than the wind and the rain.

I looked at my watch and saw that the linguist had been on radio watch for less than twenty minutes and had managed to wake up half of the team with his concerns about the PSIDs and the imaginary chopping sounds. His popularity as a new team member was wearing thin, but in his defense, I remembered how unsure of myself I had been the first time that I pulled radio watch out on the DMZ. Knowing that you are responsible for the absolute safety of seven sleeping men is serious business. Now none of us could get back to sleep, wondering if the lance corporal's concerns were legitimate. Zero two hundred came, and Keaveney, already wide-awake and angry, took over. The rest of the night passed without incident.

When first light came over the eastern rim of the A Shau Valley, patches of blue sky meant that the rain was leaving us. The team was awake, and after finishing breakfast, we cleaned our weapons, reapplied our camouflage and waited for the word to move out. Bishop told Keaveney and me to retrieve the PSIDs and claymore mines that Silva and Kegler had planted.

The best way to find the PSIDs was to follow the wires from the harbor site to the sensors. Since the wire was no longer than one hundred feet, it would not take long to complete the job even though we had not been the ones who had put them in place. Keaveney left his M-79 with Kegler and took the point man's rifle in place of the 40-millimeter.

The first brown pair of claymore wires ran out of the harbor site and over a steep rise about sixty feet away before turning downhill toward the ridge line. Keaveney moved slowly forward then signaled "freeze" when he reached the hidden sensor. Looking to his left and right, he then motioned for me to come forward, slowly, and join him. The sensor and claymore had been well hidden, not more than four feet from a well-used trail. Fresh sets of boot prints were outlined all along the trail, and steps had been dug out, making for easier footing. Keaveney decided not to pull the claymore up, and leaving the PSID and claymore mine where they had been hidden, we moved back to the harbor site and told Bishop what we had found.

We had spent the night less than one hundred feet from the edge of a trail that was being used by the North Vietnamese. The lance corporal had been right after all! There was no doubt that the chopping sounds that he had heard were made by the shovels of the North Vietnamese soldiers as they cut out steps along the rising trail. The sensors had picked up the movement of the NVA during the night, but we had become so accustomed to the sensors going off during the rains that we had chosen to ignore the possibility of the enemy moving so close to us during a rainstorm.

Bishop contacted Zulu Relay and reported the situation, saying that he intended to move the team closer to the trail to monitor traffic using the trail during the day. Then he talked with the linguist and reassured him, telling him that he had been right in waking us up while he had been on watch. Having been considered as excess baggage since joining the team, he was now viewed a little differently.

Keaveney's decision to leave the claymore mines and PSIDs in place had worked to our advantage, and as we set up to observe the trail, we knew that we were protected from anyone approaching us. By 1100 we had received no new sensor readings, and Bishop decided that it would be wise for us to move parallel to the trail. By the number of fresh boot prints we had seen in the mud, we knew that a large unit had passed during the night. We also knew that the

North Vietnamese usually rested during the day, and they moved at night to avoid observation from the sky. By paralleling the trail we stood an excellent chance of finding their base camp and then requesting close air support to come in to destroy them.

Bishop was on the PRC-77 radio talking with Zulu Relay when he passed the word to Lieutenant Singleton and me to move down the hill and get the two PSIDs and claymore mines. We left our packs with the rest of the team, and with the lieutenant in the lead, we began to move forward to the trail. When we were about fifty feet away from the trail's edge the lieutenant signaled to me to move up to where he had stopped. When I drew up next to him he said, "During the night I left the harbor site to make a head call. I think that I went close to the trail, but I didn't know that it was there. I didn't cover it up real well, and I left a lot of shit paper laying around on the ground."

I wasn't pleased to hear what he was telling me, considering that his dumb move could have cost us our lives if his mistake had been spotted by one of the North Vietnamese soldiers who might have strayed off the trail for the same reason. "If you know where the spot is, then go and cover it up, I'll cover you from here, sir." He moved off to the left of where I was kneeling, and I watched him as he followed the wire down the hill toward the place where the PSID and claymore mine were hidden. He didn't appear to stop and cover anything up and returned quickly, with the sensor and the claymore mine.

"Doc, I'll cover you while you get the other PSID and claymore. If you find the spot where I took the dump will you cover it up?" I nodded yes, and moved off to get the second PSID while Lieutenant Singleton moved forward to cover my left side, protecting me from anyone approaching from that right side of the trail. I had only moved about thirty feet away from him when I spotted white paper laying on the green jungle floor. Here was his little mistake for all the world to see!

The second claymore mine and PSID were hidden not more than twenty feet away. I could see down the right side of the trail for about twenty feet and moved to where the PSID was hidden, then I looked back to where I had last seen the lieutenant. He was signaling to me. His right hand moved quickly from his mouth to his ear—he could hear voices coming toward us from his left side. Then he pointed to his rifle, signaling that he was going to shoot, and he ducked down behind a large bush, close to where the first claymore mine had been hidden near the trail. I couldn't see him, and I had no way of knowing what he planned to do.

I moved quickly to my right and sat down in a bush not more than five feet from the edge of the trail. No other place that I could see offered better concealment. Bishop, Keaveney, Howard, Silva, Kegler, and Furhman were hidden sixty feet behind me and had no idea of what was about to happen. I had no way of knowing how many NVA were approaching or how fast they were traveling.

I turned the selector switch of my M-16 to full automatic and unstrapped my .45 from its shoulder holster and waited. I prayed that, with any luck, it might be only two or three North Vietnamese soldiers moving along the trail and that the lieutenant would let them pass by. Then I heard their voices.

I sat absolutely motionless, my eyes fixed on a point off to my right, hoping to get some glimpse of whomever was approaching. The voices got closer, still coming from the right side of the trail and close to where the lieutenant was hiding. I knew that if he did open up on them their attention would be turned toward him, and I could come out of the brush and be able to fire at them from their blind side. Still the voices got closer but there was no firing from the lieutenant. Great, I thought, he was going to let them pass by, and once they had gone by me, we would rejoin the team and get the hell out away from the area.

The voices were getting closer, but I still could not see anyone approaching. I began to wonder if they had spread out, or if they were approaching me from behind. Still, I didn't move. My mind was racing with thoughts of what to do. I could hear them coming toward me, still on the trail, and I was sure that they were close enough to me to have passed by Lieutenant Singleton.

My rifle was cradled in front of me, but pointed forward toward anyone who would approach me from the front. But what if they came toward me from the side? I wouldn't be able to see them. The voices came on. In a few seconds whoever was talking would pass right in front of me. Then there was silence. They had stopped moving. Why had they stopped talking? Had they seen Singleton? Had they seen me? Had they seen the results of Singleton's early-morning head call and white papers strewn all around? That must have been the reason. Now what were they going to do?

I caught the movement off to my left side; it was a dark green color moving very slowly toward me. The colored movement was turning from side to side. I recognized it as the outline of a pith helmet. He was not more than ten feet away from me. I tried to make myself small without moving. I just wanted him to go away, but the helmet continued to come forward slowly until it was almost directly in front of me. Then the outline of his face began to form around the lower edge of the helmet. His left hand reached forward and began to part the branches of the bush. He leaned forward. . . .

The orange muzzle flash was the last thing that he ever saw. The blast of my M-16 going off on full automatic knocked the North Vietnamese soldier backward and down on the left side of the trail. I rolled out of the bush beside the trail to my right, hoping that he had been the first soldier in the group.

I knew that I hadn't emptied my magazine when I fired, and I looked for anyone else moving toward me. Then I saw him move. The second soldier had dropped to the ground only a few feet behind the first one. He began to rise up to throw a Chicom hand grenade toward me, and I fired one round, hitting him in the left side of his chest. The impact of the bullet knocked him down, and he fell to the left of the trail. His grenade rolled over the edge of the trail without exploding. He rolled up onto his feet and started to run back down the trail in the direction of Lieutenant Singleton. I saw the lieutenant as he stood with his rifle aimed at the North Vietnamese soldier, and I fired again. This time the North Vietnamese soldier fell forward and didn't move.

Suddenly the ground between the lieutenant and me exploded. I couldn't tell if it was caused by several grenades going off, or if it was due to the impact of Keaveney's 40-millimeter rounds. The lieutenant and I both hit the deck. The sound of automatic fire came from where the team was hiding. As quickly as it had started, it stopped.

The team had heard the first rip of my automatic fire followed by my second shot and had started to run down to join me and the lieutenant when they noticed three North Vietnamese soldiers moving up the trail and began to take them under fire. The North Vietnamese suddenly turned around and ran back down the trail. Kegler and Keaveney moved over to where I was kneeling and asked if there were any more of them. I told them that I didn't think so, but I told Keaveney to watch the trail to our right side in case someone turned up to get into the firefight. Kegler and I moved over to where the first North Vietnamese soldier had fallen.

He was laying face down on the trail and the back of his dirty green shirt showed the exit marks of four bullets. When he was hit the force had thrown him backward, and his rifle and helmet had been thrown over the edge of the trail, landing ten feet from his body. As Kegler covered me, the memory of the booby-trap class at Field Memorial School came back. I placed my hands on his shoulders, picked him up, and then dropped him back to the ground. No booby trap. Kegler moved in next to him, and we turned him over and searched his pack and his pockets. We found a plastic wallet and another small plastic package, but there were no rank insignia or other unit designators sewn onto his clothing. His body stunk heavily with the stale smell of wood smoke, and when this rotten odor combined with the sticky-sweet smell of his blood and hit my nostrils, I began to dry heave.

Kegler helped roll the dead soldier's body over and we took a closer look at his physical condition and his uniform. Still feeling sick to my stomach, I placed my fingertips onto his eyelids and closed them. I felt sorry for him.

We left him where he had fallen and ran to where the second dead North Vietnamese soldier lay, face down beside the trail. Bishop and Silva had already checked him out for the possibility of a booby trap, and, finding none, they had cut away his pack to examine the contents for possible information. His pack told an interesting story. This second NVA had been a medic. His rucksack was full of medical equipment and the medicines and bandages he carried were labeled in Vietnamese. He looked to me to be no older than twenty, was in good physical shape, and the smell of him meant that he, too, had spent many lonely nights inside of a bunker warmed only by a wood-burning fire.

Bishop looked at me and asked, "Who shot him?"

"I shot him, Bishop, my first magazine is full of tracer rounds, and if you take a look at his chest you'll see that the only mark that's on him is this orange-colored entrance hole at the base of his neck."

I hoped that my explanation to Corporal Bishop would settle what I believed was going to be a problem between the lieutenant and me over "who shot John?"

What difference did it make now? There were much more important issues to deal with than getting involved over claiming responsibility for a kill. Dead is dead.

Corporal Bishop had been in constant contact with Zulu Relay since the first rounds had been fired. They knew what was happening almost as quickly as it happened, and the Marines at the radio-relay site were letting the company know that we were in contact.

Our position was compromised as soon as the first rounds had been fired, and now we were in danger of being chased by the North Vietnamese. We knew that they had used the ridge trail and that three of them had run from the firefight, but we had no way of knowing how many of them might be approaching us from either end of the trail. Bishop summed it all up in a few words. "Let's get the hell out of here, and we'll talk about all of this later."

As we ran back up the hill to where our gear was staged, we heard what sounded like a soft cry. We froze in place because the sound was very close by. Could another North Vietnamese soldier have been wounded and crawled away? Bishop and Keaveney moved forward toward the bushes where the noise had come from. As Bishop moved in closer he discovered the lance corporal curled up, crying.

"Doc, get up here and see what's wrong with him."

I moved up to find the linguist crying and shaking badly. I asked him if he had been hurt. He looked up and said, "No, I'm not wounded. I'm just scared that we aren't going to get out of this."

Bishop leaned forward and said, "If you don't get up and get your shit on, now, you *ain't* gonna get out of this!"

The hasty ambush had lasted less than a minute. Our searching of the two dead soldiers and their packs had taken less than three minutes, and now we were racing to get our packs on and move off the ridge line and away from the ambush site. Kegler led us off the ridge to the far right side of where the ambush had taken place, and as soon as he disappeared from our line of sight, we could hear his M-16 firing short bursts. The sound combined with the *clack* of AK-47 rifle fire.

The shout of "contact front" was heard by all of us, and we immediately moved into our positions, ready to fire. Kegler came running back past us, and when he hit the deck, he yelled that he had walked up on a group of six North Vietnamese soldiers running toward us on the trail. When he fired at them, they had jumped off the trail and run down the side of the steep ridge, shooting back at him as they fled for cover.

Bishop dropped his radio pack and removed his claymore mine, rigging it with a timed fuse, and returned to the center of our formation between Keaveney, Lieutenant Singleton, and the linguist. He told Kegler to move us off of the ridge line and away from the old ambush site. As Kegler moved out, the claymore mine exploded, and our pace quickened. We were moving at a dogtrot to get out of the area when Kegler signaled "freeze" and knelt down, firing his rifle downhill. Bishop radioed back to Zulu Relay that we were "in contact, again." As he moved past me, he told me to keep my eye on the linguist in case he "freaked out."

Kegler moved back up toward Bishop and told him that he had

fired at another group of North Vietnamese soldiers headed our way. This time the only place left for us to go was over the ridge line. We had reorganized to our normal order of march, with Kegler still in the lead. It was becoming more difficult to maintain our dispersion as we moved down the hill.

We knew that at least two groups of North Vietnamese soldiers were approaching us from two different directions, and by moving off the ridge line we were in danger of having Chicom hand grenades thrown down on us from above. We needed to stop moving and to find a concealed position that would allow us to hide, to wait, and to listen for signs of anyone approaching.

Kegler and Bishop had done a fine job of keeping cool while the team had made two point-to-point contacts with the North Vietnamese soldiers, and the Marines at the Zulu relay site were kept aware of what was happening to us, but when Bishop radioed his request for assistance, he quickly learned that our close air support was not available due to the weather conditions at Phu Bai—they were socked in with heavy rain, couldn't see to fly, and the rain was headed inland, toward us.

As we made our way down the steep mountainside, Kegler brought us to a small point of level ground, big enough for us to form up in a small but well-concealed defense. We stopped to wait and to listen.

With any luck, the North Vietnamese had not seen us move down the ridge line, and it would take them awhile before they would organize themselves and come looking for us, but we were certain that once they found their dead companions on top of the ridge-line trail, they would make every effort to flush us out of hiding.

Bishop took a cigarette out of his pack and lit up. It was time to ask some questions about what had put us into this situation in the first place. Bishop asked, "Doc, what happened when you went out to take in the claymores?" I explained to him exactly what had happened, beginning with the lieutenant's story about his late-night head call, and then I told him about the hasty ambush that should never have taken place. Bishop recorded some of the details in his notebook. We knew that it would all be discussed with Major Lee, Captain Hisler, and Lieutenant Coffman back at Phu Bai.

By the time that the conversation had ended, we all had settled down enough to realize just how lucky we had been. The events on the ridge line happened so fast that all of us, including the linguist, had forgotten about being afraid and had done exactly what we had practiced during our immediate-action drills. Our luck was based on our individual responses from the countless hours of practicing lifesaving, immediate-action drills.

As we sat close together, waiting and listening, we watched Kegler as he removed one of the plastic pouches that he had taken from the pocket of the first dead NVA soldier. He unfolded it, and holding it close to his face, he opened it and quickly vomited. The pouch contained *nuoc mam,* a sauce used by the Vietnamese to flavor their food. It was made from fermented fish guts, and like a good cabernet wine, the older it was, the better it was, according to those who used it. Kegler was obviously not one of them, and the odor had made him ill.

I had kept the dead soldier's wallet, and after watching Kegler's performance, I opened it quite carefully. It contained several unused stamps and several red paper bills. I asked the linguist if he knew what the value of the money was. After looking at the bills, he said that the stamps might be worth more than the dollarlike bills. Also, folded inside of the plastic wallet were several pages of an unfinished letter, and tucked between the pages of the letter was a pale blue handkerchief with two interlocking hearts embroidered in the center. The name of the dead man's wife was neatly stitched into one of its corners. I put the handkerchief and the letter back into the wallet and gave it to the linguist for him to read later.

At least an hour had passed by since we had formed our defensive position, but we had neither seen nor heard anything. Not wanting to push his luck, Bishop decided that we would stay put, and he relayed his information back to the Marine communicators at Zulu Relay. It was probably just as well that Bishop had elected to remain in place. There was no question that every man's nerves had been strained. We had been close to the enemy many times before. We had even killed them scientifically with artillery fire and close air support as we had been taught, but coming face-to-face with the North Vietnamese was not our mission. To do so was an open invitation to die quickly. They owned the valley, and we were unwelcome visitors in their backyard. Ultimately we would pay the price for what we had done.

We ate our evening meal cold, then cleaned our weapons and arranged the schedule for the night's radio watch. I don't think that any of us was capable of sleep. Too much had happened too quickly to allow for a good night's sleep. We had each seen how quickly death could come.

The dead soldier's wallet, his unfinished letter and unused stamps, and the little blue handkerchief were no different from anything that each one of us carried in the bush. Now, those personal articles were in the hands of an enemy stranger and would never be used or find their way back to his family. We wondered if any of the stuff in our pockets would meet a similar fate.

Close to midnight, Bishop was on radio watch, and what he heard disturbed him enough to make him wake up the entire team. We sat and listened to the sound of hammering coming from high up on the ridge line and assumed that the North Vietnamese were burying their dead. The sounds of their construction went on for more than an hour before it stopped. By first light we had received word to move toward the southern edge of our reconnaissance zone and be prepared for an extraction.

The dark rain clouds had again rolled into the A Shau Valley, and their appearance meant that the likelihood of an early-morning helicopter extraction would be no better than a fifty-fifty proposition. The only positive aspect of the approaching rainstorm was that the noise of our movement would be covered and the NVA's ability to see us would be reduced.

Our position for extraction, known as our third base, was more than a thousand meters from where we had remained hidden the day before. To get into position for extraction would take at least two hours of humping over steep terrain. We moved out before 0600. By 0700 we had moved into a steep draw where we stopped to rest and to listen for several minutes. We had only to cross over one last finger before we would be in a position close enough to our extraction point that we could wait for the approach of our extraction bird. The orientation and steep sides of the draw made radio reception poor, and as we began to move out of the draw Lieutenant Singleton happened to lean against a large, dead palm tree for support. The rotted tree gave way, and as it fell, a large section near the top of the palm broke away and came crashing down onto the linguist's right leg. He had tried to deflect the chunk of palm from hitting him, but it did no good. His foot was completely covered by the big section of dead palm when I got to him, and he was in a great deal of pain. In the hope of getting his mind off of his painful injury, I said, "I knew you wanted to get out of this place alive, but why wait until the last minute before getting a self-inflicted injury?" He didn't appear to see the humor in what I was telling him.

With his K-bar, Lieutenant Singleton helped me dig the linguist's foot from beneath the palm. It took us almost ten minutes before we could pull the little lance corporal away from the tree.

We laid him down to look at the extent of his injury. His foot was broken, and there was no way that he would be able to continue to climb up and out of the draw.

Bishop came down to where the lieutenant and I sat with the linguist. "What can we do?"

"Well, Bishop, the way I see it, there's only one thing we can do. One of us will have to kill him because no one wants to carry him and all of his gear out of here." Corporal Bishop knew that I was kidding, but by the look on his face, the linguist wasn't so sure. "All we really can do, Bishop, is divide up all of his gear within the team and carry him."

The climb out of the draw took at least half an hour, and when we had reached level ground we stopped. Even though the linguist was small, he felt like he was made out of lead. We had practiced carrying one another during our immediate-action drills back in the company areas at Quang Tri and at Phu Bai, but the drills never lasted for more than a few minutes, at best. To pick up and carry an injured man became an immediate burden on the entire team. Our rate of travel was slowed to a crawl, we had instantly lost twenty-five percent of our security and firepower, and if we began to take turns carrying him, it would exhaust every man within a few hours. During the rest, Keaveney moved up beside me and said, "Maybe you were right the first time, Doctor, when you suggested that one of us should kill him."

Once we cleared the draw, Bishop's primary radio was working fine, and he was talking with Zulu Relay while the rest of us took advantage of the break. But the news that he received was not what he had expected to hear. He was told that only the weather bird was available for any possible extraction, but the weather bird had taken three new pilots along for an orientation flight, making our team extraction impossible. Bishop had passed on the information concerning the injury to the linguist, and now a decision had been made that he would be the only one extracted by the weather bird, due to be in our zone within twenty minutes. We had no choice in the matter. The wounded man was a burden, and we had to get him out of the valley. All that remained for us to do was to get him near the LZ site and onto the weather bird as soon as it touched down.

As we continued to move slowly downhill, the pilot of the weather bird came up on our primary radio frequency. The pilot was inbound to our position, and he said that he would be overhead within ten minutes, but unfortunately we were in a place that would allow for only a jungle penetrator to be used to extract; the area wasn't large enough to allow for the Huey to make a landing. Bishop contacted the pilot and, fortunately, they had a penetrator on board and had used it many times before.

As soon as we had a visual sighting of the weather bird, we got the linguist to stand up and dressed him in all of his gear, minus his grenades, ammunition, and any food. We also handed him all of our camera film, and the papers and equipment that we had taken from the two dead North Vietnamese soldiers.

The Army weather bird came straight in toward us with the jungle penetrator hooked up and ready to go. As the steel device was lowered to the ground, we carried the lance corporal to a point directly beneath the helicopter hovering forty feet above us. When the penetrator had grounded itself, Lieutenant Singleton quickly pulled down the three steel blades, locking them into place. The linguist took his position on the seat, and we tied him securely to the cable. We gave the Huey's crew chief a thumbs-up and watched as the linguist was lifted up and away from us. The bird and the lance corporal were gone in seconds. It was the last time we ever saw him.

Kegler had been looking for the best route out of the area, and within a few minutes the heavy rains began again. We headed up onto the high ground to continue watching for signs of the North Vietnamese.

To see the lance corporal leave was encouraging, as it was to know that we had such good support that others would risk their lives for the safety of one of us.

We continued to elude the North Vietnamese for two more days before finally getting extracted by the weather bird on the afternoon of 31 December 1969.

SIGNIFICANT
—— MISCELLANEOUS ——

CORPORAL MOSS WAS AN ASSISTANT TEAM LEADER IN our platoon when he was told that he would be taking his team into the A Shau Valley along with Gunnery Sergeant Bilodeau. The company gunny was accompanying Moss to observe and record his ability to function as the team's new leader. The gunny had served several combat tours in Vietnam and was highly respected by the Marines in 3d Force. When he returned from the patrol, he would give Lieutenant Coffman and Major Lee a detailed report on Moss, and if it was favorable, Corporal Moss would be designated the new team leader. This test and evaluation process was done with every new team leader.

Five Marines from the third platoon were available for this patrol, but Moss was looking for a sixth Marine to be a rifleman when a private first class reported into the company for duty. This PFC had been with the grunts south of Da Nang when he had been evacuated to the hospital called NSA Da Nang (Naval Support Activity) to recover from an infection. From there he was sent as a replacement to 3d Force Recon. I happened to be in sick bay on the day that the PFC arrived and I reviewed his medical record while he checked in, and his record told the story of his past.

The PFC was tall and lanky and wasn't too shy to mention that he was not checking in by choice. He made no bones about his dislike for recon and said that he would rather be back at NSA than with a bunch of crazy bastards. None of the other corpsmen paid much attention to the PFC's comments, but Hospital Corpsman First Class Goddard told him that it would be in his own best interest if he kept his remarks to himself. His attitude was certain to get him into trouble.

The PFC was assigned to the third platoon, and within a matter of hours, he found himself slated to go to the A Shau Valley with Corporal Moss's team. They would leave the next morning.

As was customary, those of us who were not scheduled to go to the bush went across the dirt road to the airstrip to say good-bye to the departing recon teams. We all smiled at how fast the PFC had been sucked into the system. There he stood, hunched over with a fifty-pound pack on his back and fear in his eyes.

Corporal Moss's team duly departed Phu Bai, due to be gone for only four days. We felt that by having Gunny Bilodeau along, Moss's chances for success were much better than average. The gunny knew the bush and would help Moss pass his test.

Three days later, and somewhere close to midnight, I was seated with Bishop and Keaveney in the enlisted club drinking beer when the club manager announced that all members of 3d Force Recon Company were to "double time your asses back to the company compound." Such an announcement could only mean one thing, serious trouble.

When we returned to our squad bay, Staff Sergeant Williams and Sergeant Garcia told us to immediately get our gear together because we were now part of a reaction force that was being formed to rescue Corporal Moss's team. According to "rumor control," the Zulu radio-relay site had not heard from Moss's team for several hours, and there could be only three reasons for that—the team had been ambushed; the team was in an area where their communication was useless; both of the team's radios didn't work.

If the team was in an area where comm was poor, they would know to move out of that area as quickly as possible to reestablish the comm link with the radio-relay site. The likelihood of both the team's radios not working was next to nil, which meant that the possibility of Moss's team having been ambushed was very real.

Rumors continued to spread as to the other possibilities for the team's disappearance, but the bottom line was quickly established—if Corporal Moss's team could not be raised on either one of its radios, then a reaction force made up of Marines from within the company would be flown into the last known area where the team's location had been plotted, and we would begin searching for the team. We knew nothing more than that, and that the reaction force was expected to be ready for departure from the flight line within thirty minutes.

As the pilots of the helicopters that would take us into the A Shau Valley were being briefed, we stood in line for a final gear inspection by Staff Sergeant Williams. There was a great deal of excitement at the prospect of a forty-man force flying into the A Shau Valley at first light to find and rescue Corporal Moss's team. Of course, the possibility of finding the North Vietnamese waiting in ambush for us was a bit of a sobering thought.

Captain Hisler came out in front of our reaction force and told us to gather around him so that he could pass on some word. He began by saying that the requirement for the reaction force had ended. There would be no heliborne rescue mission into the A Shau Valley; Corporal Moss's team was now known to be safe and secure. He went on to thank us for our rapid response. It was good news to hear, but as we stood outside in the darkness, we all wanted to know why Moss's team had been down on the comm net for such a long time.

What had happened was easily explained by our company executive officer. Moss's team had traveled through some very difficult terrain during their days of patrolling, and on their third day in the bush, the team had set up in their harbor site to rest and to sleep. They were located close to where they had planned to be extracted. But during the night, some unnamed team member, who had been tasked to be on security and radio watch, had fallen asleep. That was why no one answered the radio calls from Zulu to the team. The entire team had been so fatigued from three days of hard humping that sleep had come too easily.

The last resort used to raise the team from their suspected sleep was to request that the Army fire three 155-millimeter rounds from the guns at Fire Support Base Bastogne to a position several thousand feet above the team's last plotted location. If the team was asleep, the overhead detonation of three 155 shells would awaken all of them immediately.

The plan worked. The team came to life, and Moss then contacted Zulu Relay to find out the reason for the unrequested night firing. When the situation was explained to Corporal Moss and then repeated to Gunnery Sergeant Bilodeau, the individual who had been on watch and fallen asleep, leaving the safety of the entire team exposed, was "adjusted" by the company gunny. We knew what that meant, and given the disposition of Gunnery Sergeant Bilodeau, we shuddered at the thought of anyone having to face him over such a serious screwup.

When the afternoon extraction bird was due to land at Phu Bai, several dozen recon Marines stood by, waiting to find out who the guilty party had been. The Hueys settled down onto the airstrip, and all doubt as to the identity of the culprit was removed when a badly battered Marine was carried off the Huey and over to sick bay by two of Moss's team members.

The Marine had committed the unpardonable offense. He had fallen asleep, leaving his teammates exposed to the possibility of discovery, attack, and capture, and had not had the common sense to get help from anyone in his team. The "physical awakening" that he had received in the bush for his stupidity was slight in comparison to having his sleeping throat slit by an NVA soldier. The Marine departed the company that same day, and we were happy to see him go.

The short adventure of Corporal Moss's team in the A Shau Valley served as a constant reminder and an example to all of us. Our missions were serious business, and it was only good teamwork that insured our individual survival. But the actions of one thoughtless individual could spell disaster for an entire team.

Shortly after that incident, another team experienced an unusual event. A team from the fourth platoon was operating in the A Shau Valley in January when they made a point-to-point contact with four North Vietnamese regulars.

The point man for the recon team, a lance corporal named Breen, made an untimely decision to capture the entire group. Breen aimed his rifle at the lead man and shouted, "*Chieu hoi*," a Vietnamese phrase for "surrender." The first NVA soldier dropped his SKS rifle and put his hands straight up in the air, but when Breen moved a little closer, thinking he had the situation well in hand, the second enemy soldier in the group stepped out from behind the point man and shot at Lance Corporal Breen with a pistol, hitting him once in each of his legs. Breen fell over backward on the trail, the lead NVA scooped up his weapon, and the four NVA ran back down the trail away from Breen.

The team's position was compromised; Breen was lucky not to be captured. He was medevaced out of Vietnam, his attempt at being a hero having backfired.

Life within the company area was not as regimented as in many other military organizations. When the members of a team returned from a mission, they went immediately to a debriefing session to articulate what had occurred in the field in an hour-by-hour rehash of information. Following the debrief session, the men cleaned their weapons, cleaned their equipment, and then slowed down to read mail from home, write letters, or just take some time to play cards or listen to the radio. Life in the company area was really a series of mental peaks and valleys because each team member knew that it would only be a matter of one or two days before the cycle would repeat itself, and his team would be fragged for another mission. As soon as the order to get ready for the bush was given, the mental process was accelerated and thoughts of card games, music, letters home, and quiet reflections on life in general gave way to the seriousness of patrolling.

——— BAD WATER ———

DURING THE FIRST WEEK OF JANUARY 1970, SNAKEY was one of three reconnaissance teams that was flown into the A Shau by helicopters of the Army's 2/17th Air Cav. Our team's four-day mission was to observe a road located on the northwestern floor of the valley. The road was suspected of being used as the main thoroughfare for the North Vietnamese Army as it moved from the safety of Laos into South Vietnam.

This mission was also the last patrol for our point man, Lance Corporal Kegler. On our return from the A Shau Valley he would begin checking out as the first step of his long-awaited journey back to Texas.

Checking out was not a long process, and the administrative paperwork could probably be accomplished in less than a day, but the unwritten policy of our company was to allow anyone checking out for the World to have about five days of grab-ass time in the rear to prepare himself for the trip home. The tremendous psychological benefits of this policy cannot be overstated as, otherwise, many men found themselves back in the World having less than two days' time to separate themselves from combat in the jungle and to readjust to life on the streets in "Hometown, USA." If anyone had earned the right to five days of grab-ass time, it had been Kegler. He had walked point in a Force Recon team for more than a year, and we wanted to see him leave in the vertical position, not in the horizontal.

We had also acquired a new team member for this short patrol, a young Marine I'll call Joe Dokes. Since Lance Corporal Silva's name had finally been approved for a well-deserved, five-day R & R, Swift was tapped to take his place and to hump the secondary radio.

Corporal Bishop had voiced his concerns about additional people being sent out on patrol, and after the linguist incident, he had been promised that it would not happen again. But the need for a secondary radio operator was valid, even if Dokes had never been out on patrol. We assumed that if Dokes wanted to go to the bush as badly as he had indicated, then he would listen to our instruction and do exactly as he was told.

The pace of our company's patrolling in the A Shau Valley had quickened, and four days in the bush was considered more than adequate time to observe the assigned area. Our sister teams had constantly reported hearing vehicle engines and seeing their lights along the roads during the night, but for whatever reason, the decision makers who occupied spaces higher up in the chain of command were not convinced that the North Vietnamese were driving trucks through the A Shau Valley. Our comment to this reasoning was simple—reading about the A Shau Valley was one thing, walking in it was another.

We hoped to be able to catch one of the truck convoys as it moved along through the valley, and if the unpredictable weather was on our side, we would be able to call in some close air support to attack the nightly NVA traffic.

Kegler, Bishop, me, Keaveney, Dokes, and Furhman made up our single-file order of march when we moved out of the small helicopter landing zone and headed for the high ground. Bishop wanted to cross over a ridge line that separated us from the road before it became too dark to travel. Having enough daylight to make the climb and to get ourselves into position would mean a full day of climbing. The OP that Bishop planned to use was located on the forward slope of a hill which overlooked the road, and from there we would watch and report on anything that might be traveling through the valley. We had brought along two Starlight scopes and extra binoculars that would allow us to watch the road throughout the night.

The climb up to the ridge line took the better part of the day, with rest stops every few hundred meters. It soon became obvious that the difficult hump was taking its toll on the team and particularly on Dokes. We had become accustomed to long, slow climbs with heavy packs, but we frequently rested for short intervals and drank large amounts of sugar-water to compensate for our loss of energy. Dokes was scared and new to all of this, and his mental strength had not been tested to the limits that he was now experiencing.

Furhman was positioned as our team's tail-end charlie, which required him to walk backward most of the time. With Dokes slowing down the pace because of fatigue, Furhman began to literally walk into him. That situation was unacceptable because good individual dispersion helped to ensure our survival in the bush. To bunch up was an invitation to an enemy ambush, and the point was finally made clear to Dokes by Keaveney.

We had started to move up a rock-covered draw, and the angle of the climb was becoming sharper with each step. At one point, Keaveney turned to check on Dokes, but he was nowhere in sight. Keaveney signaled, I stopped, and Bishop stopped Kegler. We waited for several minutes hoping that Dokes and Furhman would come into view, but it didn't happen. It was now up to Keaveney to go back down the draw, locate Dokes and Furhman, and get them back in line.

Keaveney carried not only his pack and his M-79 grenade launcher, but he had two canvas pouches, originally designed to protect plasma bottles, as carrying cases for his 40-millimeter grenades. His pack weight probably exceeded sixty pounds, and for him to climb back down the draw to find Dokes was testing not only the limits of his strength but of his responsibility for Dokes.

The rest of us had halted in place on the rocks of the draw, and within five minutes we heard movement as Dokes, Keaveney, and Furhman came into view. Dokes was moving quickly in front of Keaveney and he was not stopping to rest. Bishop gave them the signal to stop, and went down the draw to find out from Keaveney what had happened.

Keaveney explained to Bishop that after the last rest, Dokes had started to move up the draw and became too tired to continue, but rather than call a stop, he signaled only to Furhman to stop and then proceeded to sit down and light up a cigarette as the rest of us continued moving up the draw. Furhman had no idea that we had moved forward, and Dokes was sitting on a rock smoking when Keaveney came upon him. Without saying a word, Keaveney drew his .45 Colt from his hip holster and placed the barrel of the big automatic in Dokes's ear. He then whispered, "Dokes, if you ever sit down again, I'll blow your goddamned head off your fuckin' shoulders." Dokes took the hint and didn't stop until he saw Bishop's signal. That was our first indicator that Dokes might be another problem child.

There was little for Bishop to do with Dokes, who was scared to death that Keaveney would carry out his threat, and he moved back to his position in file. Then Furhman moved up to where Dokes stood and added his own comment, "If Keaveney doesn't find a reason to blow your greasy little head off, I will."

We crossed the ridge line ahead of schedule, and Kegler walked us down the opposite slope and onto a rock ledge that overlooked the valley floor. The brown outline of the old road was partially visible from our location, so we staged our packs behind the ledge and began to watch the road, two men at a time.

As Bishop radioed back our location and our plans for the evening, Kegler took Dokes out to the observation point, knowing better than to leave him alone with either Furhman or Keaveney.

The night passed without our having seen any trucks moving along the road, but we did see numerous dots of light on the hillsides of the valley, and we plotted each sighting, sending the information back to Zulu Relay. Our second day began with heavy, cold rains, and the prospect of our team being extended in the bush if the downpour continued. We felt secure in our OP and took the time to make hot cocoa and coffee in order to keep warm and to pass the time. By late in the afternoon, we had seen no movement along the road, and Bishop contacted the relay site with his plans to move to a different location early the following morning.

The second night brought only colder temperatures and continued heavy rain. The rock ledge did not allow for a good runoff, and by midnight we were trying to sleep close together in several inches of cold water, and there was little we could do to improve our situation. But here was a rare opportunity to change out of our wet socks and put on two pairs of cherished dry socks.

Only rarely did we find the time or the place to remove our boots when we were in the bush, and when the opportunity did present itself, it was done individually and fast. Oddly, of all the fears associated with being out in the bush, none of us ever wanted to be caught exposed with our trousers down or our boots off.

After checking each man's feet, I gave Bishop a thumbs-up, and we moved out of our night's harbor site, soaking wet but wearing dry socks, a small victory achieved under adverse conditions. We knew that the pleasure of dry socks would last for only a short time. The first knee-deep stream would make sure of that. But for the meantime, dry socks were a small source of joy.

We began our move toward a new observation point that required us to move downhill toward the floor of the valley. There was a natural shelf that Bishop had seen on his map, and he wanted to look at the shelf as a possible helicopter landing zone that we could use for our extraction, scheduled for late in the afternoon of the following day. The map also indicated that a small pond, fed from two small streams above it, was located at the far end of the shelf. Most of us had used up a considerable amount of water during our climb on the first day, and what water had remained in our canteens since then had been used for hot cocoa, coffee, and dehydrated food.

Our move across the level shelf took several hours of slow patrolling, and by noontime we had stopped to rest and to observe the area around us. One of the interesting things that Kegler had noted as we moved across the shelf was that several large trees had been marked. They had been cut close to their base and the cuttings looked like two parallel lines with a long slash dividing them. We had seen other markings on trees in the A Shau Valley, but we had no idea what they meant. Our concern was their age and who had made them. The marks that Kegler had spotted were fresh. His eyes had picked up the yellow shavings at the base of the trees, and the bright color stood out in contrast to the green and brown of the jungle floor.

Keaveney sketched the markings in his notebook, to be saved and discussed at our debrief session at Phu Bai. Maybe someone in the intelligence shop could find out what they meant.

We found the first stream that fed the little pond and crossed it, knowing that the second stream was less than one hundred meters ahead. When Kegler signaled back to Bishop, we stopped and waited while the two of them talked about moving nearer to the pond to check for boot prints or other markings around the pond's edges.

Kegler moved us across the stream, and we began to climb to a position that overlooked the small pond. We staged our gear, and Bishop explained that he did not want our boot prints to give away our presence. Two of us would go down to the pond to see if the mud around the pond could tell us about any recent activity.

Bishop told Keaveney that he would take me with him. Keaveney would set up to observe the area, and we would use the place to rest until nightfall. Anyone who was out of water was to give Bishop and me one canteen that we would fill from the feeder stream when we returned from reconning the pond.

From our elevated view, we could see two places where bushes came right to the water's edge. We would approach the pond using the bushes for concealment, check out any tracks that we might find, and return to our OP site with canteens of fresh water.

As Bishop looked at the tracks that were in the mud, I filled one of my canteens from the pond and returned it to its pouch. I figured that it would take less time to fill the canteen from the pond than it would take us to fill six other canteens from the small feeder stream. When we had finished checking out the pond, we filled the canteens from the stream and returned to the OP.

Bishop contacted Zulu Relay, plotted our position, and told them about the shelf as a possible extraction point for the next day's events. After he finished, he signaled us to move in close so that he could talk quietly about what he had seen at the pond.

"There were several sets of small boot prints along the water's edge, and there were tracks that looked like they were made by pigs there, too. I also saw two sets of the biggest cat tracks that I have ever seen. They were almost two hands across. If what made those tracks is still in the area, then we will go on a two-man watch tonight. Tigers and NVA in the same grid square isn't a good sign."

Since being threatened Dokes had done exactly what he had been told, but the thought of having to deal with a tiger in the grid square where we were to spend the night had a marked effect on him. He asked Keaveney if he could clean his weapon, something he had had to be reminded to do during the past two days. Then he spent half an hour on preventive maintenance of his radio. Dokes was alert and watchful to the point that it began to annoy the rest of us. Finally, Keaveney had another talk with Dokes to assure him that if he did what he was told to do, his chances of getting back to the rear were good.

The rain had stopped during the afternoon, and we prepared ourselves for another night of watching. We could see the moon as it was reflected in the water of the little pond, but seeing it so early in the evening meant that there would be no light after midnight. At 0100 Keaveney and I began our second shift, watching the road and plotting the points of light that we could see on the hillsides. Just after our first time check with Zulu Relay, we heard the first growl of the tiger.

There was no need for us to ask one another what had made the great noise. It wasn't even close by, but the sound was unforgettable. It began as a low moan and increased in a resonating volume that could be heard for quite a distance as it echoed off the rock walls of the A Shau Valley. There was no doubt in the mind of any man who could hear that sound, whether he was North Vietnamese or American, that a tiger was moving in the valley. There was no need to wake up the other members of the team; they had all heard the sound. We listened as the growls continued, and they became weaker as the tiger moved away, but that did not satisfy any of us, particularly Dokes. We passed the radio handset over to

Furhman and Kegler at 0230, not needing to wake either of them. By first light we had all spent a restless night napping. Bishop had heated some water with a piece of C-4, and the smell of coffee caused the rest of us to sit up and exchange looks of satisfaction at having survived the night without a visit from our feline neighbor.

Dokes passed the radio handset over to Bishop, who started to write down message traffic from Zulu Relay. When he was finished, we moved in around him as he explained what was happening.

"The extract bird will come in early and get us out of here at noon. They want us to go to Zulu Relay for a week's stay on top of Hill 8683. After we eat, we'll move toward the shelf and wait for the extract bird."

News of the early extract was welcome, but the word about staying on top of Hill 883 was a different matter. The radio-relay site was manned by less than a dozen men, and the company had been rotating teams out of the valley to the site to protect the radio equipment from attack. It was a stationary position; there was no patrolling off the hilltop, and the daily routine was restful but boring. A week on top of one hilltop was all we had to look forward to.

Our mission to observe the road junction ended when two Hueys came into view shortly after noon. We had reported the lights, the tracks around the pond, the markings on the trees, and hearing the tiger, but we had seen no movement of North Vietnamese. To us, the mission had been a partial success at best, strengthened only by the fact that we had come out of the A Shau alive.

The second Huey carried Major Lee. He frequently visited Zulu Relay to inspect improvements to the defenses made by whomever was the senior Marine on the hill. That position rotated with our platoon staff sergeants, and as we landed we were greeted by SSgt. Byron Tapp, platoon sergeant of the fourth platoon and a former grunt.

Staff Sergeant Tapp had planned for our arrival, and two communicators acted as guides, showing us where we were to drop our gear before giving us a tour of the site. We watched as the first Huey left Hill 883, taking with it one of the six-man teams from the fourth platoon that had finished its week of security duty. They very quickly scrambled onto the waiting Huey, leaving no doubt about their being glad to get off the little hilltop.

Staff Sergeant Tapp had been at the relay site for almost three weeks, and he took great pride in showing us the work that had been done by his Marines to make the place such a fortress.

The two-niner-two radio transmitter was protected by at least six layers of green sandbags. Trench lines led from the comm bunker and connected each firing position. The trenches, we were told, would protect us from incoming mortar rounds. Over one hundred claymore mines had been planted into the sides of the hilltop. One .50 caliber (heavy) machine gun had been donated by the Army and was emplaced on the western side of the hill. The wreckage of the two helicopters, reduced to chunks of melted metal after they had burned, was still plainly visible. It stood in mute testimony to the men who had flown in them, and it reminded us of the price that had been paid only several weeks earlier to establish our little outpost on the Laotian border.

When Major Lee was satisfied that the new defensive improvements had been completed, he congratulated Staff Sergeant Tapp and the Marines who had remained on the hill on the good work and then flew back to Phu Bai. Staff Sergeant Tapp then explained the ground rules of life at Zulu Relay. Our presence was well-known to the North Vietnamese. They had watched our helicopters resupply the relay site each week, and they probably knew exactly how many of us were defending the hill. He said that they probably had watched as each of the claymore mines was planted and that they knew exactly where the .50 caliber machine gun was positioned, too. The picture that he painted didn't sound as though it was in our favor to be there, but then he explained why we could hold out on the hill.

It was almost impossible to hit the peak of the hill with a mortar round; it was too steep. Any incoming rounds would either hit the side of the hill or pass harmlessly over the top. The trench lines were dug almost chest deep. The dirt from the extensive trench system had been used to fill the countless sandbags around the comm bunker, and we were told that we would improve on that each day. Tapp said that the best part about being at Zulu Relay was that we would not have to whisper as was normal for us when we were in the bush; the worst part of spending a week on Zulu was that there was only one makeshift head, located on the steepest part of the hill. He advised us to use the wooden-ammo-box head only at night. The possibility of an NVA sniper picking us off as we sat on the ammo box did not have to be explained more than once. He completed his talk about Zulu Relay by reminding us to keep off the edges of the hill and that strict light discipline was to be observed after

1700 hours. We were then turned back over to our team leader for any additional instructions.

Keaveney and I were to share a two-man fighting hole that was positioned on the western side of the hilltop with a view straight into Laos. We dropped our packs at the entrance to the hole and went to work making ourselves comfortable. Eight wires led to the claymore hell boxes that had been hidden inside of our hole. Next to the hell boxes was a C-ration box with a diagram of where the claymore mines were located below and in front of our position. We studied the ground to our front in preparation for the night. Then, as we had extra time on our hands, I decided that it would be a good time to make a canteen cup of hot coffee. Using the water that I had drawn from the pond the day before, I filled the canteen cup and heated it with C-4. By the time the water was hot enough, Keaveney had left the hole to talk for a while with Bishop. I smoked a cigarette and enjoyed the view, sipping my coffee until it was gone.

By nightfall I had begun to feel sick and told Keaveney about it. He only kidded me and said that our in-country R & R was enough to make anyone sick. By midnight I had broken into a heavy sweat and began to puke my guts out. I drank the rest of the water from my canteen, hoping that it would settle my gut, but the water did little to help. After a few minutes I had vomited up the water and began to dry heave. The only thing that I could taste was bile. By that time I knew that whatever I was suffering from was not a simple case of the flu. After covering myself with my poncho liner, I took my temperature. Using my flashlight, I saw that the thermometer read 103 degrees. I shook the mercury down and did it again, same reading. I asked Keaveney to get Bishop.

Bishop knew that I wasn't bullshitting him; my poncho liner was soaked with my sweat. He felt my forehead with his hand. "I'll tell Staff Sergeant Tapp about this 'cause they're going to have to get you outta here tomorrow." When he returned, Tapp was with him, and I explained again that I had no idea what could be wrong. All I knew was that I had never felt so sick before and that all I wanted to do was sleep.

By morning I was shaking badly, and Keaveney made some hot cocoa. I swallowed a mouthful and immediately threw it up. Then I took my temperature. The mercury showed 104.4 degrees. By the time Staff Sergeant Tapp came over to our hole, I was beginning to see double.

"There's a medevac bird due to land here in ten minutes. Take the doc down to the LZ with all of his gear and get him out of here.''

When the Huey landed at the 85th Evacuation Hospital in Phu Bai, I was placed on a stretcher and taken into the emergency treatment room. A nurse came over to the stretcher and asked me how I had gotten burned. Burned? I tried to figure out why she had thought that I had been burned. It was the camouflage paint. She hadn't ever seen anyone wearing the dark green paint before. It was an honest mistake, and I was in no condition to argue with her.

Blood samples were taken, and I was placed in a hypothermia bed, which had a mattress covered with plastic tubes that circulated cold water underneath the green sheets. An Army doctor came to examine me, and after asking me a bunch of questions, he hooked me up to two IV bottles of D5W (5% dextrose in water), one bottle to each arm. He said that the bed would break my fever and once it went below 99 degrees, I would be placed in a dry bed.

Because my temperature was so elevated, it was to be taken every fifteen minutes. But I complicated matters by not being able to get out of the bed fast enough to relieve myself. It didn't matter, they had seen it all before. I was stood up between two Army medics and washed off with a hose of warm water and then returned to the hypothermia bed. Within minutes I became unconscious.

When I came to, I knew that I was in the dry bed. It felt warm, and I hoped that they would just leave me alone and let me die. I also knew that the spasms had not left me and that I would foul the dry bed within a few minutes. It was only a matter of time.

I was told by a doctor that I was suffering from amoebic dysentery and had contracted Type A hepatitis as well. All I knew was that I was suffering; I only wanted someone to walk up to my bed and kill me.

The first person who I recognized was Captain Hisler. He and Major Lee and First Sergeant Henderson had come to the hospital to visit the first day that I had been admitted, but I was asleep when they arrived. On their second visit, I was conscious and was really pleased to see them. They had brought along some letters from my sisters. I saved them for a better time.

I remained at the 85th Evacuation Hospital for eight days, losing seventeen pounds, mostly to fever and to dysentery. The doctors were not sure what had caused the illness until one of them asked about my gear. They took a sample of the water from my canteens and discovered that the water I had taken from the pond was contaminated. Their laboratory showed that decayed meat had been in the water. Pig meat.

According to the intelligence people in Da Nang, the North Vietnamese had trapped and staked bush pigs to the bottom of the ponds in the A Shau Valley and had marked which ponds were unusable, protecting their own people from using the fouled water. That explained the markings that Kegler had found along the shelf, and it also explained why I was the only one to have become so sick. The other canteens had all been filled from the feeder stream.

On the seventeenth of January, I was picked up by First Sergeant Henderson and Staff Sergeant Williams for a two-mile jeep ride back to the company area. Bishop, Keaveney, and Furhman were all in the squad bay when I returned, having just come off of Zulu Relay that afternoon.

MY MATE

I've been sittin' starin', starin' at 'is muddy pair of boots,
And tryin' to convince meself it's 'im.
(Look out there, lad! That sniper—'e's a dysey when 'e shoots,
'E'll be layin' of you out the same as Jim.)
Jim as lies there in the dug-out wiv 'is blanket round 'is 'ead,
To keep 'is brains from mixin' wiv the mud;
And 'is face as white as putty, and 'is overcoat all red,
Like 'e's split a bloomin' paint-pot—but it's blood.

And I'm tryin' to remember of a time we wasn't pals.
'Ow often we've played 'ookey, 'im and me,
And sometimes it was music-'alls, and sometimes it was gals,
And even there we 'ad no disagree.
For when 'e copped Mariar Jones, the onc I liked the best,
I shook 'is 'and and loaned 'im 'arf a quid;
I saw 'im through the parson's job, I 'elped 'im make 'is nest,
I even stood god-farther to the kid.

So when the war broke out, sez 'e: "Well, wot abaht it, Joe?"
"Well, wot abaht it, lad?" sez I to 'im.
'Is missis made a awful fuss, but 'e was mad to go,
('E always was 'igh-sperrited was Jim)
Well, none of it's been 'eaven, and most of it's been 'ell,
But we've shared our baccy, and we've 'alved our bread.
We'd all the luck at Wipers, and we shaved through Noove
   Chapelle,
And . . . that snipin' barstard gits 'im on the 'ead.

Now wot I wants to know is, why it wasn't me was took?
I've only got meself, 'e stands for three.
I'm plainer than a louse, while 'e was 'andsome as a dook;
'E always *was* a better man than me.
'E was goin' 'ome next Toosday; 'e was 'appy as a lark.
And 'e'd just received a letter from 'is kid;

And 'e struck a match to show me, as we stood there in the dark,
When . . . that bleedin' bullet got 'im on the lid.

'E was killed so awful sudden that 'e 'adn't time to die.
'E sorto jumped, and came down wiv a thud.
Them corpsy-lookin' star-shells kept a-streamin' in the sky,
And there 'e lay like nothin' in the mud.
And there 'e lay so quiet wiv no mansard to 'is 'ead,
And I'm sick, and blamed if I can understand:
The pots of 'alf and 'alf we've 'ad, and *zip*! like that—'e's dead,
Wiv the letter of 'is nipper in 'is 'and.

There's some as fights for freedom and there's some as fights for
    fun,
But me, my lads, I fights for bleedin' 'ate.
You can blame the war and blast it, but I 'opes it won't be done
Till I gets the bloomin' blood-price for me mate.
It'll take a bit o' bayonet to level up for Jim;
Then if I'm spared I think I'll 'ave a bid,
Wiv'er that was Mariar Jones to take the place of 'im,
To sorter be a farther to 'is kid.

Rhymes of a Red Cross Man
(Robert Service)

DEATH IN THE A SHAU VALLEY

I HAD BEEN CHOSEN TO ATTEND THE COMPANY'S prescuba school during the last week in January 1970, along with ten other Marines in 3d Force. My health and strength had steadily improved after having been released from the 85th Evac Hospital, and I was ready to learn a new skill and pick up an additional sixty-five dollars per month as a diver.

The training schedule at prescuba school was designed to weed out all but three of us who would then be sent to the U.S. Naval Ship Repair Facility, located at Subic Bay in the Philippines. The Navy's scuba school would then give them three weeks of training. Quotas for the school were considered to be extremely difficult to come by, and I considered it as quite an honor to have been picked for this class.

We began our training with a daily trip to an old swimming pool that was outside Phu Bai, where we were introduced to a rigorous swimming program that was part of the weeding-out process. After hours in the heavily chlorinated pool, we then spent hours in the classroom learning as much about the fundamentals of diving as was possible. The method to the madness of our scuba instructors was to teach us all that they could, prepare us mentally and physically for the school, and then select the three fortunate individuals who would leave Vietnam for three weeks in the glorious Philippines.

As our training at prescuba school continued, so did the constant patrolling of the A Shau Valley. On the morning of 5 February 1970, a team from the fourth platoon was scheduled to go out on a short mission in the A Shau. One of the team radio operators was a lance corporal named Tommy Sexton. Sexton came from Columbia, South Carolina, and he was known within our small company as a friendly, reliable, and solid individual and a fine athlete. Bishop, Keaveney, and I had walked over to the ammunition bunker and watched as Sexton and his fellow team members drew their allocation of ammunition. Once that was done, they would sit and wait near the bunker for the arrival of their insertion helicopters. Lance Corporal Sexton was joined by his teammates, Corporal Hutchinson, Lance Corporal Savage, and Corporal Cantu.

There was a heavy ground fog that particular morning, and with a little extra time to wait for the birds, Sexton asked if we would take some photographs of him and his teammates before they left for the A Shau. We agreed to waste our camera film on members of another platoon and laughed and teased them about all the extra gear that they were taking with them for only a three day hot-dog mission. (We used the term "hot dog" to describe what was usually considered to be an easy mission—get in, look around, get out.) After their helicopter departed for the A Shau, I left Bishop and Keaveney to attend my daily prescuba school classes which would last until late in the afternoon. But on this particular day in February our classes ended abruptly around 1000 hours.

Word was quickly passed throughout our small company area that one of our teams was engaged in a firefight with an NVA unit. No specifics were given as to who might be wounded or how many North Vietnamese might have been killed, but the news of any one of our teams in contact was a major event.

As the morning turned into early afternoon, little additional information had come from the company's operations office to explain to us what was happening in the A Shau Valley, but sometime close to 1500 Major Lee and First Sergeant Henderson left the compound in their jeep and headed for the Army's 85th Evacuation Hospital, located on the far side of the airstrip. As the CO's jeep pulled away, Captain Hisler came out of the operations office and told us what he knew about what had happened.

"The news that I have for you men isn't good. Corporal Hutchinson's team was ambushed earlier today and he, Cantu, and Savage are reported now as having been killed. Lance Corporal Sexton brought in close air support to protect the other members of the team, and some of them are wounded as well. The CO and first sergeant have gone over to the 85th Evac to meet the incoming medevac bird. When he returns, I'm sure we'll find out all there is to know about what happened."

The captain's words were met with silence from those of us who heard him. As we walked back to the squad bay the talk was of disbelief and of great sorrow. The company executive officer wouldn't say that Hutchinson, Cantu, and Savage were dead unless it was true. We waited for the CO and first sergeant to return. When they drove into the company compound Lance Corporal Sexton was with them.

That evening Corporal Bishop, Paul Keaveney, and I walked over to the fourth platoon's squad bay to talk with Lance Corporal Sexton. He was sitting on his rack when we walked in, and Bishop asked him if he could use some company. Sexton had probably repeated his account of what had happened that day in the A Shau Valley a dozen times before we spoke with him, and we were no better than the rest of the of the Marines in the company for asking him to repeat it. His recollection of the day's tragic events was clear as he repeated his story. "Why I'm still alive, I'm not sure. I guess I owe my life to my day/night flare and my K-bar. When the gooks opened up on us, I got knocked over backward, and I knew that I was hit, but I didn't feel anything. There was no real pain. I put my hand up to my chest where I felt the bullet hit me, and when I looked at my hand, it was colored orange. I couldn't figure out why it was orange until I looked at my knife and flare. One AK-47 round went right through my day/night flare and then that bullet went through the leather sheath and broke the K-bar blade in half while it was still in the sheath. The orange color came from the powder in the flare."

Lance Corporal Sexton was still visibly shaken by what had happened and by the fact that he was the only one to have survived the ambush without having been killed or wounded. He went on to tell us what had happened during the initial part of the ambush and how he had stacked the bodies of Hutchinson, Savage, and Cantu around himself for protection as he stayed on the radio, requesting close air support. He said that it was a miracle that the gooks didn't overrun his tiny defensive position, but his two wounded teammates kept firing their weapons at where the attacking enemy firing was coming from, and he thought that must have kept the NVA from trying to capture them. They had thrown all of their own hand grenades and took the ones from the bodies of their dead teammates to use against the NVA.

There was a lot more to Lance Corporal Sexton's story than he cared to share with us. It was obvious to see that it upset him to recall watching three of his best friends die and protecting two wounded teammates from additional injury. He wonderd why he alone had been spared injury or death in the ambush. He knew that his life was saved initially by his K-bar knife and day/night flare being worn over his heart and secondly by his own ability in keeping a cool head on the radio while all hell was breaking loose around him.

During the time that Lance Corporal Sexton and his wounded teammates were engaged in their life-or-death firefight with the North Vietnamese, Sexton was able to contact friendly close air support on his radio and requested that the helicopter gunships and fixed-wing aircraft bring their fires to bear on the enemy position.

We had been told that when 3d Force Recon Company was given the mission of patrolling the A Shau Valley in December of 1969, the detailed planning between the Marine Corps and the U.S. Army tasked the Air Cav soldiers at Camp Eagle with providing an immediate-reaction force, known as a Blue Team, to assist us in situations like the one Sexton's team had experienced. The Blue Teams consisted of a reinforced Army grunt platoon that would be quickly flown into the area where the small reconnaissance team was in contact and, by using their heavy firepower and helicopter gunship support, secure a landing zone and assist in getting the recon team out of the area. That was exactly how Lance Corporal Sexton and the two wounded members of his team were taken out of the A Shau Valley.

The deaths of Hutchinson, Cantu, and Savage were a stunning blow to the officers and men in 3d Force Recon Company. The reality of how quickly life could turn sour was made apparent by the events of that day. Tommy Sexton was promoted meritoriously to the rank of corporal, and his ability to protect the surviving members of his team earned him the nation's second highest award for extraordinary heroism, the Navy Cross.

The following day, February 6, 1970, it was Team Snakey's turn for a three-day hot-dog mission in the A Shau Valley.

An Army Air Cav observation helicopter had spotted a well-used trail that ran next to a series of fresh bomb craters. The trail was described as being "one foot deep and two feet across." The team's mission would begin with its being inserted by helicopter on a small plateau near the trail. Snakey was to find out who was using the trail and where they were headed. After Corporal Bishop had received the initial briefing, he gathered together his team.

Sergeant Arthur Garcia, our platoon guide, would be the point man for the team and carry his M-14 rifle. Corporal Bishop would walk second, carrying his own PRC-77 radio, as the team leader. Furhman would walk behind Bishop, followed by Keaveney who carried his M-79 grenade launcher. A new team member, Private First Class Murray, was the fifth man in the team. Murray was known to us simply as Nic because he was new in country. Lance

Corporal Silva would walk at the rear of the column as tail-end charlie.

Knowing that Sexton's team had been the target of an NVA ambush only the day before and in the same general location, there was a noticeable change in the attitude of the team.

Sergeant Garcia had a premonition that there was going to be trouble on the mission. After he had gotten all of his gear ready for the field, he began to throw away old letters, extra junk that he had kept in his footlocker, and then he cleaned up his living area. This busy attention to his personal gear caught the attention of Silva, Keaveney, and me, and when we asked what he was doing, he said that he "didn't feel right about the mission. If I don't come back from this one, I want my shit in order when it gets sent home." He went back about his business, and we went to talk with Bishop. Ironically, at the time that Sergeant Garcia was dealing with his problems, Furhman (who had been recently promoted to lance corporal) was listening to a tape recording that he had received in the day's mail. During December his wife had given birth to their son, and at a family gathering at Christmas time, his family had recorded the sounds of the family's party. Included in the tape were the sounds of his infant son. Hearing the baby noises of his child and the laughter of his family back in York, Pennsylvania, had a great effect on Furhman. He wanted us to listen to the tape, which we did, but then his mood changed. He told us that he "didn't feel good about going to the bush" and he wondered if there was any way that he could get out of it. It was unusual to hear that sort of talk coming from him; he had never balked at going to the bush before.

Having witnessed Garcia's change in attitude and then listening to Furhman talk along the same vein, I explained it away as a result of their thinking about Sexton's ordeal only a day earlier. Who wouldn't have the same reservations about going into an area that was known to be crawling with North Vietnamese?

I talked with Corporal Bishop and told him about the obvious changes in Sergeant Garcia and in Lance Corporal Furhman. He listened to my concerns because he knew how the mental attitude of anyone of us was important to the team as a whole. There was absolutely no room for daydreaming or soul-searching when we were in the bush. He thanked me for confiding in him and told me not to worry about it.

By 2000 the team was packed and prepared for the next morning's mission. Bishop, Silva, Keaveney, and I sat outside on the back steps of the platoon squad bay and talked about the mission.

By then the atmosphere inside the squad bay had changed—Sergeant Garcia and Lance Corporal Furhman appeared to have resolved their feelings. There had been no more talk about the uncertainty of the mission, only resolve to get on with it. We ended our conversation with the standard phrase of the time, "It don't mean nothin'," and then returned inside to sleep.

Dawn on 7 February found Snakey and one other team finishing breakfast at the mess hall. I walked back to the company compound with Bishop, Silva, and Keaveney. Sergeant Garcia and Nic Murray had finished breakfast and were getting ready to carry their gear across the road to the ammo bunker. Furhman had elected to write some letters home rather than eat, and he was moving to get his gear on when we walked into the squad bay. He handed me a stack of letters and asked if I would make sure that they got into the outgoing mail sack.

I walked with Bishop and Keaveney over to the ammo bunker and waited with them until the two Hueys from 2/17th Air Cav arrived with their two Cobra gunship escorts to take the team into the A Shau Valley. I was joined by Staff Sergeant Williams and First Lieutenant Coffman. They both knew what was on my mind when I said, "It really feels strange for me, watching them load up and not being with them. This is the first mission that I haven't gone out on with Bishop, Keaveney, Silva, and Furhman."

Lieutenant Coffman lightened the moment when he said "Not to worry, Doc, they'll be back in four days and they'll tell you all about it when they get back." As the engines on the two Hueys began to increase their rpms Staff Sergeant Williams, Lieutenant Coffman, and I gave the team a thumbs-up. They returned the gesture and lifted off from the Phu Bai airstrip. I walked back to the squad bay with Staff Sergeant Williams, picked up my scuba school notebook, and went down to the training section's classroom to prepare for a written examination.

Just before 1100, Staff Sergeant Williams came into the classroom and spoke to one of the sergeants who was administering the test. He pointed to Lieutenant Singleton and then to me, and then he motioned for the two of us to join him. As we got up from our seats, Staff Sergeant Williams walked outside.

"I have some bad news, sir, and I think that you and the doc ought to hear about this now, that's why I came down to the classroom. Team Snakey walked into an ambush about half an hour ago, and they're in real bad shape. As far as I know there are three dead, and a couple of them may be wounded, but that's all I know right now. I don't know the names of who was killed or who was wounded, but they want you over at the operations office, and they want Doc to be ready to go to 85th Evac as soon as the team is pulled out. They said that an Army Blue Team is in the air now, headed for the team's position.''

Lieutenant Singleton took off for the S-3 office, and I stood with my platoon sergeant unable to believe the words he had just spoken. He put his arm around my shoulder and said, ''Doc, I know how much those guys mean to you, and I'm sorry to have to be the one to tell you. Major Lee and Captain Hisler told me to come and get you and bring you over to the CP.''

I walked with Staff Sergeant Williams toward the company's command post and was met outside by Captain Hisler. He too looked very sad. ''Doc, I know that you've heard the bad news about Bishop's team. I want you to come with me when we get the word, and we'll go across the airstrip to the 85th Evac Hospital to meet the incoming medevac birds. You can go back to the squad bay, and I'll have a runner come and get you.''

When I walked into the squad bay, I was met by Corporal Snowden, an assistant team leader in our platoon. He had already heard about the ambush, and he sat on the end of his rack, crying. I didn't have to speak to him, there was nothing that I could say. I wanted to know who was still alive and who had been killed. There were so many questions that remained unanswered. When would the team be extracted? Could whoever was still alive hold out until the Blue Team arrived? How could this have happened? When would we go over to the hospital and find out the answers to these questions?

I heard the sound of the jeep's engine as it came up to the front door of the squad bay. First Sergeant Henderson was behind the wheel, Captain Hisler riding shotgun. I quickly hopped in the backseat, and we wasted no time in heading for the medevac pad at the 85th Evacuation Hospital. By this time Captain Hisler and the company first sergeant knew the names of who had been killed in the ambush, and it was Captain Hisler who told me.

''Doc, when we get to the Army hospital, you and I will meet Keaveney when the medevac bird lands. He's been shot up pretty bad, but it sounds as though he'll make it. The first sergeant will bring Silva and Murray back to the company area for a debriefing as to what the hell happened out there. Corporal Bishop, Lance Corporal Furhman, and Sergeant Garcia were killed. After we get to talk to Keaveney, you and I will make sure that our three KIAs are taken care of the right way.''

It is difficult to describe the emotions that ran wildly through my mind. I was pleased to know that Silva and Nic Murray had survived the ambush, and I felt relieved knowing that the "Ol' Man" had survived, too, but I couldn't believe that Bishop, Furhman, and Garcia were all dead. I wouldn't believe it until I had seen it for myself.

Several Army Hueys were approaching the hospital's landing zone as we entered the compound. The first sergeant stopped the jeep within thirty feet of the first Huey as it touched down. An Army medic ran out to the Huey with a stretcher, and we watched as Keaveney was helped out of the medevac bird. We were out of the jeep and next to him in seconds, and he was trying to walk toward us and away from the medic. His right trouser leg was stained brown from dried blood, and both of his arms had been placed in slings across his chest. He still had his fighting gear on, minus only his rucksack and M-79 grenade launcher. He was pale white, but he didn't appear to be in any great pain.

His first words were apologetic. "Doc, I'm sorry, but Bishop and Furhman didn't make it." I motioned for the Army medic to get to where we were standing, and he brought the stretcher with him.

"Here, Keaveney, lay down on this stretcher and we'll get you inside. How bad are you hit?"

Keaveney said that he wasn't sure how bad it was, but he knew that he had been hit first in his right leg and then he had been hit a second time in both of his arms, his hip, and his right side.

By this time, several more medics had run out to meet the incoming medevac bird, and Keaveney was carried inside to be examined by one of the Army's doctors.

As the second Huey touched down, I watched Private First Class Murray and Lance Corporal Silva jump out and walk toward the company first sergeant. They had no trouble in recognizing First Sergeant Henderson; being six feet eight inches tall had its advantages. He motioned to them to get over to the jeep and asked them if they were all right. Silva assured him that they were fine and both he and Nic only wanted to get back to the company area.

While the company first sergeant took care of Nic Murray and Silva, Captain Hisler and I ran over to the second bird. We were joined by the first sergeant. We took the bodies of Arthur Garcia, Ted Bishop, and James Furhman out of the helicopter. The medevac helicopter crewmen and Army medics knew, somehow, that it was not their place to do this. We placed each body on a green canvas stretcher, and then carried them into the emergency room of the field hospital.

Keaveney was told that he needed to be X-rayed, and I walked beside him as he was wheeled to the X-ray room. This was my first opportunity to talk with him. ''Do you want to tell me what happened, or do you want to wait and talk about it later?'' I asked.

''No, that's okay. I can talk about it. We must have landed right in the middle of them, but they suckered us in. We landed right next to a bomb crater, and there were signs all over the place.''

''What kind of signs?''

''You know, there were boot tracks, and the brush was broken down like a bunch of people had just walked through the area.''

''Did you see any of them?''

''No, that's the weirdest part. They didn't shoot at us when we landed, they just waited for us to get close, and that's when they ambushed us. Big time.''

''How did you manage to walk into an ambush, Keaveney?''

''When we landed, we formed up in a three-sixty to protect the LZ. Bishop had good comm, and when our Huey left, we gave ourselves some time to get our hearing back. Then we started to move out. Well, you know the order of march. Garcia was up on point with his M-14, and Bishop was walking behind him. Furhman was in front of me, and Nic Murray was behind me and in front of Silva, who was tail-end charlie. We stopped to do a map check and to get one last comm check with Zulu Relay. We started to go up a finger, and by the time we had spread out to match the terrain, I could see that we were on a gook trail. I tapped Furhman and told him to tell Bishop to get Garcia off the damn trail. When Bishop moved up to Garcia, there was a burst of automatic fire, and I got hit in the leg. It knocked me backward, and I fell off to the side of the trail. Bishop came back down to where I was, and I asked him where the firing was coming from. I had gotten spun around and wasn't sure of the direction. I got up, and then I knelt down and fired my first round in the direction that Bishop had pointed to. After the first HE round went off the gooks assaulted, and sprayed the area with automatic fire. That's what got Garcia, Furhman, and Bishop. When I fired my second round, the gooks were less than ten feet away. I heard a safety on an AK-47 as the gook flipped it off, that's how close they were. I got hit that time, too. I sat up and fired my third round at where that second burst of automatic fire came from and hit the gook point-blank. That's when all of the firing stopped. Why they didn't sweep in over us, I don't know. After the firing stopped, I crawled forward and picked up Bishop's rifle. Silva came up to where I was, and then he crept forward to check on Garcia, Bishop, and Furhman. When he came back, he had Bishop's radio and Garcia's M-14. He took the radio from Murray and gave it to me, and then he got on the air net and raised the gunships that had escorted us in. They were back over us in less than five minutes. I talked to one of the Cobra pilots, and he said that he could see me and that he was taking heavy ground fire from a position higher up on the finger.

"Silva was talking to the fixed-wing guys, and they came in so close that you could see the pilot's face when he made his first low-level pass. All I cared about was that they didn't blow us up when they cut loose."

I was joined by Captain Hisler, who had made sure that Silva and Murray were okay, and he asked Keaveney about the Army's Blue Team. Amazingly, Keaveney had not gone into shock although he had been hit in his legs, both arms, and in his side close to his hip. I picked up his web belt from the stretcher as he was being X-rayed and showed it to Captain Hisler. His .45 holster had been hit by one AK-47 round, and the bullet had passed through the holster, hit the magazine in the .45, and one of the bullets had exploded inside of his .45 while it had been on his hip!

Keaveney went on to explain how the Army Blue Team had come in to help get the team extracted.

"Silva was on the secondary radio when we heard that the Blue Team was headed in for our position. We watched as they came by, and finally Silva gave them a mark to let them know that we were right below them. They landed in the same place that we had used to be inserted. The guy leading the Blue Team came up on our frequency and said that he had a KCS (Kit Carson Scout) with them and that he wanted to send him up first, in case the gooks were waiting in ambush. I told him that if the first face we saw coming toward us belonged to a gook, we would blow the bastard away. He got the message real fast, and they sent a black medic up to where Murray and Silva and I were waiting. The medic called for a jungle penetrator, and that's how they took me out. I guess that Silva and Murray made it out with the Blue Team."

Captain Hisler explained that Silva and Murray were fine and that they had been brought back to the company area. At the same time, a doctor came into X-ray and told Captain Hisler that they were taking Keaveney down to the OR. He said that we could come back later on in the evening, when Keaveney would be out of surgery and waiting to be medevaced out of country.

I picked up Keaveney's gear and went with Captain Hisler back to the emergency-room portion of the Army hospital. We then walked with the stretcher bearers as they carried the bodies of

Sergeant Garcia, Corporal Bishop, and Lance Corporal Furhman to Graves Registration. After the captain had signed a receipt for their uniforms and equipment, we said our good-byes to each of them as they began the journey home to their families. Shortly afterwards the company first sergeant returned to the 85th Evac Hospital and brought Captain Hisler and me back to the company compound.

I saw Silva and Murray at the back end of the squad bay, and they were surrounded by half a dozen Marines from the other platoons. Silva and Murray handled the situation well. It was difficult for them to be the center of attention and have to relive what had happened to them that morning, but Silva was calm as he reflected on Sergeant Garcia's action.

"When Keaveney told Furhman to stop Bishop, that was what kept us all from being killed. Garcia broke up the ambush when he started to fire his M-14. It sounded just like an M-60 going off, and that was why the gooks went after him. I heard him fire out at least two full magazines before they assaulted. These weren't trail runners. They were hard-core NVA in full uniform, helmets, and packs. When Keaveney fired his last round, he hit their automatic weapons man point-blank." There was only silence after Silva finished telling the group how the Army's Kit Carson Scout had refused to come up the trail to where the team was positioned. Silva had been on another radio talking with the Army Blue Team. When the Kit Carson Scout had been told how close the NVA were, he must have figured that he could "get it" from either side, and so he had refused to go up to where Keaveney and Silva were waiting. When Silva said that they meant to kill him as soon as he showed his face, nods of agreement and understanding passed through the group.

Staff Sergeant Williams came into the squad bay and told the rest of the Marines to get out of the squad bay and leave us alone. He wanted to talk with Nic Murray to make sure that he was all right. The mission had been the first one for Murray, and according to Keaveney and Silva he had handled himself in the ambush without any problems. He did what Silva had told him to do, and his inexperience in the bush had not added to the situation, and for that they were grateful.

Staff Sergeant Williams talked with Silva and Murray and me for at least an hour before letting us go. He expressed his personal feelings for Bishop, Garcia, and Furhman by telling us that he had never served with any better Marines in his fourteen years of service. He knew that we would miss them, too, and that there was no way that the company could replace their experience. His grief at the loss of three of his men was sincere. He finished his talk to us by saying that the company had planned a memorial service for Cantu, Hutchinson, and Savage for the next afternoon. Now, the names of Sergeant Garcia, Corporal Bishop, and Lance Corporal Furhman would be added to the memorial service list of those who had been killed in action.

Sometime close to 2200, Staff Sergeant Williams came into the squad bay and told me to get dressed and come with him to the SNCO barracks. The staff NCO barracks was sacred territory where sergeants and below were not welcomed. As I walked with my platoon sergeant, I wondered what I had done that required my presence in their living spaces. Seated inside were the company first sergeant, Gunnery Sergeant Bilodeau, Staff Sergeant Tate, and Staff Sergeant Tapp. They had asked Staff Sergeant Williams to get me to join them in a small tribute to my dead teammates. Captain Hisler and First Lieutenant Morris, both of whom had been staff sergeants, were seated with them. A quart bottle of Old Granddad whiskey was being passed around as kind words were being said about the Marines who had been killed. I was honored to be with those Marines and to know that they thought so much of Bishop, Furhman, Garcia, Cantu, Hutchinson, and Savage. When the bottle was passed to me, I drank deeply and hoped that the stiff drink would help me to sleep. They wanted to show their sorrow at the loss of those fine Marines, and they wanted me to know that I was not alone in my feelings of helplessness. I stayed with them until I was drunk, then Staff Sergeant Tapp walked with me back to the darkened squad bay. I remember only how quiet and lonely the barracks were as I waited for sleep to wash over me.

The next morning I was told to report to First Lieutenant Morris, the 3d Force company adjutant. He asked me to write a euology that I would be asked to read during the memorial service scheduled for 1100 hours. I asked him if it were possible to get Keaveney out of the hospital so that he could be present at the service. He told me that when he had called to check on Keaveney's condition, the people at the 85th Evac had said that Keaveney would be confined to his bed until his medevac flight took him to Japan.

When I finished writing the words that best expressed my feelings, I gave the paper back to First Lieutenant Morris. He read what I had written, said that it sounded good and proper, and then he told me that I was going to be leaving the company the following day. I had been selected to attend scuba school, and I would leave Da Nang for the Philippines with a Lance Corporal Thompson and First Lieutenant Singleton the following morning. I asked him if I could speak to Captain Hisler. He checked to see that he was in his office and then motioned me to go inside.

Captain Hisler and I had talked many times in the past, and he had always treated me fairly. He knew that I wouldn't ask to speak to him unless I felt that it was important. I told him that I thought Keaveney should be present at the memorial service. Hadn't he been with Bishop, Garcia, and Furhman when they died? I knew that Captain Hisler had always gone with Major Lee and the first sergeant to visit any member of our company who was hospitalized, and I asked him if I could go with him when he went to check on Keaveney. He knew how important it was. Then he said that I was to check out with Staff Sergeant Williams, we'd leave in a few minutes.

As we started to drive out of the company compound, First Lieutenant Morris ran up to the jeep and hopped into the backseat. His office was adjacent to the captain's, and I'm sure that he had heard my conversation and my request to get Keaveney out of the hospital. Whether or not the hospital staff would approve of us kidnapping Keaveney for a few hours was another matter.

When we arrived at the 85th Evac Hospital, Captain Hisler checked with the information office to find Keaveney's ward. He walked onto the ward and discovered that the "Ol' Man" had two IV bottles hooked up to his arms, but he was awake and alert and pretty glad to see us standing around his bed. I explained to him what we intended to do and asked him if he felt strong enough to walk, then his eyes grew wide in disbelief. "I got shot to shit only twenty-four hours ago and now you want to take me on a jeep ride? Hell yes, I'll go. Where's the jeep?"

Captain Hisler had driven the jeep to the door closest to the recovery ward, and without the hospital staff realizing what was happening, we loaded Keaveney, in his blue pajamas and still hooked up to the two IV bottles, into the running jeep.

The memorial service was set for 1100 hours, and we arrived at the little air wing chapel with five minutes to spare. Every member of 3d Force Recon Company, minus three recon teams that were still in the A Shau Valley, sat in the chapel. In front of the altar were positioned six M-16 rifles. A bayonet was fixed to each rifle and each inverted rifle was held in place by a sandbag. The bush cover of each Recon Marine who had been killed covered the butt of an M-16.

The memorial service didn't last a long time, but each Marine who had been killed was given a euology by one of his teammates. When it was my turn to stand up, Silva held the two IV bottles as they dripped into Keaveney's arms. I spoke on behalf of Corporal Bishop. I still remember exactly what I said.

"Ted Bishop was the best team leader in our platoon. He cared about each one of us in his team, and he was always a friend to each one of us. Ted Bishop was a kind man, and he believed in God. He has left us too soon. He has gone to a place that we know is a far better place than where we have been lately. We all will miss him, and we are each better and stronger for having known him. He taught us well, and for that we will always be thankful. Good-bye, Ted, and thanks."

After the service was over, we put Keaveney back in the jeep and drove him over to the platoon squad bay. He wanted to get some personal gear that he had left in a footlocker. As we stood inside of the squad bay, he talked with Silva and Nic Murray, knowing that he would probably never see either one of them again. He was due to fly to the naval hospital in Yokosuka, Japan, later in the day. I handed him the broken clip from his .45 and hoped that he would be able to carry it with him as a reminder of a bad day in the A Shau Valley. There wasn't too much other talk about what had happened. Corporal Snowden, Lance Corporal Draper, and Staff Sergeant Williams wished him well as he climbed back into the jeep and returned to his bed on the ward at the 85th Evac Hospital.

The squad bay was quiet when I returned from leaving Keaveney at the hospital. Staff Sergeant Williams, along with Silva and Murray, was busy inventorying the personal gear that had belonged to Garcia, Bishop, and Furhman. I asked if I could help. It was not easy for any of us to handle and package their gear without the constant flow of memories interrupting the work. Individually, each of us was trying to accept what had happened; it was not something that could be shared.

The following day I left Vietnam to attend the Navy's three-week scuba school course in the Philippines. I was told that three weeks in the P.I. would help to get my mind off what had happened. It didn't.

RETURNING TO VIETNAM

IN MARCH OF 1970, I RETURNED TO VIETNAM AFTER having graduated from the Navy's scuba school. During our last week there Lieutenant Singleton had managed to finagle orders for three of us from 3d Force Recon to attend jump school, courtesy of the United States Navy. The Navy was running a jump school at Cubi Point, and their Paramedic Rescue Team #1 had helped in arranging for us to make five static-line jumps while we were waiting to return to Vietnam. On my last jump from a CH-53 helicopter, fast-moving ground winds caused my chute to oscillate, and I was slammed into the deck and knocked unconscious for half an hour. I was flown to the hospital at Clark Air Force Base and spent a week on a ward recovering from a severe concussion. First Lieutenant Singleton and Lance Corporal Thompson left me at the hospital and departed the Philippines for Vietnam, via Okinawa. That was the last I saw of them.

Once the doctors at Clark Air Force Base were convinced that I had recovered from my concussion, I was given a new set of orders to Okinawa for further processing back to my platoon with 3d Force Recon Company, in Vietnam. I wanted no more time in the Air Force hospital.

When I arrived in Da Nang, I now had learned enough about the in-processing business to ask the order-writing clerk to get me hooked up with a military flight that would take me back up to the company at Phu Bai, but when he researched the location of 3d Force Recon Company, he told me that I wouldn't have to head north; the company was no longer located at Phu Bai but had recently moved south to Da Nang. Luck was with me—he was headed to the 1st Marine Division headquarters that morning and could drop me off at 3d Force.

Our jeep pulled up to the sign that read: 3D FORCE RECON-

NAISSANCE COMPANY III MAF, and I was glad to see some of the old familiar faces as I pulled my seabag out of the back of the jeep. I walked into the hootch where the S-1 shop had hung their sign and reported to Staff Sergeant Schemmel and First Lieutenant Morris.

"Well, no shit, Doc, where the hell have you been?" It had been more than a month since I had been with the company, and I explained to the company adjutant what had kept me from making it back with the other Marines from scuba school. When I finished telling him all about my diving experiences in the Philippines, he said that First Lieutenant Coffman had left word that I was to see him as soon as I returned to the company. He pointed out the operations hootch and said that I would find Igor inside.

When I entered the plywood hootch, the lieutenant was sitting outside on the back steps, smoking a Salem and eating a large bowl of ice cream. He motioned for me to come over and sit down.

"Where the hell have you been hiding, Doc? We've been waiting for your sorry ass to get back here ever since that peckerhead lieutenant left you behind in the Philippines. There's a lot that has happened to 3d Force in the last month, and you need to be brought up to speed."

Over several cigarettes, Lieutenant Coffman explained that 3d Force Recon Company was being deactivated. "There are a number of reasons as to why all of this has happened. All of them are bad. General Nickerson was our greatest supporter, and he has left country for duty in Washington, D.C. The casualties that the company took in January and February made it difficult to keep experienced six-man teams in the bush, and the North Vietnamese Army was staging hundreds of fresh troops along the Laotian border every day. The gooks were getting better at finding us because they began to bring in scout dogs, radio-direction finders, and two of their own NVA recon units: 11A and 11B Counter-recon Companies. I know that our job is far from over, but the face of this war is changing so fast that the grunts and close air support cannot respond to all of our sightings. The South Vietnamese are too afraid to go into the A Shau for fear of getting their asses kicked.

"We got the word just after you left that we would be disbanding as a company. Major Lee has gone down to be the Ops O with the 7th Marines and to work for Colonel Charlie Cooper. Captain Hisler went back to Quantico. Singleton came back to pick up his personal gear, and he's gone back to the States, too. We are training ARVN rangers down near An Hoa, but there are only twenty of us left. The rest of the guys who wanted to stay and run the bush have been sent over to 1st Force Recon Company.''

As Lieutenant Coffman polished off his sacred bowl of vanilla ice cream, I told him about the Philippines, scuba school, and jump school. Then he ran off a list of the names of those Marines who had gone over to 1st Force and they included Lance Corporal Mackawa, Lance Corporal Dave Draper, and Lance Corporal Morgan, all men who had been in my platoon. He told me that our platoon sergeant, Staff Sergeant Williams, was now the SNCOIC of the division enlisted club. All of those changes were hard to accept, but there was nothing that could be done to change what had already happened. He softened the blow about leaving the company by telling me that I could stay with the company for one week and make a couple of training jumps out of CH-46s. It would be the last time that 3d Force would get to jump in Vietnam. Following the week that I spent with the cadre force from 3d Force Recon Company, I was finally given a set of orders to report for duty to the commanding officer of 1st Force Recon Company.

The last gathering that 3d Force Recon Company had was a surprise party that we threw to honor ourselves. Major Lee attended, as did Lieutenant Coffman, Lieutenant Morris, and Lieutenant Hodge. Staff Sergeant Tapp and Staff Sergeant Williams showed up. Corporal ''Grape'' Vineyard, one of the company's more famous team leaders, even got to play drums with the band. It was a great time, but it was a very sad time. We drank toasts to our commanding officer, to the executive officer, to Hutchinson, Savage, Cantu, Bishop, Garcia, and Furhman, and to ourselves. We drank until we cried, and then the party was over. Third Force Reconnaissance Company was cadred to zero strength the next day.

That next morning I was driven over to 1st Force Recon Company to begin another tour of duty with a Force Recon Company. Those experiences will be the subject of my next book.

——— EPILOGUE ———

DURING THE THREE AND A HALF MONTHS THAT THE recon teams from 3d Force Reconnaissance Company operated in the A Shau Valley and on the Laotian border, the company suffered sixteen Marines wounded and nine Marines killed at the hands of the North Vietnamese. These numbers may seem relatively small in the grand scheme of life, but only eight six-man teams were operational during that time. Our recon teams accounted for 267 dead North Vietnamese soldiers during that same period.

Third Force Reconnaissance Company was later awarded the United States Army's Valorous Unit Citation for the period of 7 December 1969 to 16 February 1970, during which time the company accounted for more than three thousand enemy casualties, using supporting arms and close air support, this according to the accounts from North Vietnamese POWs and captured documents. In the long history of the Vietnam war this Marine Corps Force Recon Company was one of only two Marine units to receive the prestigious award.

It has been more than twenty years since I returned from Vietnam, and over those years I have been asked many questions by people who are genuinely interested in that war. What was it really like? What made duty with 3d Force Recon Company so special? Did you have good leadership? Did everyone who served in Vietnam see combat? What was it like to experience combat at nineteen? Did all of your training prepare you well for combat?

Similar questions are now being asked by the sons and the daughters of the men and women who served in Vietnam, and they are being asked by people who have a great curiosity concerning our involvement in that war. Those questions deserve honest answers.

The young men and women who will someday be tasked with

defending democracy on some foreign shore might do well to study the written history of those men and women who fought in the war in Vietnam. The answers to their many difficult questions lay there. There is a common thread that runs through the fabric of our American military history, and when that thread, called combat, is carefully unraveled it also tells us a great deal about ourselves.

I cannot speak for every man and woman who served in Vietnam; their individual tours of duty, I'm sure, were different than mine. But I do feel qualified to speak on behalf of those Marines with whom I served in 3d Force Recon Company because I knew them very well. Their story deserves to be told and to become a part of our unique military history.

In addressing the question of what made life in 3d Force Recon special, the answer is—desire, devotion, leadership, and courage. The young men who put camouflage paint on their faces, who carried heavy packs and went out in six-man teams to locate the North Vietnamese soldier, wanted to be there. They were doing what Marines have asked to do since the day they joined the Corps—to patrol aggressively against an enemy, to operate tactically in small units, and to return from their patrolling, together. They desired that type of duty, and once they were trained for it, and then given a taste of it, their desire became devotion. They were devoted to one another, to their team, and to the company. It was an unspoken devotion that carried us through very difficult times.

The leadership of our small company could not have been any better. Our commanding officer, Maj. Alex Lee, had spent thirty-nine months of operational combat time in Vietnam. He had commanded two different rifle companies in heavy combat and had served as the operations officer of two different battalions in combat. He was a qualified test parachutist with 421 military jumps, and a qualified test diver for underwater equipment. Some of his personal decorations include the Legion of Merit, the Silver Star, the Bronze Star, three Navy Commendation Medals, the Navy Achievement Medal, and two Purple Hearts. Today, he is still considered a genius at small-unit tactics.

Our executive officer, Capt. Norman R. Hisler, was a prior enlisted Marine. He had extensive combat experience in a rifle company during the Korean War and had served two tours in reconnaissance units in Vietnam, two years of duty as a drill instructor at Parris Island, and had been the assistant ground reconnaissance officer at MCDC, Quantico, Va.

Our operations officer, 1st Lt. C. C. Coffman, Jr., had twenty years of service when he came to 3d Force Recon Company. He, too, was a prior enlisted Marine. He had been awarded the Navy Cross, as a sergeant, two Silver Stars, four Bronze Stars, one Air Medal, one Navy Commendation Medal, two Navy Achievement Medals, and seven Purple Hearts. He had served in the Korean War, Lebanon, the Dominican Republic, and Vietnam. He was qualified as a parachutist, scuba diver, Army Ranger, and special operations officer.

Our company adjutant, and one of the company's platoon commanders, 1st Lt. Wayne Morris, had ten years of prior Marine Corps enlisted time. He had three tours in Vietnam, and had been awarded the Bronze Star.

The officers of 3d Force Reconnaissance Company were the very best the Marine Corps had to offer. They were respected and admired by every Marine in the company. We were proud of them.

That pride of being in 3d Force Recon was built on the strongest bond that holds an organization together—loyalty. The loyalty in 3d Force Recon Company went up and down our chain of command. There was the loyalty of one Marine to another, loyalty to one's team, to one's platoon, and that loyalty fostered a sense of honor at belonging to the company.

We expected just two things from our officers and from our noncommissioned officers—leadership and courage. They never failed us in either respect. To stand in the face of a numerically superior enemy force and to remain calm under fire was the mark of the type of Marine who was in 3d Force Recon, officer and enlisted man alike.

What was expected of us, the team members? First, we were expected to be mentally alert. We were expected to be dependable, to use common sense, not to take unnecessary chances, and to look out for each other all of the time. We did that, and in doing so, it gave us an advantage that lesser organizations didn't have.

The Marines of 3d Force Recon Company were not outwardly patriotic and, as most combat veterans will quickly admit, there was little if any talk about patriotism, democracy, the flag, or the great American way. What was important to us was to see the next day.

The Marines of 3d Force Recon were sentimental. They cared about each other in a way that brothers care only about brothers. They felt the loss of a wounded or killed Marine as any family member would mourn the loss of kin. They felt proud when a member of their team left Vietnam to return home healthy. We were tight. We were a family.

Operating deep in enemy-controlled territory demanded that our individual and team training be the very best possible. It was.

Every man knew how to read a map and how to use a compass. Every man knew how to use the team's radio. That radio was our life link. Every man knew how to call for and adjust long-range artillery fire and how to use close air support. Every man knew the fundamentals of first-aid and lifesaving techniques; they practiced them. Every man practiced those skills that were the most difficult to master until he was confident in himself and in every member of his team. Our recon team was built around that type of confidence. Confidence bred courage.

No one in our company ever seemed to wallow in self-pity, because we shared the same common experiences. No one benefitted at the expense of his teammate. We simply took the worst that the war in Vietnam had to offer, and we made the most of it. Sure, our life was difficult, but we looked upon it as a great and exciting challenge. We had fun with it.

There were many individual qualities that have stood as the trademark of a Force Recon Marine—to be creative, observant, resourceful, alert, disciplined, innovative, knowledgeable, honest, and funny. A sense of humor was almost mandatory; it had to be in an all-volunteer organization such as ours that demanded the utmost from each man.

To experience seeing the enemy close up was *not* the most difficult experience of all. We were never afraid of the North Vietnamese soldier. We respected him. We were concerned only by their vast numbers in comparison to our own small teams. But our ability to use supporting arms and to use close air support gave us a multiple advantage over their numerically superior forces. We were taught simply to kill them scientifically. To us our missions were a deadly game of hide-and-seek. The price that was paid if we were found was usually our lives. The rules were the same for both sides.

Did everyone in Vietnam see combat? The answer to that question is a flat no. I can only speak about what I saw while I was there, and I know that there were people who never heard a shot fired in anger during the time they spent on the ground in Vietnam, and I am pleased at their having been spared.

Combat is fast, unfair, cruel, and dirty. It is meant to be that way so that the terrible experience is branded into the memory of those who are fortunate enough to survive. It is up to those survivors to ensure that the experience is recorded and passed along to those who just might want to try it.

I hope that in my telling of the story of being with "the swift, silent, and deadly," I have done just that.

——— APPENDIX ———

The Navy Cross

COFFMAN, CLOVIS C., JR.

Citation: For extraordinary heroism in action against Communist Forces while serving as a Platoon Leader with Company C, First Reconnaissance Battalion, First Marine Division in the Republic of Vietnam on 10 October 1966. Sergeant Coffman was leading a thirteen-man patrol assigned the mission of observing a valley near Long Bihn, Quang Ngai Province for enemy activity. Early in the afternoon, while leading his unit from their observation post to a helicopter landing zone, the patrol came under a heavy small-arms and grenade attack from an estimated thirty-five to fifty man enemy force. Reacting immediately, Sergeant Coffman skillfully organized and directed the return fire of his out-numbered unit. Fearlessly disregarding his own safety, he repeatedly exposed himself in order to deploy his force and deliver maximum fire power against the attackers. On one occasion during the ensuing fierce action, he observed a wounded Marine lying helpless forward of his position. Courageously he went to his stricken comrade's aid. Although wounded himself, he killed three of the enemy at point-blank range in order to reach the stricken Marine. Sergeant Coffman was successful in his effort to return his stricken comrade to friendly lines. When the patrol's medical corpsman was disabled by wounds, he skillfully administered first aid to four seriously wounded Marines. Sergeant Coffman directed fixed-wing and armed helicopter attacks against the enemy with devastating accuracy, with the result that helicopters were able to land and extract the force. Although wounded, he remained until all of his men were safely embarked, resolutely defending the landing zone. As the last rescue helicopter was loading, he and another Marine held the landing zone alone, killing four of the enemy in close combat. Only after all of his patrol were embarked, did he board the aircraft and depart the embattled area. By his courageous devotion to duty, and extraordinary leadership, Sergeant Coffman reflected great credit upon himself and the Marine Corps and upheld the highest traditions of the United States Naval Service.

SEXTON, CHARLES T.

Citation: For extraordinary heroism while serving as a Radio Operator with the Third Force Reconnaissance Company, Third Marine Amphibious Force in connection with combat operations against the enemy in the Republic of Vietnam. On 5 February 1970, Corporal Sexton was a member of a six-man reconnaissance team which was patrolling deep in the A Shau Valley when it came under a heavy volume of small-arms and automatic weapons fire from approximately fifty enemy soldiers occupying well-concealed emplacements in the dense elephant grass. During the initial moments of the attack, three Marines were mortally wounded and two were seriously wounded. After a rapid assessment of the precarious situation, Corporal Sexton directed the fire of his two wounded companions and moved about the fire-swept area to collect hand grenades and ammunition from his fallen comrades. Utilizing his radio, he then reported the situation to his commanding officer and requested assistance. For the next several hours, while the enemy attempted to encircle and overrun his position, Corporal Sexton repeatedly adjusted helicopter and fixed-wing air strikes on the hostile unit, hurled hand grenades, shouted encouragement to his wounded companions, and simultaneously furnished a running commentary to his company commander until a reaction force arrived to lend support. His heroic and determined actions were an inspiration to all who served with him and undoubtedly saved his fellow Marines from further serious injury or even death. By his courage, superb leadership, and valiant devotion to duty in the face of grave personal danger, Corporal Sexton upheld the highest traditions of the Marine Corps and the United States Naval Service.

Silver Star

PAUL S. KEAVENEY

Citation: For conspicuous gallantry and intrepidity in action while serving as a Reconnaissance Man with the Third Force Reconnaissance Company, First Marine Division in connection with combat operations against the enemy in the Republic of Vietnam. On 7 February 1970, Lance Corporal Keaveney was a member of a reconnaissance team which was conducting a patrol in the A Shau Valley in Thua Thien Province when the Marines came under intense fire from a numerically superior North Vietnamese Army force, pinning down the team and wounding four Marines, including Lance Corporal Keaveney. Despite his painful wounds, he moved to a vantage point along the trail from which he could more clearly observe the movements of the enemy and from which he could more accurately deliver fire with his grenade launcher. With complete disregard for his own safety, Lance Corporal Keaveney boldly stood in full view of the hostile force on three separate occasions, and fearlessly remained in his precarious position while the enemy concentrated their fire on him, and delivered his grenade launcher fire with such devastating effectiveness that the North Vietnamese were prevented from advancing down the trail toward the Marines' position. Each time he stood, he was struck by hostile small-arms fire but, undeterred by his serious wounds, he would again resolutely stand to deliver fire. When the nature of his wounds finally rendered him unable to fire his weapon, Lance Corporal Keaveney obtained the radio from the operator, thereby freeing a fellow team member to more actively engage the enemy while he requested helicopter gunship support and medical evacuation helicopters. His aggressive fighting spirit and valiant actions inspired all who observed him and were instrumental in the defeat of a numerically superior North Vietnamese Army force. By his dauntless courage, bold initiative, and unwavering devotion to duty in the face of great personal danger, Lance Corporal Keaveney upheld the highest traditions of the Marine Corps and of the United States Naval Service.

About the Author

Bruce H. Norton, raised in North Scituate, Rhode Island, enlisted in the United States Navy in 1968 and served as a hospital corpsman at the Naval Hospital, Newport, Rhode Island, and with both 3d Force and 1st Force Reconnaissance Companies in combat in Vietnam from 1969 to 1970. Following an honorable discharge from the United States Navy in 1972, he attended the College of Charleston in South Carolina and received a B.A. in history. He was commissioned a Marine second lieutenant in 1974. Now a major, he has served as an infantry platoon leader, reconnaissance platoon leader, infantry company commander, battalion executive, and operations officer. In 1986–1988, he was the first operations officer for the Marine Corps' Maritime Prepositioned Shipping Program (MPS) at Blount Island, Florida. Major Norton is currently assigned as an operations officer at the Marine Corps Recruit Depot, San Diego, Calfornia. He and his wife, Deaine, reside in Poway, California.